TO THE LETTER

TO THE LETTER

A Handbook of Model Letters for the Busy Executive

Dianna Booher

Jossey-Bass Publishers
San Francisco

For this, my seventh book on business communications, I'm once again indebted to many of the people who have previously shared their corporate experiences with me. Participants in my writing workshops have very willingly expressed their reactions to the letter guidelines in this book, as well as provided their models of effective writing.

Particularly, I want to thank clients such as IBM, Hewlett-Packard, Exxon, Conoco, Tenneco, and many others who have been willing to allow my research among their employees.

I would also like to express my gratitude to Facts on File Publications and to Britannica Training and Development, Inc., for allowing me to reproduce the MADE format and organizational tips.

Jossey-Bass books and products are available through most bookstores. To contact Jossey-Bass directly, call (888) 378-2537, fax to (800) 605-2665, or visit our website at www.josseybass.com.

Substantial discounts on bulk quantities of Jossey-Bass books are available to corporations, professional associations, and other organizations. For details and discount information, contact the special sales department at Jossey-Bass.

For sales outside the United States, please contact your local Simon & Schuster International Office.

 Manufactured in the United States of America on Lyons Falls Turin Book. This paper is acid-free and 100 percent totally chlorine-free.

Library of Congress Cataloging-in-Publication Data

Booher, Dianna Daniels
  To the letter : a handbook of model letters for the busy executive
/ Dianna Booher.
   p. cm.
  Reprint. Originally published: Lexington, Mass. : Lexington Books.
©1988.
  ISBN 0-7879-4479-3
  1. Commercial correspondence—Handbooks, manuals, etc. 2. Form
letters—Handbooks, manuals, etc. I. Title.
HF5726.B724 1998
 651.7'5—dc21   98-7628

CONTENTS

CONTENTS

CONTENTS

Dear Busy Executive:

In spite of today's high-tech environment, nothing has replaced the impact of the personal letter . . . even if it's delivered by electronic mail.

A good letter can

--motivate other people to do what you want them to do

--create a spirit of cooperation and "team play"

--maintain friendly relations with important contacts

--convey a difficult message in a tactful and courteous way

--create a dynamic, positive impression of you and your organization.

You can write effective letters without taxing your energy and your patience. With the techniques in this book, letter writing will become a powerful tool you call on routinely to accomplish your business and personal goals.

For many years my work has involved helping people write more effectively. I've used this experience to create 365 model letters with 1,578 alternate phrases for customizing to suit your personal style, the reader's personality, and the occasion.

There are model letters for even the most difficult situations--apologies, complaints, condolences, credit problems, employee terminations, crisis management, delays due to misfortune, neutral references, and more.

You choose the model that fits your situation, plus any alternate phrasing you wish, and customize the letter so that it sounds like "you."

You can even photocopy a model letter, write in alternate phrasing, and have an instant letter ready to submit for typing or to put into your word processor. (The publisher has specifically authorized photocopying of the model letters to make the book easy to use.)

To get started, just select a topic that interests you and try your hand at using the model letter.

You'll be pleasantly surprised at how easy it is to write letters that say what you want to say in a concise, organized, and friendly way.

Dianna Booher

INTRODUCTION

ESSENTIALS IN COMPOSING YOUR OWN LETTERS OR CUSTOMIZING OURS

Your writing characterizes you and your company in much the same way your telephone voice does. Consider your own reaction to a phone call from someone you've never met: The caller has a deep, full, gravellike voice. Do you imagine a large-framed male about fifty, with dark hair and perhaps a full beard? On the other hand, when the telephone voice is shaky, high-pitched, and stammering, do you imagine a non-assertive, wimpy-looking character?

Those telephone-voice characterizations may be highly inaccurate, as you've probably discovered on seeing those callers in person. Nevertheless, most of us continue to jump to such conclusions.

In much the same way, your letter writing characterizes you. Your customers, clients, and colleagues may not be able to watch you make decisions, manage time, or negotiate a sale, but they see the result of your work. That result, in the form of a letter or memo, is what finally circulates around your organization and the client's.

Also, the higher you go in the corporate structure, the more your letters circulate and the more important your communication becomes. Effective letters can do much to sell your organization and your own skills.

Letters

- help you conduct business productively

- substitute for personal visits

- impress clients and customers with your product or service

- maintain your network of associates

- create or maintain your reputation

- generate goodwill.

SO WHY DO WE HATE TO WRITE LETTERS?

"I hate to write, but I love to have written" is the sentiment often tossed around among profes-

sional authors. Letter writing can be a time-consuming, agonizing process.

We've all heard the general rules about effective letter writing: Be concise. Be courteous. Be conversational. Be clear. Be informative. Be positive. Use small words, short sentences, and short paragraphs. Avoid clichés. Avoid sexism. So much for good principles. (If you need more explanation about these generalities, you may want to see one of my earlier books, *Would You Put That in Writing?*)

This book, however, takes these rules a step further in giving 365 models and 1,578 alternate phrases in 154 categories to serve as concrete examples: Of courteous letters to a client who owes your organization money. Of positive statements in a "no" message to a client. Of handling public relations functions with the press. Of complimenting a speaker on an effective presentation. Of referring a prospective employee to a colleague. Of turning down a job applicant.

Effective letters don't just happen; they take thought. When I ask participants in my writing workshops to list problems they have as communicators, the most frequent responses I hear are "getting started" and "knowing exactly what I want to say and in what order." Once writers analyze the audience and set out their own purpose and plan, they generally have no problem drafting an effective letter.

Therefore, the aim of this book is to provide the models to start your thinking process.

HOW TO USE THIS BOOK

1. Skim the table of contents for your subject category of interest.
2. Turn to the pages dealing with that subject and read the model letters given there to start your thinking process about content to be included in your own letter. Consider your audience, your purpose, and your own personality.
3. Refer then to the "Guidelines and Alternate Phrases" heading that begins the models in each subject category and read the additional suggested phrases.
4. Select the model letter and any alternate

phrases you want to use to customize the letter to your personality and situation. (Some models and alternate phrases are generic enough to be used as is. In other letters, you will need to add, delete, or rephrase sentences or paragraphs to refer more specifically to your reader and situation.)

5. Turn to Appendix A for answers to any questions about letter format such as complimentary closings, subject lines, copy notations, and so forth.

6. Keeping the book at hand, dictate your own letter and drop in your customized phrases. If you prefer to customize the letter by hand rather than by dictation, use the form in Appendix B with its prompting questions. (You may want to duplicate this form and keep copies at hand to help you customize and dictate all your letters so there is no miscommunication with your typist about the final document.)

7. Save a copy of each letter you customize so that eventually you will have your own model letter collection reflecting your own personality.

SELECTING A STYLE TO SUIT YOUR PERSONALITY

At this point, you may be asking: If I'm using a book of models, how can I possibly make my letter any different from the next person's?

Learn the thinking process behind letter writing and then let your own personality come through in your own phrasing.

An appropriate writing style is one of those terms difficult to define, but easy to recognize. For example, examine the four versions of the following announcement:

We are pleased to announce a new awards program for our employees.

We are extremely pleased to make you aware by way of this announcement that we are currently beginning a new awards program for all our loyal, dedicated employees who have consistently performed well (and continue to do so) over the years.

Please be advised that an innovative system of awards for all personnel is herewith being instituted by management.

Employees! A new awards program!

You see what I mean about personality being reflected in an individual's writing style? Some people have a lifeless, cold, impersonal style. Others have a warm, conversational, even colorful, style.

Let's delve into the subject of style in a little more detail. Notice how each of the following letters varies depending on writer, reader, subject, and purpose.

Why is this letter passive, stuffy, and impersonal? First, the surname salutation sets up a formal tone. Also, the opening sentences make this a "company" transaction, not a personal one. You'll notice that the writer has been "assigned" to accompany the new sales rep.

The passivity of the writer comes across in his use of passive-voice verbs: "it is suggested," "it is recommended," "pricing will be discussed," "questions should be directed." (Passive: *The orders will be reviewed by my staff.* Active: *My staff will review the orders.* Passive: *Your business is sincerely appreciated.* Active: *We appreciate your business.*)

In fact, the writer has practically taken himself out of the letter altogether; the reader should direct questions to "his office" rather than to him. He uses very few personal pronouns. Note, too, the stuffy choice of words such as "peruse." Finally, he chooses one of the most formal closings possible, "Yours truly."

What is your impression of this writer and his attitude toward his "assignment" to introduce the new employee to colleagues?

Dear Mr. Jones:

Amco would like to take this opportunity to welcome you as an employee. Our company has determined you to be a valuable asset and is anticipating your contribution to the organization over the years.

As Tom Massey, regional director, has requested, I have been assigned to accompany you to the next staff meeting in Milwaukee and introduce you to the other sales representatives from across the country.

Before our June 6 trip, it is suggested that you familiarize yourself with the shop operations here. Secondly, it would be appropriate to set up meetings with old customers to inform them that their accounts will now be serviced by you. Any current orders these customers have, of course, should be taken on these visits.

Pricing and general administrative duties will be discussed during the course of the trip to Milwaukee. It is also recommended that you peruse the attached agenda prior to the meeting.

Any further questions about our upcoming trip to the regional sales meeting should be addressed to my office directly at 459/244-2345.

Yours truly,

Harold Hart
Sales Representative

How would you characterize this writer? Notice that he uses a warm, personal greeting. His comments seem to be team player to team player rather than boss to subordinate. He also uses the direct approach: "I suggest" and "please call" rather than awkward and passive phrases such as "it is suggested" and "calls should be directed." He uses the colloquialism "how you fit into the picture" and the witty understatement "we wouldn't object if you took a few orders." Also, notice the frequent mention of people in his writing—you, our, I. Finally, the first-name salutation and the informal closing add warmth.

This writer sounds agreeable and ready to help the new employee be successful.

Dear Robert:

We would like to welcome you as a part of the Region 6 sales team. Tom Massey tells me that you are a super salesman; therefore, we're eagerly anticipating your contribution to our team efforts this year!

As Tom may have mentioned to you, he has asked that I accompany you to the next staff meeting in Milwaukee and introduce you to the other salespeople. Therefore, I'll look forward to meeting you on June 6 and will do my best to give you an overview of the regional goals and how you fit into the picture.

In the meantime, I suggest that you familiarize yourself with the shop operations here and then set up meetings with present customers to let them know that you will now be handling their accounts. Of course, we wouldn't object if you took any orders on these initial, get-acquainted calls!

Our traveling together should also give us time to discuss any other questions you may have, such as pricing matters and general administrative duties. Also, you may want to review the attached agenda before our staff meeting.

I'm looking forward to getting to know you and working with you to make ours the top team in the nation. Until I see you on June 6, if you have further questions about travel arrangements for Milwaukee, please call me directly at 459/244-2345.

Cordially,

Harold Hart
Sales Representative

Notice that the writer has dropped the "dear" and addressed the reader directly in a chatty style. The closing is equally cordial and informal. Energy and excitement come through in the punctuation and in the short sentences and sentence fragments: "Welcome aboard." "But more about that later." "Looking forward to meeting you."

Notice also the personal warmth that comes through in the short, direct, informal phrasing:

". . . questions about what to do and how to do it."

In these three versions, we've gone from the stuffy "peruse," to the formal "review," to the informal "look over." The colloquial phrases give the letter an informal tone: "run around," "go-ahead," "lifeline," "uncharted customer waters," "show you the ropes."

This writer seems to be a fun, energetic, helpful sort of guy who rarely meets a stranger.

Robert,

Welcome aboard! We're excited about having you on the Chicago team and are ready to go for the big win next December on awards night.

As a new team player, I'm sure you have some questions about what you are supposed to do and how you're supposed to do it. Well, I've got a few answers for you.

Tom Massey, regional director, has given me the go-ahead to accompany you to the next staff meeting in Milwaukee and introduce you to the other reps there. In case Tom hasn't told you, these Region 6 guys are great to work with and will be eager to show you the ropes. In fact, they have even been known to throw out a lifeline for a fellow team member in uncharted customer waters! But more about that later.

Because all good sales reps have a plan, here's one I think will be beneficial for you before the Milwaukee meeting: First, familiarize yourself with the shop operations here. Second, try to set up meetings with old customers to let them know you're the "new kid on the block" and will be giving them great service on their accounts. Of course, we wouldn't be offended if you took a few orders on this initial go-around!

As for questions you probably have about the pricing and general administrative duties, we'll get to those on the way to Milwaukee. You may also want to look over the attached agenda for the staff meeting.

If you have any trouble with travel arrangements, give me a call directly at 459/244-2345, and I'll see what I can do. Looking forward to meeting you.

Regards,

Harold Hart
Sales Representative

INTRODUCTION

There's no doubt this writer is direct, personal, and informal. The question is, has he become too familiar and flippant? Notice he uses a nickname—but what if Robert doesn't like to be called Bob?—and has dropped the closing altogether. The opening paragraph has a standoffish, maybe even arrogant tone: Are you as good as the rest of the sales team? Let's see you prove it.

Additionally, note the air of superiority: "I'll be your sponsor." "Just hold any questions." Also, he no longer "suggests" that the new sales rep familiarize himself with the shop and call on customers; instead, he turns his statements into commands: "Familiarize. . . ." "Call. . . ." "Take orders. . . ."

Finally, note the familiarity that he's taken in making a derogatory remark about the airlines and even about his fellow employees. How does he know the reader's brother-in-law is not CEO of one of the airlines or a sales rep from another region? Will such negative comments offend?

Bob,

Tom Massey tells me we have a new sales rep aboard. Let me tell you that the pace is fast and that your colleagues in Region 6 are outstanding sales people. We hope you will be eager to join the fast track with us.

I'll be your sponsor to the upcoming June 6 Milwaukee staff meeting. At that time, I can make appropriate introductions to other sales reps across the country. Some you'll want to get to know much better, and some are your typical you-know-whats found in every organization.

Before the trip, you should do three things: 1) Familiarize yourself with the shop operations here. 2) Call on old customers to tell them that you will be handling their accounts now. 3) Take orders from existing customers.

Just hold any questions you have about pricing and general administrative duties until we fly to Milwaukee. If the airline pulls their usual screw-ups, we'll probably have a couple of hours' delay on one end or the other. If you've got a minute, you may want to glance over the attached agenda for the staff meeting--in case they decide to stick to it for a change.

Call me at 459/244-2345 if you have any problems.

Harry

INTRODUCTION

Regardless of how you react to the previous four letters, you can see how writing style conveys personality. Rarely do you want to choose a dull, impersonal tone such as in version 1 or a sarcastic, flippant tone such as in version 4. But either of versions 2 or 3 would be appropriate on occasion, depending on a specific reader, content, and purpose.

To sum up, when choosing an appropriate style, consider sentence length, punctuation, word choice, passive and active verbs, salutations, and closings.

The general trend in business writing today is to be conversational, courteous, and direct. But that trend has to be tailored to your purpose and your personality.

Basically, then, getting started with the appropriate style in letter writing involves five key steps:

STEP 1: CONSIDER YOUR AUDIENCE.

Are you writing up, down, or laterally? How well do you know your reader? Are there any hidden audiences? How will your reader use this information?

STEP 2: PLAN YOUR MESSAGE IN THE **MADE** FORMAT.

M: What is the key *message* of interest to this reader?
A: What *action* do you want the reader to take?
What *action* do you plan to take next?
D: What *details* need elaboration? Who, what, when, where, why, how, how much?
E: What *enclosures* have you sent along to make the message clearer or the action easier?

STEP 3: ANTICIPATE SPECIAL PROBLEMS IN YOUR READER'S REACTION AND ADJUST YOUR PLAN.

Is this a touchy subject? If so, do you need to be more tactful? Have you eliminated any "fight" words or buzz terms and phrases that will unnecessarily offend? Are you sure this is an appropriate subject to write about, or should you talk face to face or by phone? Do you have the right audience? Perhaps you should not write at all.

Is this a disappointing message? If so, perhaps you should bury the key message at the end of the letter and first lead your reader through your reasons for the message.

Is this a low-priority message? Can you improve the tone to make it more motivational, adding either an incentive for action or a consequence for inaction? Can you mention the name of someone with more clout in the organization? Can you use a more upbeat tone?

Do you need to persuade or simply to inform? If you want to persuade, have you given incentives and adequate evidence or reasons? Is the tone motivational? If you simply want to inform, have you been direct, clear, and concise with the message?

Should you be passive or direct? If you want to be passive, have you used passive-voice verbs and vague generalizations? If you want to be direct, are your verbs active and your words unambiguous? Is the action to be taken specific? Have you eliminated any "fight" words?

STEP 4: DRAFT YOUR LETTER.

STEP 5: EDIT FOR GRAMMAR, STYLE, CONCISENESS, AND CLARITY.

Most of the models in this book will exemplify a personal, direct, conversational style. Others are formal, forceful, and even threatening. Whatever your audience or subject demands, you'll find several alternate sentences and phrases provided with each category model. I suggest that you make each letter reflect your own personality and then begin compiling a personal sample-letter book for yourself and others in your organization.

Your image, your time, and your productivity depend on an effective writing style.

The Letters

ACCOMPLISHMENTS/To Document to Colleagues and Superiors

GUIDELINES AND ALTERNATE PHRASES

GIVE THE BIG-PICTURE MESSAGE OF YOUR OVERALL CONTRIBUTION TO THE COMPANY OR DIVISION.

PRESENT THE SPECIFIC FACTS TO BACK UP YOUR CLAIMS.

INTERPRET THE SIGNIFICANCE OF YOUR ACHIEVEMENTS.

We've had the highest overall growth rate in the last decade.

This is a 22% increase in our newest product line.

This marketing effort brought in 68 new clients, the most significant "new-business" effort in the past two years.

This additional program means that we now have 85% of our work force trained in supervisory skills.

BE BOTH MODEST AND CONFIDENT IN TONE.

THANK OTHERS FOR THEIR HELP IN ACHIEVING THE GOAL.

To each one of you, my sincerest thanks.

To each one of you: You have gained my utmost respect.

Without the expertise of our engineering staff, this new model would still be "chasing around in my subconscious."

I thank each of you for your individual contributions to the project.

With your continued support and input, we plan to continue this same pattern of achievement.

Dear Herb and Colleagues:

By now I am sure many of you have heard rumors about our most recent circulation figures for the year ended June 30. The good news specifically:

Daily	678,344
Sunday	877,455
Post Parade	957,875

These numbers represent significant gains (23%) from a year ago. Our competitors have experienced reductions from previous statements, leaving us with a total daily lead of more than 224,000 and a total Sunday lead of more than 344,000.

The competitive business supplement hasn't even gotten off the ground--even with our model marketing efforts to follow. Our growth is even more remarkable when you consider that barely four years ago, we trailed on our Sunday circulation by 41,000 and on our daily circulation by 23,000.

This achievement represents extraordinary effort by many people in every department--particularly those who conceived the phenomenally successful advertising campaign for the Post Parade. Our Circulation Department has depended on them every step of the way as we forged ahead with both sales and service matters.

We know that the competition will be even more intense in the future, but with your help we intend to surpass ourselves and set our own unparalleled growth records for next year.

For all these accomplishments in the past twelve months, I offer my sincerest thanks and congratulations to everyone who has had a part in reaching this goal. Onward!

Sincerely,

GUIDELINES AND ALTERNATE PHRASES

FOCUS ON THE POSITIVE RESOLUTION OF THE PROBLEM.

DISARM THE READER BY ADMITTING A CAUSE FOR COMPLAINT RATHER THAN GLOSSING OVER THE PROBLEM.

EXPLAIN BRIEFLY AND POSITIVELY HOW THE MISTAKE OCCURRED.

> Although we take great pride in our thorough methods for safe packing, someone apparently let this package slip by without the usual precaution.

> Computers and people do make mistakes—both goofed this time.

> I simply did not relay all the complete details to that department. Please accept my apology for that oversight.

SOUND EAGER, NOT BEGRUDGING, TO MAKE THE ADJUSTMENT AND REGAIN THE CUSTOMER'S GOODWILL.

> Thank you for bringing this to our attention.

> You are right about our error. We are happy to. . . .

> We are very embarrassed. You must think that we have to work really hard to mess up things so badly! We are doubly chagrined because you are a special customer to us, and we highly value your business. Please bear with us; we will get the order right this time and make sure that we improve our service to you in the future.

> When any company serves as many customers as we do, there will inevitably be errors from time to time. Nevertheless, even one is distressing to us—particularly when that customer is as good as you have been.

> Thank you for pointing out the error so promptly, before it caused all of us even more problems.

> Thank you for giving us an opportunity to correct the situation to your satisfaction.

MAKE AN ADJUSTMENT APPROPRIATE TO THE ERROR. THAT IS, DON'T APOLOGIZE PROFUSELY FOR A MINOR PROBLEM. SUCH EFFUSIVENESS SOUNDS INSINCERE. LIKEWISE, DON'T GLOSS OVER SERIOUS ERRORS; SHOW APPROPRIATE CONCERN AND MAKE AMENDS.

MENTION ANY SAFEGUARDS YOU'VE TAKEN TO PREVENT A RECURRENCE OF THE PROBLEM.

REESTABLISH RAPPORT WITH THE CUSTOMER—ASSUME THAT ALL IS WELL AGAIN.

Dear Ms. Smith:

We are pleased to tell you that we have rescinded our proposed changes to the mileage requirements for travel awards valid for use to and from Singapore. We have listened to our customers and are not too big to admit we have made a mistake. As a result, we can still offer the four first-class tickets you wanted to claim for your frequent-flyer mileage.

At the time you were denied those tickets we had just recently made the decision to change our policy and had not received any feedback from customers. Consequently, we are happy you wrote again and gave us an opportunity to provide the extra tickets due you under the old terms.

I know the delay in getting your tickets must have created some anxiety on your part about your planned family vacation, and we are sorry for the misunderstanding.

Please do have a nice, enjoyable vacation with these tickets. Thank you for choosing our airline for all your travel needs.

Cordially,

GUIDELINES AND ALTERNATE PHRASES

SHARE SOME OF THE BLAME FOR THE PROBLEM, IF POSSIBLE.

We always try to have our sales people emphasize the importance of following the instruction booklets carefully. Apparently, Mr. Smith was not emphatic on that point.

Although we try in every way possible to make sure the warranty terms are clearly understood, evidently we failed in this case. But please note in the first paragraph of the contract letter. . . .

I should have reminded you of our earlier discussion as soon as I was aware there might be a problem.

Perhaps I should have phoned you personally to make you aware of the situation rather than simply conveying the details to your assistant.

TELL BRIEFLY AND POSITIVELY HOW THE MISUNDERSTANDING OCCURRED.

We have no other explanation about the damage other than that it must have occurred after delivery to your site. Can you provide further documentation that the problem was ours? If so, please write again.

Because our documents say the merchandise was received at your address and signed for by Mr. Brown on June 10, we can only suggest that the weather damage occurred after that time.

STATE TACTFULLY WHAT YOU CAN AND CANNOT DO ABOUT THE MISUNDERSTANDING. BE SIMPLE AND CLEAR.

We, therefore, cannot replace the equipment, but we will be happy to repair it at a cost of $XX. Please let us know what you decide.

Since we cannot replace the item, please let us know what other actions you'd like us to take. Should we repair it and send you the bill, return the merchandise to you as it is, or simply discard it here?

Because the terms of our agreement were not met, we must decline to offer the discount. I'm sure you understand that we cannot show partiality to one customer without making other customers feel they have been treated unfairly.

Although there is the temptation to make an exception in your case, that would simply not be fair to others involved.

ASSUME THAT THE READER, ONCE HE OR SHE UNDERSTANDS THE CORRECT FACTS OF THE MATTER, WILL ACCEPT YOUR POSITION AND CONTINUE THE BUSINESS RELATIONSHIP.

We trust that you understand the reasons behind our decision and hope we can continue to serve you in the future.

I'm sorry we can't help you with this particular request, but under the circumstances, I think you'll agree with our position.

I'm sure you understand our plight in this whole matter. Again, thank you for discussing the matter with us.

I think you will understand our position. If, however, there are other circumstances of which we're unaware, please write again and we will certainly want to do whatever is appropriate then.

Thank you for giving us an opportunity to explain our situation and position to you.

We value your goodwill and want to continue doing business with you as we have over the years.

We value your business and want to continue to serve you in the future.

We look forward to your giving us another opportunity to serve you.

Dear Mark,

We fully appreciate your patience and desire to work with us in resolving your color print problems with the J267 printer. We regret the misunderstanding that leaves you without the $200 diskette that would enable your printer to function as expected with the graphics program you purchased from Harborough Company.

Although we do have a contractual agreement to market Harborough's graphics program, we have no legally acceptable way to provide you with the $200 diskette you need to make the printer work. We have made further calls and completed our research into the problem and have concluded, just as you did, that the special diskette is all you need to perform your printing tasks.

We realize that this is an additional expenditure you had not planned on. However, we are sure you understand that we have no authority to offer you this diskette from Harborough.

Please do let us know what other arrangements you are able to make with the graphics company. We are eager to have you turn out the fine quality printing jobs that our printer can provide.

Sincerely,

Dear Mr. Jones:

We have received your request for an extension of your support on the System 8888. We know how infuriating Murphy's Law can be, and you must be experiencing that frustration just now--three weeks after the support ends, you have questions about a new application.

But our free support service provided with purchase must fall within a three-month period beginning with the date of installation of your CPU. Our records indicate an installation date at your site of May 5, 19--; therefore, we regret that your free support service expired August 5, 19--, just before you ran into difficulties. If I'm wrong on these dates, please let me know immediately.

There is, of course, no problem in extending our support service to you for any length of time you desire. I've taken the liberty of enclosing an extension agreement in case you decide to do that.

Thank you for letting us serve you, and we have been happy to answer your computer questions during the past months. We hope you're enjoying the equipment and benefitting from the increased productivity of your word processing staff.

Cordially,

Dear Ms. Thatcher:

We received your letter asking us to investigate the overgrowth of pecan trees on your property and have looked into the matter.

Our inspector tells me that the trees to which you refer are not actually on our 10′ × 10′ regulator-station site, but are instead actually located on your private property.

When such trees are cut down, there is always the possibility of damage to other above-ground structures. Therefore, as you can understand, we would not want to be responsible for any such damage to your private property and have a policy that we cannot provide this tree-cutting service for private-property owners.

As I'm sure you'll agree, throughout the many years of our lease of the regulator-station site, we have always given special attention to its appearance and have kept it in very satisfactory condition. We regret that the overgrown trees have now made it unsightly from your kitchen window.

Attached is a list of companies in your area that can provide you with this tree-cutting service. I hope this is helpful.

Sincerely,

GUIDELINES AND ALTERNATE PHRASES

MENTION THE OCCASION YOU'RE CELEBRATING.

We've passed a milestone and we're celebrating. This month marks our fifth year in the Brownville business community.

We'd like you to join us in celebrating our fifteenth anniversary.

EXPRESS APPRECIATION FOR THOSE WHO HAVE HELPED YOU GROW. YOU MAY OFFER A COMMEMORATION GIFT, A PRODUCT OR SERVICE DISCOUNT, OR SIMPLY A GOODWILL STATEMENT.

Through the years, we have continued to appreciate the goodwill and business of customers such as you.

We want to take this opportunity to recognize and thank the valued customers who have expressed confidence in us and who have been so loyal to our products.

To show you how much we have appreciated your business over the years, we want to offer you a 15% discount on any supplies you order during August. To receive this discount, simply present this letter with your order.

We are mailing separately a copy of *Financial Recordkeeping* as a small token of our appreciation for your business over the years.

END WITH A CHALLENGE FOR THE FUTURE.

We pledge to you our continued very best service. You deserve it.

Thank you for helping make this a great ten years. We plan to keep your needs in mind as we grow.

We plan to keep on listening to your needs, and we will never forget that your ideas and business have helped keep us on target.

We will continue to offer you the best accounting services in the state. Thank you for your patronage.

Dear Mr. Tonette:

We've just flipped the calendar page to our anniversary date--this month marks our tenth year in business in this community. We didn't want to let the occasion pass without telling you that your patronage means a great deal to us.

In looking back over our shoulder from that first day until now, we first remember the good customers such as you who have placed their confidence in us and have been so loyal to our products and services. We are well aware that our growth is due, in large part, to your trust in us.

We plan happily to continue in the years ahead to provide you the service you've come to expect. Thank you for your part in our success.

Sincerely,

ANNIVERSARY DATES/Of Individual's Service to Your Firm

GUIDELINES AND ALTERNATE PHRASES

MENTION THE ANNIVERSARY FIRST AND WHAT YOU PLAN TO DO, IF ANYTHING, TO COMMEMORATE THE OCCASION—A CERTIFICATE, LUNCHEON, BONUS GIFT.

In an effort to convey our heartfelt thanks for your 20 years with Helco, we have prepared a book of congratulatory letters from your friends and associates.

My, how time flies when you're having fun. You may not have noticed, but we at Helco have had much pleasure working with you for the last 20 years.

Another 20 years and what do we have to show for them? We at Helco can say that we've profitted wonderfully from having a dedicated, talented employee such as you with us through the years. We hope the feeling of satisfaction and friendship is mutual.

Jill, how about joining us for lunch on Friday, May 6, at 12 noon? Oh, one more thing—you're the guest of honor! Congratulations on your 20-year anniversary with the company.

What do you do when you have an employee who is productive, talented, creative, loyal, and an all-around nice guy? Well, in lieu of a 90-day trip around the world, we offer our heartfelt thanks for the privilege of working with you the last 20 years.

INCLUDE AT LEAST ONE OR TWO SPECIFIC ACCOMPLISHMENTS OR CONTRIBUTIONS. MANY WRITERS THINK THAT VAGUE, GLOBAL COMMENDATIONS SOUND BETTER THAN SPECIFIC ONES. NOT SO. THE MORE SPECIFIC, THE MORE SINCERE THE COMMENDATION SOUNDS.

I sincerely appreciate the long hours, the furrowed brow over projects gone awry, the creativity in problem-solving, and the can-do attitude you have displayed through the ups and downs of these 20 years.

We have especially appreciated your willingness to work on any client project that came along. In fact, I can't think of a single project you refused—and all have been handled with such class!

I want to thank you especially for your dedication to the needs of our customers. We've noted so many occasions when you've stayed after hours to handle a crisis, when you've called in from vacation to answer customers' requests, and when you've even driven across the city in a severe thunderstorm to handle an on-site problem.

Your telephone skills have created just the impression we have wanted to convey to our clients. In fact, your telephone conversations have often had better response than some of our on-site sales calls! We thank you sincerely.

LOOK FORWARD TO THEIR FUTURE. WHAT KIND OF ACHIEVEMENTS OR ACCOMPLISHMENTS DO YOU EXPECT ON THEIR BEHALF?

If the past is any indication of the future, we know that your contributions will lead us to many more profitable, enjoyable years in the computer industry.

Please keep that same congenial spirit as we move into the next decade together.

Our thoughts are with you today; employees like you keep us in business.

Best wishes for 20 more good ones!

Dear Cheryl:

We are pleased to commemorate your twenty years of service as a part of the Helco team by asking you to be the guest of honor at a 12 noon, May 6, luncheon at the Houstonian.

Our success and expansion into a three-state region are directly attributable to employees like you who have stayed with us through the years, learned our customers' needs, and then "pulled out all the stops" to see that they got what they wanted. Specifically, I recall your invaluable help in getting the media attention we needed to go into the Atlanta market.

You have shown our new employees what continual education means to the business by always being one of the first to avail yourself of new training seminars. We also have appreciated your willingness to offer your time to professional groups outside the organization working to improve the way we do business.

We're looking forward to the luncheon and more time to express our deepest appreciation for your contribution to the company, as well as your gift of friendship to those of us who work closely with you. Best wishes in the years ahead as you lead the way to more markets and better customer service.

Cordially,

ANNIVERSARY DATES/Of Client's or Customer's Business

MENTION THE REASON FOR THE LETTER—THE ANNIVERSARY DATE.

Fifty years is a long time to maintain the excellent reputation your company has.

During these last 20 years, your company name has become almost a household word in our community.

Congratulations. We've just been informed that you're celebrating your thirtieth year in the automotive business.

GIVE AT LEAST ONE SPECIFIC COMPLIMENT: EITHER MENTION AN ACCOMPLISHMENT OR TWO, OR STATE WHAT YOU APPRECIATE ABOUT THE COMPANY.

We've particularly appreciated your considerable effort to pay us so promptly each month.

Your prompt delivery of equipment is one of the things that always stands out in my mind—we appreciate such effort to meet our special needs and timetables.

Your service people have always demonstrated a highly professional manner and courtesy toward our staff.

Your sales staff has always proved so knowledgeable about any questions we've had through the years.

EXPRESS YOUR APPRECIATION FOR THEIR PATRONAGE.

Thank you for your business.

We appreciate your attitude about doing business.

We consider you a friend as well as a customer.

Clients such as you make our job easy.

Thank you for the confidence you've placed in our company.

We appreciate your trust and confidence through the past 20 years.

I can't think of a single client relationship I've enjoyed more.

We value your business a great deal.

You have our heartfelt gratitude for your patronage.

Please know how very much we appreciate your business.

LOOK FORWARD TO A CONTINUED BUSINESS RELATIONSHIP.

We look forward to a continued, mutually beneficial relationship with you during the coming years.

We will continue to do everything possible to maintain your trust in our expertise.

We wish you continued success.

Best wishes to you and your staff for the decade to come.

We wish you every success as you continue to grow.

Best of everything to you as you expand your services in the years ahead.

A pleasant relationship with clients such as you is one of the things that makes our business so enjoyable.

We look forward to many more years together.

Dear Ms. Stein:

I received the notice of your anniversary date in last week's mail. Congratulations on your exceptional growth during the last ten years.

As one of the old-timers in the community, I can remember when you began operations here in Belfast. If I remember from our earlier conversations, you were in a 43-foot trailer, with less than 12 members enrolled. As I understand it, your membership now exceeds 150,000 and is increasing by an average of 100 each week. Your living-donor program and fund drive stand out as two of your most noteworthy accomplishments during the last few years. In summary, you have grown from a small-town service to national recognition.

All of these successes, I'm sure, are due largely to the fine employees working continuously to make sure the membership's needs are met--almost before the members themselves even perceive a need.

I'm proud to be associated with such a fine organization. You richly deserve such success and recognition.

Sincerely,

GUIDELINES AND ALTERNATE PHRASES

ANNOUNCE THE MERGER, ACQUISITION, OR RESTRUCTURING UP FRONT.

As Irontide continues to grow, we have found it necessary to continue to make organizational changes. These changes are beneficial for all our employees because we have opened new opportunities for advancement.

The many rumors you have heard do have some basis in fact—we are pleased to announce that. . . .

PROVIDE DETAILS TO THE MOST PRESSING QUESTIONS EMPLOYEES WILL HAVE.

We will continue to operate under the name of Irontide.

This acquisition will, of course, dictate significant restructuring of our marketing division. I've outlined below the major reporting changes. . . .

Please rest assured that your jobs will in no way be affected.

Your retirement funds are entirely secure, and we have plans to continue our policies as in the previous years.

We will, of course, be making some structural changes within our marketing effort—expanding our staff, not reducing it.

Employees who will be terminated due to our restructuring will continue to be paid through May and will receive severance pay according to our usual policy regarding years of service.

Medical and hospitalization coverage for these employees will continue through August.

Our Personnel Office will provide out-placement assistance, including resumé preparation, interview techniques, and aptitude testing.

PROMISE TO PROVIDE OTHER DETAILS AS SOON AS THEY BECOME AVAILABLE.

Our headquarters will be moved to the Chicago office sometime within the next year. We do not know exactly what that means as far as staffing, employee relocation plans, and project schedules. However, as soon as we complete our studies and make these decisions, we will keep you informed.

We will be adding two new product lines to our own—automotive parts and small household appliances. Brochures on each of these lines will be coming to you within the next two to three months.

BE OPTIMISTIC IN TONE.

We think you will be as happy about the merger as we are, and we look forward to expanding our operations all over North America.

Rumor has it that most of our employees are quite eager to complete the final transactions that will make us the largest retailer in the state.

Keep up the good work. There's a bright future ahead.

I'm sure you will continue to be as capable and productive in this new venture as you have proved to be in the past. With your help, we will continue to serve our customers in the way they've come to expect.

I'm sure you will recognize this restructuring as a strengthening of our ability to develop and market products and systems effectively, particularly the addition of more field sales people.

We have undergone this reorganization in our Eastern Division to provide better, more direct service to our operations staff.

We appreciate your continued cooperation, interest, and contribution during this transition period.

To All Employees of Irontide:

Today, Grafton, Inc. announced that an agreement has been reached with certain investors to acquire the stock of Irontide. This agreement is subject to several conditions that must be met before the acquisition is final, and this negotiation process may require up to five months. Until this agreement is final, there will be no organizational changes within our company.

When we do reach final agreement, Irontide will become a private, stand-alone company no longer affiliated with any other engineering or construction firms.

The investor group has requested that existing management of Irontide remain with the company after the transaction is complete. Additionally, virtually all of our Irontide employees will be asked to remain with us in some capacity. Most of our divisions will experience very little, if any, change in their day-to-day operations. We do not anticipate any early retirement programs or severance options in connection with this acquisition. We also expect all benefits to remain as they now are.

The next few weeks will be busy, exciting, and challenging ones. Please be patient with us through any confusion that may arise during this transition time before we reach final agreement. We will keep you informed of all the events and plans as we learn of them ourselves.

Sincerely,

Dear Fellow Employees:

We are in the process of making a number of changes in our worldwide manufacturing operations that will require us to establish an after-tax profit reserve of about $555,000,000.

As you can imagine, this decision to establish a restructuring reserve has been given thorough and deliberate consideration by the company's management. We are convinced that it's the right thing to do for the overall health of our company. As a result of this reserve, we can become more cost competitive and continue to bring innovative products to our customers.

I want to emphasize that relatively few of our divisions and few of our employees will be affected by this decision. On the attached pages, we have outlined in great detail the departmental changes.

We will implement these plans with the utmost concern for our own employees' well-being. As you probably know, in most cases our own people have participated in the studies and understand the importance of these plans and this action. At the few sites where our studies are still incomplete, we will continue to listen to our own staff and work closely with them, keeping you informed every step of the way.

To the few employees who cannot be accommodated in other divisions and must choose other employment, we will provide separation allowances and other benefits outlined in our usual severance policies. Finally, we pledge those leaving the company every reasonable assistance in finding suitable employment.

In closing, let me say that I am pleased to make this restructuring announcement. We have a fine company--a company with people who have the highest values and interest for their colleagues. I'm confident you will come to share my enthusiasm for this decision.

Yours truly,

To the Burford-Hymil Organization:

Our company officials and those of Freeman Inc. announced today that an agreement has been reached on the merger of our two companies, to be effective May 9. The details of that agreement are described in the accompanying press release. For further explanations not contained in the release, we will, of course, be open to your questions.

I simply want to tell you how pleased I am about this merger. Freeman Inc. is a fine company, a company with values and people similar to our own. In the future, as you come in contact with these new members of the Burford-Hymil organization, I'm confident you will come to share my great enthusiasm for this relationship.

Sincerely,

GUIDELINES AND ALTERNATE PHRASES

GIVE EXPLICIT DETAILS ABOUT TIME, PLACE, AND SCHEDULE.

You are cordially requested to attend the Farnsworth Engineering, Inc. shareholders meeting at 7:00 p.m. on August 17, 19--, in the company's headquarters office at 15567 Acton Avenue, Memphis, Tennessee.

Farnsworth Engineering, Inc. will hold its annual shareholders meeting at. . . .

You are cordially encouraged to attend the annual meeting of shareholders that will be held in our offices in Houston, Texas, on May 4, 19--, at 10:00 a.m. For those of you who cannot be present at this 34th annual meeting, we urge that you participate by indicating your choices on the enclosed proxy and completing and returning it immediately.

INCLUDE THE PURPOSE OF THE MEETING OR PROXY VOTE.

The meeting is being held to. . . .

The purpose of the meeting is. . . .

The agenda items are as follows: . . .

Matters to be discussed at the meeting are: . . .

In addition to acting on the election of directors and ratification of the appointment of auditors, you are being asked to approve amendments related to our Restated Certification of Incorporation.

Our agenda calls for a discussion and/or action on the following items: . . .

MAKE IT EASY FOR THE READER TO COMPLETE ANY PROXY FORM CORRECTLY AND TO RETURN IT PROMPTLY.

Please sign, date, and mail promptly the enclosed proxy in the envelope provided.

So that your stock ownership may be represented at the annual meeting, please complete, sign, date, and return the enclosed proxy form promptly. By doing this, you are assured of representation. Should you attend the annual meeting, you retain the right to vote in person even though you may have previously mailed in the enclosed proxy form.

Gentlemen and Ladies:

The annual meeting of Varlco Incorporated will be held on Wednesday, May 6, 19--, beginning at 12:00 noon in the Congress Room of the Artral Hotel located at 3100 Breckenridge, Building 6, Duluth, Georgia.

The meeting is being held for the following purposes:

- To consider amending investment advisory agreements
- To propose a distribution-of-funds plan
- To review compensation of senior executives
- To transact other business that may properly come before the meeting

The trustees have fixed the close of business on March 5, 19--, as the record date for the determination of shareholders entitled to notice of and to vote at the meeting.

If you are unable to attend the meeting, please promptly sign and return the enclosed proxy. Thank you.

We look forward to meeting you on May 6.

Yours truly,

Dear Shareholder:

You are cordially invited to attend the annual meeting of shareholders that will be held at our corporate headquarters, Dallas, Texas, on June 6, 19--, at 12:00 noon. For those of you who cannot be present at this meeting, we urge that you participate by indicating your choices on the enclosed proxy and returning it as soon as possible.

We have also enclosed an agenda listing important matters on which action is expected to be taken during this meeting. It is important that your shares are represented at this meeting, whether or not you are able to attend personally. Accordingly, please sign, date, and mail promptly your proxy in the envelope provided.

On behalf of the Board of Directors, thank you for your encouragement, cooperation, and participation.

Sincerely,

Dear Member:

If you will be unable to attend the 19-- annual meeting on Sunday, June 23, 19--, at the Georgia World Congress Center, Atlanta, Georgia, please complete the following:

I hereby appoint the 19-- Corporate Secretary as my proxy to vote in my name, place, and behalf. This proxy is valid only for the following purposes:

   Amendments to Bylaws, Article VII
   Amendments to Bylaws, Article IX

_____   I VOTE FOR the amendments.
_____   I VOTE AGAINST the amendments.

Signature _____
Printed name _____
Membership number _____

Please return the proxy in the enclosed postage-paid envelope.

Yours truly,

GUIDELINES AND ALTERNATE PHRASES

GIVE A STATE-OF-THE-COMPANY SUMMARY STATEMENT, INCLUDING NEW PRODUCT OR NEW SERVICE INFORMATION, FINANCIAL POSITION, MARKETING MATTERS, PROPOSED NEW VENTURES, LEGAL CONFRONTATIONS.

———————————

EXPLAIN NOT ONLY WHAT HAPPENED, BUT WHY.

———————————

RELATE THE COMPANY'S PERFORMANCE TO THE INDUSTRY AS A WHOLE AND GIVE PROJECTS REGARDING THE FUTURE.

———————————

SHOW MODEST PRIDE IF YOUR COMPANY HAS HAD A SUCCESSFUL YEAR.

———————————

We want to congratulate our employees for their dedication to this new. . . .

We think this attitude has been a successful one in enabling us to. . . .

This approach has turned out to be quite beneficial to. . . .

The risk and hard work of prior years has paid off handsomely this past quarter.

COMMUNICATE MANAGEMENT PHILOSOPHY ABOUT MAJOR EVENTS SUCH AS NEW OR ONGOING MARKET CHANGES, NEW-PRODUCT INTRODUCTIONS, LEGAL BATTLES, ACQUISITIONS, DIVESTITURES, OR CHANGES IN SENIOR MANAGEMENT.

———————————

MENTION ANY COMPANY CIVIC COMMITMENTS.

To Our Shareholders:

Financial Highlights

We submit herewith the Annual Report of The Procter & Gamble Company for the 1987 fiscal year which ended June 30, 1987.

Net sales for the year amounted to $17.0 billion, an increase of 10% over net sales of $15.4 billion for the previous year.

Net earnings for the year amounted to $327 million, and earnings per share amounted to $1.87 per share. Excluding the impact of the reserve to restructure manufacturing operations which we wrote to you about in June, net earnings amounted to $786 million, an increase of 11% over net earnings of $709 million for the previous year. Pre-tax earnings excluding the restructuring reserve were up 21% over the comparable amount a year ago. Earnings per share excluding restructuring were $4.59 which compares with $4.20 for the previous year.

Dividends of $2.70 per common share were paid during the year. The comparable amount for the previous year was $2.625 per share. This marked the 31st consecutive fiscal year of increased dividend payments.

Sesquicentennial Anniversary

This year marks the 150th anniversary of the partnership formed by the Company's founders, candlemaker William Procter and soapmaker James Gamble. We are proud of our long and successful history. As we look to the future, we are committed to do what's right for the long-term interest of our Company so that it will prosper through another 150 years.

Restructuring of Manufacturing Operations

In June, we reported to you that we had established a restructuring reserve for the Company's worldwide manufacturing operations. After final review, this resulted in a pre-tax charge against the fourth quarter of $805 million that reduced net earnings by $459 million, or $2.72 per share. The restructuring program primarily focuses on consolidations of manufacturing operations which result in the conversion or disposal of some plants, buildings and equipment in the United States and abroad.

A significant part of the program includes a sharp curtailment of Duncan Hines cookie manufacturing operations in the United States and Canada. This cutback in resources behind the ready-to-serve cookie business is related directly to the infringement of the Company's patented technology by three major U.S. cookie manufacturers and the injury this has done to our cookie business. We are continuing to pursue these lawsuits in U.S. District Court.

Over the long-term, the restructuring program will result in a stronger, more competitive company and will set the stage for more vigorous growth in the current year and beyond. The program will have a positive impact on cash flow and will not inhibit the Company's ability to pay dividends.

Acquisitions

Earlier this month, the Company announced an agreement to purchase all shares of the Blendax Group subject to governmental agreement. Blendax is a major European manufacturer and marketer of health and beauty aids headquartered in Mainz, Germany. It holds important market positions in the Federal Republic of Germany and Austria. Blendax's products include dentifrice, toothbrushes, oral care appliances, bath and shower foams, hand and body lotions, shampoos, hair colorings and deodorants. Its experienced organization of over 2,000 employees will give the Company an expanded presence in European health and beauty aid markets.

In mid-June, the Company's Richardson-Vicks subsidiary signed an agreement to purchase the worldwide rights to Bain de Soleil, the second largest selling sun care line in the U.S. The line comprises a full range of sun care products for tanning, sun protection and moisturizing.

United States Business

Net earnings from operations in the United States excluding the effects of restructuring totaled $711 million, a 12% increase over the previous year. A new unit volume record was established for the domestic consumer products divisions despite a business climate that was particularly competitive throughout the markets in which we do business. Termination of investment tax credits by the Tax Reform Act of 1986 had a negative impact on net earnings this past year. However, beginning July 1, 1987, the drop in the federal statutory tax rate from 46% to 34% under the Act will more than offset the loss of these tax credits.

Notable volume and market share increases were achieved in the dentifrice and deodorant categories, led by Crest Tartar Control toothpaste and Secret anti-perspirant. In the mouthwash category, Peppermint Scope was expanded broadly as a companion product to Original Mint Scope. Two new and unique health and beauty aids were expanded into national distribution: New Pert Plus, which replaced original Pert, is the first hair care product that delivers complete cleaning and conditioning benefits in one product. Peridex, a prescription mouthwash, is the first product to carry the American Dental Association's seal of acceptance for control of plaque and gingivitis.

There was significant growth in the coffee and fruit juice business. A record market share boosted Vacuum Folgers coffee to leadership in its category. Record unit volumes of Citrus Hill Select orange juice were shipped, and the stage was set for future growth by expanding Citrus Hill Plus Calcium nationally in orange juice and grapefruit flavors. Its calcium source marks an important breakthrough in family nutrition. Patent approval on the product is pending. The American Medical Women's Association accorded special recognition to Citrus Hill Plus Calcium as an effective source of dietary calcium, which also marked the first product acceptance citation by this professional organization.

Record unit volume was attained in paper products, led by Charmin bathroom tissue, Bounty towels, Always feminine sanitary pads and liners, and Pampers disposable diapers, all of which reported significant growth over the previous year. New Always Slender for Teens was expanded nationally late in the year and is directed specifically at the teenage catamenial market. In June, Luvs Deluxe diapers with improved containment and ultra thin padding were expanded into national distribution.

In the laundry and cleaning products segment, a number of reformulated and companion products to existing Company brands were expanded successfully to national distribution.

- Liquid Cascade dishwashing detergent is generating new volume in tandem with powder Cascade, the dishwashing market leader.
- Liquid Cheer detergent offers all-temperature cleaning versatility just like Cheer powder detergent.
- Dash detergent was repositioned as a lemon-scented economically priced detergent.
- New, fresh-scented Lemon Comet joins regular Comet in the cleanser category.

Our industrial and institutional businesses made significant progress this past year, most notably from improved margins on wood pulp that helped to restore profitability to more satisfactory levels.

International Operations

International operations achieved net earnings of $197 million excluding the effects of restructuring. This represented an increase of 38% over the prior year. This was the second straight year of strong earnings growth. The growth was broadly based geographically and by product line, and included the effect of favorable currency exchange rates.

The soap and detergent business in Europe recorded significantly improved margins. New or reformulated products expanded our brand line-up in many major markets. Additionally, we are very encouraged by the growth of the citrus beverage business in Germany where we introduced improved products with unique technology that retain more of the natural juice flavors. In most countries improved versions of Pampers contributed important unit volume growth. This progress was particularly noteworthy in Japan where our market share improved in a disposable diaper category that has grown substantially.

During the past year we completed the integration of the Richardson-Vicks international business with P&G operations. Revised divisional structures and the combining of companies in many countries are providing efficiencies and presenting new opportunities for business growth to the unified organizations.

Geographic expansion activities continued during the past year. A joint venture became operational in Egypt, and a joint venture was established in Turkey with the Mintax Company. In Colombia, the Company acquired a controlling interest in Inextra, a local manufacturer of soaps and detergents.

Research and Development

Last year, the Company invested $576 million in research and development expenses, a 20% increase over the previous year. Expenditures included basic research with emphasis on relevant new technologies as well as applied research to develop new products and to maintain the vitality of existing brands. Worldwide, about 6,000 employees--or over eight percent of the Company's total enrollment--are engaged in research and development activities.

Olestra

Following twenty years of extensive research, the Company has developed an important new food ingredient. In May, the Company's petition for approval of a new calorie-free ingredient to replace fat in everyday foods was accepted for processing by the U.S. Food and Drug Administration. Olestra, its proposed generic name, will let consumers reduce their intake of fat and calories. Products containing olestra cannot be marketed until the FDA reviews and approves its use, but we are very much encouraged by this first step in making these important nutritional and health benefits available to the public.

Capital Expenditures

Last year, capital expenditures amounted to $925 million, or slightly below the expenditure level of the previous two years. Product and process improvement projects to existing manufacturing capacity and cost savings projects accounted for over sixty percent of these expenditures.

Financial Strength

The Company maintained its strong financial position in 1987. All of the past year's cash needs were provided by internally generated funds. Coupled with considerable unused debt potential and ready access to capital markets here and abroad, we have a great deal of financial flexibility in funding the future growth of the business.

*   *   *

The commemorative booklet inside the front cover of this report reviews how "Excellence through commitment and innovation" has characterized the Company's operations since it was founded in 1837. It is particularly appropriate in this sesquicentennial year to pay tribute to the men and women of Procter & Gamble, both past and present, who have contributed to that record. They are primarily responsible for the past achievements and growth of the Company through the years, and it's because of them, now 73,000 strong, that you can share our confidence in the future.

Respectfully,

John G. Smale
Chairman of the Board and CEO

John E. Pepper
President

GUIDELINES AND ALTERNATE PHRASES

EXPRESS YOUR CONGRATULATIONS.

Congratulations on another great year so well documented in your annual report. The diversity of your projects and the scope of your activities are really impressive.

Although I'm sure you as CEO are never fully satisfied with the way things are going, you can take real pride in the kind of results that your company achieved last year. Congratulations.

Your recent annual report shows remarkable achievement. There are few organizations in the U.S., or in fact in the world, that are able to show the progress apparent in your report. Additionally, I think it has been achieved in one of the most difficult, highly competitive industries in the world. My sincerest best wishes.

Your annual report is certainly an outstanding presentation of interesting and diversified operations. I read it from cover to cover and want to compliment you and the other decision makers on a job well done.

Someone obviously deserves a lot of credit for the evident stability and paced growth of earnings detailed in your latest annual report. Since the man at the top gets the blame when things go wrong, the praise for the good should belong to you as well. Sincerest congratulations.

As a happy and proud stockholder, my heartiest congratulations on a fine year and quarter just past.

Congratulations on a successful year-end result. Your dramatic increase in earnings over the previous year is astounding. I'm afraid some of the rest of us are going to be scrambling this next year.

BE SPECIFIC IN YOUR PRAISE, MENTIONING AT LEAST ONE DETAIL ABOUT THE COMPANY'S ACHIEVEMENTS.

It appears that the Casper project will present a great challenge for the coming year. Best of luck with it.

I am delighted to see the extent of your participation in the Asian project. You have the dedicated management and special equipment that will prove this a success.

I thought your letter to the shareholders was very informative; it outlined your policies very clearly with regard to the lending operations.

I noted the impressive increase in new work contracted in the second quarter. This amount of backlog, with your new bidding procedures, certainly bodes well for the future.

I was delighted to see that the new recruitment policies we discussed last year are paying off handsomely.

I agree with your statement that. . . .

I was especially interested in some of your comments about profitable contracts and your shying away from the "monuments." That philosophy is close to our own.

Congratulations to you on acquiring Spencer Inc. The transaction makes a really logical "fit."

I'd like to compliment you on the brightness of your photos. The offshore pictures and the photographs of the Arctic were of particular interest to me. In fact, I felt cold all over.

I think your new design services will really broaden the capabilities of your company, and of course, you already have such a fine reputation in related fields.

Your earnings look very good indeed. I hope that some of the new business and the backlog will all be profitable. Volume is important.

You and Frank and the others are doing a fine job, and it looks to me as though you have turned things around—particularly in the software division.

BE SINCERE; EFFUSIVE FLATTERY SOUNDS STILTED AND INSINCERE.

Dear Jean:

Congratulations on your outstanding annual report. I don't mean only your financial results!

The report itself is an impressive document that reflects well on your management skills. The balance of text and photographs was good. I was especially impressed with the description of your various product lines. Your company being so varied, such a series of short descriptions could easily turn into a laundry list. Instead, these descriptions molded themselves very nicely and gave the reader an excellent overview of your varied interests.

Believe me, I know how difficult such reports are to write. Congratulations again.

Sincerely,

Dear John:

Thank you for sending me a copy of your annual report. It looks as though you had a great year and one of which you can be very proud.

I was especially interested in your emphasis on foreign operations. On a much smaller scale, of course, we have a problem at Belton determining how much we should emphasize domestic versus foreign activities. Sometime I'd like to talk that over with you.

Hope to see you soon when you're in Atlanta again.

Sincerely,

Dear Max:

I read your annual report with particular eagerness this time. The results you are getting are excellent, and I know this is a source of great satisfaction, particularly under the prevailing circumstances of strain and wear that seem to be the rule in most companies of the industry at this time.

It's always a pleasure to work with you and your staff. Please call on us at any time we can be of service. All good wishes.

Cordially,

Dear Jolene:

I continue to be amazed, but also quite pleased, at the growth and performance of Hartford International, and I congratulate you most heartily on the leadership you have offered in the aerospace industry.

With every good wish for your continued success.

Sincerely yours,

Dear Kenneth:

Glad to see that your company's results are so strong. Last year was obviously a very good year for Hadley International, and it looks like 19-- will be even better.

I must confess that your comment about there being "more sure profit in our backlog than at any time in the company's history" has me a bit envious!

Cordially,

GUIDELINES AND ALTERNATE PHRASES

FOCUS IMMEDIATELY ON THE POSITIVE ACTION TAKEN TO CORRECT THE SITUATION. OR, INDICATE AN APPROXIMATE TIME FOR RESOLUTION IF THERE WILL BE A DELAY TO YOUR CORRECTIVE RESPONSE.

We agree. You are totally correct, and we will pay for the damages to your garage shelves caused by our service personnel. Please forward the repair bills to my attention.

We will schedule the repair service as soon as we receive confirmation of the warranty.

ACKNOWLEDGE THE COMPLAINT EVEN IF THE CORRECTIVE ACTION MUST BE DELAYED AND TURNED OVER TO ANOTHER PERSON FOR HANDLING AND FOLLOW-UP.

We have discussed your position with Sarah Rateson, the local manager, and she will be glad to replace the lamp if you will return it to the Willowbrook store.

We have spoken to our distributor in your area about the urgency of your situation, and he has assured us that he will ship the new order by May 6.

EXPLAIN BRIEFLY AND POSITIVELY HOW THE MISTAKE HAPPENED. TO DO SO GIVES THE READER CONFIDENCE THAT YOU HAVE REALLY INVESTIGATED AND DO INDEED HAVE THE SITUATION UNDER CONTROL. IF YOU HAVE NO REASON FOR THE PROBLEM, A FRANK ADMISSION TO THAT EFFECT USUALLY DISARMS THE READER.

The information I gave you was understandably misleading. I should have been clearer about how the amount was actually calculated.

I totally agree with your sentiments about the apparent mishandling of your request. You must be down right ready to "pull your hair out" over this delay.

MAKE THE READER FEEL THAT HIS OR HER GOODWILL IS VALUED.

In the event you have a recurrence of the problem, please feel free to phone me collect.

Thank you for your patience in dealing with this matter.

WATCH UNNECESSARY "FIGHT" WORDS THAT WILL TEND TO FURTHER ALIENATE THE READER ALREADY CAUGHT IN A DISAPPOINTING SITUATION.

We have received your letter of concern (not complaint) about. . . .

Apparently, I was unclear in (not you misconstrued) my response to you.

MENTION ANY PRECAUTIONS THAT YOU PLAN TO TAKE AGAINST A RECURRENCE OF THE SITUATION.

I've made a calendar note to follow up with our sales rep again next week about your situation.

I've instructed my staff to clear all such procedures with me directly before they report to your site.

We have completely discarded the misleading set of procedures.

BE SINCERE. DON'T USE VAGUE GENERALIZATIONS SUCH AS "WE APOLOGIZE FOR ANY INCONVENIENCE THIS HAS CAUSED YOU." THE READER WANTS ASSURANCE THAT YOU UNDERSTAND THE INCONVENIENCE.

We greatly regret that you were offended by the opening remarks; I can certainly understand your embarrassment in front of your former customers.

We know what an inconvenience the malfunctioning elevators must have been—particularly during the peak traffic hours.

We regret that you had to make three long-distance calls to correct the situation. May we reimburse you for these?

36

Dear Mr. Smith:

Thank you for your August 5 letter calling attention to the rudeness with which our sales representative handled your account. We take great pride in dealing with our customers in a friendly, polite, and efficient manner; when such is not the case, we want to do our best to correct the problem.

I have spoken with the representative who dealt with you on the telephone and have taken the appropriate disciplinary actions to correct the situation.

We sincerely apologize for the delay in taking your order and the inefficient way it was handled. Please give us an opportunity to serve you again in the way you deserve to be treated.

Sincerely,

Dear Jewel:

Your brochure has now gone through our final proofing and has been delivered to the printer this afternoon. We will provide you with a blueline within the next week so that you can see the final version for yourself and make any last-minute corrections. Please let me reassure you that the brochure will be ready for your Atlanta convention, April 9. The printer has promised an earlier-than-expected completion date of March 25.

You are quite right about the unexpected delays in gathering the information and photographing your staff in all the various locations. I will have to admit that the delays were mostly due to my inadequate planning for the number of off-site photos needed to make the brochure exactly what we wanted to cover all aspects of your products and services. Not having control over staff absences, equipment failures, and others' travel schedules is frustrating; nevertheless, with my twelve years' experience in the business, I should have allowed time for such unexpected crises.

I sincerely appreciate the confidence you've placed in our staff to showcase your organization's many accomplishments and services. The brochure captures the sense of your leadership position in the industry. We appreciate your giving us the opportunity to work with you on this project.

Sincerely,

Dear Ms. Adams:

Thank you for calling to my attention the frustration you have experienced in our handling of the repairs to your System 16. I have discussed the situation with my manager, and we have scheduled a special meeting next week to come up with a plan to offer you better support service in your outlying branches. I'll phone you at least by the end of next week to give you the details of our plan to solve the problem.

The printer problem you mentioned is not so easily solved. The system you purchased is not equipped with a buffer capable of saving data during an error condition. The software package you're using does not present you with the option to continue your data-processing project because of the probability that data will be lost in the intervening process. Currently, the only option you have is to delay your word processing project until the error condition is remedied.

I might point out that our new printers do not have this limitation.

Again, I will be back to you by March 2 to give you the details of our plans to improve support services to all your branches. We appreciate your patience with our efforts to give you a most thorough, comprehensive solution.

Sincerely,

APOLOGIES/Avoiding Responsibility for Error

GUIDELINES AND ALTERNATE PHRASES

ACKNOWLEDGE THE COMPLAINT EVEN IF THE ERROR IS NOT YOURS.

We received your letter telling us about the difficulty with the swimming pool you recently purchased. We in no way can tell our local dealer how to handle situations such as yours, but we want you to know that we are very concerned. We will be following up with Mr. Hightower to see how he decides to resolve the problem.

Thank you for writing us about the situation involving your daughter's delayed registration to the upcoming seminar.

We appreciate your letting us know of your concern with the way your new Buick Regal is performing on short trips within the city.

EXPLAIN YOUR PERSPECTIVE ON THE SITUATION.

We regret that you were not pleased with the manner in which your telephone call to our office was handled. Perhaps the person you spoke with did not effectively communicate the reason she requested that you call our local office. Because your account is serviced by that local office, she knew that you would get faster, more efficient service by contacting them directly. In the future, she will take great pains to convey that benefit to customers.

Your comments about the possibility of our becoming overextended are well taken. This is definitely very much in our minds, and we're watching that possibility. Our business seems to be reaping the benefits of recovery, and we're grateful for the "problem" while also aware of a possible lag in service.

BE CAUTIOUS ABOUT ADMITTING FAULT OR LIABILITY EVEN IF YOU DECIDE TO TAKE SOME CORRECTIVE ACTION. FOCUS ON ANYTHING YOU ARE WILLING TO DO TO SOLVE THE PROBLEM.

While we do not accept responsibility for the problem, we do want to assist you by. . . .

While we regret that our instructions were misunderstood, we are in any event sorry that you were displeased with the outcome.

If our warranty was misrepresented in any way—and we do not understand that it was—we would like to make things right with you by. . . .

We have cautioned our representatives about any promises that we can't adequately warrant in writing. A copy of our warranty is enclosed for your reference if you have further questions.

WATCH UNNECESSARY "FIGHT" WORDS THAT WILL TEND TO SEVER THE RELATIONSHIP COMPLETELY.

To be serviced most efficiently, all requests should (not must) go through our office.

The postponement in resolution came about after your decision (not heated debate about proceeding) not to proceed with the steps we discussed March 3.

We know that you regret the oversight (not failure) of renewing your contract as much as we do.

MAKE THE READER FEEL THAT HIS OR HER GOODWILL IS VALUED.

Thank you for taking the time to write us.

We try never to forget that it is loyal customers such as you who keep us in business. We will continue to make every effort to deserve your loyalty.

Thank you for giving us opportunity to respond to your inquiry.

We appreciate your bringing the matter to our attention so that we could explain our situation to you.

We hope this letter has clarified the issues and that you can understand our desire to keep your business while doing what we think is fair in the situation.

Dear Ms. Bistrauff:

We have attempted several times to reach your staff by phone to discuss the issues you raised in your letter about the compatibility problem between our computer and the software package you are using. On our part, we were unaware that you had also spoken to several other people here in the office, and we didn't always know to communicate to each other that we were working on getting the same answers for you.

To avoid all future delays, may I suggest that you funnel all requests through Mark Jones or me. We will make every effort to see that you get an immediate answer.

I understand from talking to Mark that, ultimately, your problems were resolved by an outside consultant. In the situation where the proper functioning of our hardware is dependent on another vendor's software, we, of course, can't warrant that particular function will work.

The software vendor has the responsibility to support that particular function according to its claims of compatibility. Unfortunately, Vestco cannot legally modify another company's software to make it compatible, nor do we always have the expertise to do so. We regret this unfortunate situation, knowing that you feel trapped with equipment that does not adequately meet your needs.

We are glad, however, that you have found someone to solve the immediate incompatibility problem and hope you understand the legalities of the situation. We hope that you will give us another opportunity to prove that we make every effort to support our sales and service promises.

Sincerely,

Dear Mr. Howard:

I have received your January 3 letter concerning what appeared to be excessively high gas consumption amounts on your previous few months' bills. As a result, I made a special trip to Sarasota to discuss this situation with Harry Fountain, our local manager.

At that time, we did two shut-in tests of sufficient duration to show that there was no loss of gas in the houseline or in the meter. We did, in fact, remove the old meter and replace it with a new one. We also made a comparison study of four homes in your block and did discover that your home did use more gas than the others around you. This comparison study, of course, proves only that your home used more gas but did not itemize the reasons for such use, such as amount of heated water used in showering, laundry, and so forth.

We simply cannot give you a more definitive evaluation than what we have outlined above. We do hope you will continue to remain a Bestvelt customer and will take care of any outstanding balances on your account.

Sincerely,

Dear Ms. Chorton:

We received your letter about the remarks made by Dr. Frank Martin at the Business After Hours seminar on May 9.

Mr. Martin made those remarks, not as a Fullerton employee, but as a member of the national Chamber of Commerce. However, if Mr. Martin has made reckless, false, or misleading statements about our industry and the way we do business, I will certainly call them to his attention.

I have now read the full draft of his paper. Would you please point out to me exactly which statements are in error so that I may discuss them with him immediately? We do want to be as accurate and as helpful to our industry colleagues as we possibly can. Thank you for giving us the opportunity to review your concerns.

Sincerely,

G U I D E L I N E S   A N D   A L T E R N A T E   P H R A S E S

STATE THE PURPOSE OF THE APPOINTMENT REQUEST.

BE SURE TO SUGGEST A TIME, DATE, AND PLACE.

GIVE AN ALTERNATE TIME AND PLACE, IF POSSIBLE, EXPRESSING CONCERN FOR THE READER'S CONVENIENCE.

If this date is not acceptable, let me know when you're free and I'll arrange my schedule accordingly.

If this is inconvenient for you, give me a call and we'll discuss another possibility for a meeting time.

If you have an alternate suggestion, let me know. I can meet with you almost any time Thursday or Friday of next week.

GIVE ALL THE DETAILS FOR THE READER TO CONFIRM THE APPOINTMENT.

Would you mind phoning my secretary to confirm?

If I don't hear from you otherwise, I'll see you in your office on June 5 at 3:00.

LET THE READER KNOW IF THE APPOINTMENT IS MANDATORY OR A "NICE TO DO" OCCASION.

We could, of course, proceed with our plans without your input, but we do want to give you the opportunity to let us know your feelings.

We do hope you'll be able to join us.

Mr. Radaux has requested that we get together to discuss these issues before the end of the month.

MENTION ANY PREPARATION NECESSARY FOR THE APPOINTMENT.

I've enclosed an agenda. I'd like your comments particularly on the Hite project.

Please bring the Boston figures with you to the meeting.

I'm looking forward to your comments about the contract clause in dispute.

Could you be ready to present your opinion about the new hiring policy?

ANNUAL MEETINGS/Notice of Meeting Time and Place

APOLOGIES/Admitting Error

Dear Ms. Thompson:

We received your letter saying that you had not received your shipment of office supplies but had received our invoice #5889 for $348. After reviewing your order form, we have discovered that the artwork for the logo to be engraved on the binders was not included with your original order. A note attached to that order stated that the artwork was to be sent from your office "shortly." But we have never received it--thus the delay in processing your complete order.

As soon as you are able to provide us with the artwork, we will process your order and ship all your merchandise within five working days. If you prefer that we ship the other office supplies separately without the binders, please let us know (1-800-456-7890), and we will process that portion of the order immediately.

We appreciate your continued business.

Sincerely,

Dear Mr. Morris:

Your inquiry concerning our current bill to you has been forwarded to me for handling. After reviewing your account, we have determined that the use of electricity in your home seems to be within the normal pattern. We can find no evidence of an error having been made and believe that the bill is correct as stated. If you have discovered additional information about your situation and a possible error, please call or write us again and we will be happy to talk with you further.

We are appreciative of your business and are trying to keep costs as low as possible for our customers.

Sincerely,

Dear Mr. Bonnette:

We have rechecked your bill for service to May 31, using as a guide the information you sent us about your purchases. With that information, we still find your account balance to be correct at $2,244.

The $766.86 purchase that you returned for credit was reflected on last month's statement. Perhaps you did not check that previous billing record.

In reviewing your account we also found that we had erroneously calculated the interest to be $28 rather than $38. But because we have inconvenienced you in making this interest error, please forget the extra $10 owed us and we will call things "even."

We appreciate your business.

Sincerely,

G U I D E L I N E S   A N D   A L T E R N A T E   P H R A S E S

STATE HOW YOU'VE CORRECTED THE ERROR.

Enclosed is your copy of the corrected deposit slip for $500. It reflects your correct account number (233444) and the original deposit date of October 16, 19—.

We have reviewed the questions you raised about your account and have found we made an error. We have, therefore, made the appropriate adjustments and enclosed a corrected bill.

EXPLAIN BRIEFLY HOW THE MISTAKE OCCURRED.

The error was made when our clerk manually recorded your checking account deposit to another account.

The new sales representative was unaware of the extra charges for such expedited processing and shipping.

EXPRESS REGRET FOR THE BUYER'S INCONVENIENCE, BUT MAKE YOUR APOLOGY APPROPRIATE TO THE SERIOUSNESS OF THE ERROR.

We are sorry for the mistake and want to assure you that no checks were returned because your balance remained positive even without the unrecorded deposit.

We know you were greatly inconvenienced in having to make two trips to our office to supply the paperwork we needed to correct the situation. We sincerely apologize for your trouble and lost time.

MENTION ANY EXTRA EFFORT YOU HAVE EXTENDED TO SHOW YOUR REGRETS.

After we completed your order form over the phone and then checked with our supplier, we discovered that he no longer distributes the particular model you wanted. To get that model, we will order from a new vendor. The price will be $228.45. Do you still want us to process your order?

In an effort to make up for the anxiety the error caused, we've deleted the $10 service charge on your original billing.

Because your original order was delayed, we have tried to accommodate your needs by shipping the merchandise overnight express at our expense.

We have enclosed a little gift, one of our newest digital alarms, to show our regret in having made this error. Please accept it with our apologies.

CLOSE POSITIVELY, WITH A BUSINESS-AS-USUAL TONE.

We look forward to servicing all your future needs.

We look forward to hearing from you again and are eager to improve our service to you.

We value your account and hope your questions have been answered satisfactorily. If not, however, please let us know.

Thank you for allowing us to serve your needs.

Thank you for doing business with us.

We hope you enjoy the closet rack.

Dear Ms. Speck:

It's regrettable when mistakes are made. And this happens to be one time when we owe you an explanation and an apology.

Invoice #45621 for $5,667.34 has just been billed to your account after almost a year's delay. We have attached a copy of the invoice, along with the proof-of-delivery documents.

Somehow the paperwork on your order was buried in our records, and then was incorrectly billed to another account. It wasn't until the other customer called the error to our attention that we became aware of the mix-up.

With the $3,334 credit appearing in your account as of January 14, there is a balance of $2,333.34. Again, we are sorry for this delayed billing. Perhaps you were able to make good use of that money during this past year and won't be too upset at our oversight to bill you.

Please call us if you would like to discuss the matter further before sending your check.

Sincerely,

Dear Ms. Hatten:

Please disregard the additional billing you just received from our office. The billing was in error, and the cause has now been corrected on our computer. Your account is clear.

Please accept our apologies for any momentary concern this may have caused you. We appreciate your business, and we're looking forward to hearing from you when you again need our services.

Sincerely,

Dear Sheila:

I have enclosed the revised, corrected billing for the auto coverage with an effective date of February 1 rather than January 2. The down payment is $2,660, and you will make seven monthly installments of $922.33. The difference between the actual amount you paid in your returned January 29 check ($3,440) and the down payment is $780.

Please return the signed agreement, along with your new check for the down payment, to our office by February 10.

These rating changes were made after the original policy was delivered to you. Thank you for permitting us to provide your insurance coverage.

Sincerely,

Dear Mr. Jackson:

In checking our equipment recently, we discovered that the meter serving you has not been registering properly. Therefore, we have rebilled you for the months that are involved.

Attached is a statement showing the amount we originally billed you and the new, correct amount. Please note that we have deducted all the payments you've made during the last few months from the total amount shown on the enclosed rebilling.

We regret the malfunctioning meter and apologize for the inconvenience of your having to write us another check for the difference. Thank you for your understanding and your business.

Sincerely,

Dear Ms. Hargroves:

Thank you very much for bringing to our attention the computer billing problem. We will correct it immediately.

Sorry for the false alarm--you do not owe any money on your account. Please accept our apology for your trouble in having to write us.

Sincerely,

COMMENDATIONS/To a Program Chairperson or Meeting Planner

STATE YOUR GENERAL COMMENDATION ABOUT THE PROGRAM OR MEETING ARRANGEMENTS.

I want to express my admiration for your planning skills—the convention schedule and logistics could not possibly have been handled any better than during this recent AVA meeting.

Just a note to tell you that I thoroughly enjoyed the recent AVA seminar topics and speakers. Your selection was right on target for our group.

As you must have realized by now, the AVA meeting was a great success, thanks to your planning and foresight.

Last week's AVA meeting was one of the highlights of my career. Your administration of the details, the program, and the follow-up roundtables far exceeded my every expectation for the meeting. I want to commend you for making it such a worthwhile and enjoyable experience.

MENTION AT LEAST ONE OR TWO SPECIFIC DETAILS THAT WERE PARTICULARLY OUTSTANDING. FOR EXAMPLE, COMMENT ON THE PLANNING TIME AND EFFORT INVOLVED, SHARE COMPLIMENTARY REMARKS YOU HEARD OTHERS IN THE GROUP MAKE ABOUT THE MEETING, OR PASS ON FOLLOW-UP RESULTS OR SUCCESSES THAT YOU ATTRIBUTE TO THE MEETING OR PROGRAM.

As I left the room, I heard others in the group comment on your wise selection of a speaker and how applicable her comments were to the group as a whole. Such, as you know, is not always the case.

I'll have to admit that I was dreading "just another long drawn-out meeting." What a pleasant surprise to find that the agenda was well defined, that the speakers addressed the topics they'd announced, and that the accommodations were exceptional.

The delicious food, not the usual banquet fare, was served fresh and warm.

When you chose the accommodations, you certainly had people like me in mind—the large work space in each room, the exercise and jogging facilities, and the easily accessible transportation around the area.

Thanks to your attention to detail, things ran so smoothly—not a single hitch or complaint.

Thank you for your special effort in making it easy for those attending the conference alone to "network." I know having the message boards and all the special sign-up booths for dinner groups and after-hours tours required additional volunteer help, but such extras made the trip especially enjoyable for those of us traveling alone.

Dear Mr. Summers:

As you may know, this past week was my first time to attend the AVA monthly meeting and the first time to observe your group in action. I was extremely impressed.

Having spoken to such groups on many occasions, I believe that I'm qualified to express the opinion that your organization ranks among the finest in member turnout, attentiveness, and participation from the individual members, and, most importantly where you're concerned, efficiency. There's much to be said for the obvious planning behind an unhurried dinner meeting for 123 persons that can be completed in less than an hour. By my watch, that's exactly how long it took, and I congratulate you.

Such careful planning on your part shows an uncommon sensitivity to the busy schedules of those in your audience.

Sincerely,

COMMENDATIONS/To a Speaker

GUIDELINES AND ALTERNATE PHRASES

STATE THE GENERAL COMMENDATION ABOUT THE SPEAKER'S PRESENTATION.

What an informative talk you made last week!

Your session at last week's conference made my week.

If nothing else had been of personal benefit, your presentation alone was worth the price of registration for last week's conference.

Well, they certainly pulled out the big guns last week when they selected you as keynote speaker. Your aim was terrific—just what I came to hear.

Your talk last week set the stage for wonderful things to come in our company.

I appreciate the time you took to work with us last week. Your presentation was sincere and urgent, as it should have been.

From all indications, your Tuesday workshop was a success. Thank you for so willingly giving your every effort toward planning and presenting an effective, well-received program.

We want to express our appreciation for the excellent job you did in both preparing and presenting your topic to our eager audience.

BE SPECIFIC WITH YOUR PRAISE. STATE AT LEAST TWO OR THREE DETAILS THAT YOU APPRECIATED ABOUT THE PRESENTATION.

Your enthusiasm was contagious; I felt my spirits lift two notches after hearing you speak.

Not only did you give us "the facts"; you illustrated them in such a memorable way that they really took on new meaning.

The visuals you selected to reinforce your key points certainly increased the effectiveness of what you had to say. They were so professionally prepared.

And I certainly appreciated your humor. As you are well aware from the many speeches

you give on this topic each year, it's not a topic that, in and of itself, keeps people awake at night. Your presentation style made it come alive!

You did a superb job of keeping the audience's attention under difficult circumstances.

The statistics you quoted were quite alarming and should call us all to immediate action.

SHARE ANY NEW INSIGHT OR BENEFIT TO YOU PERSONALLY.

I plan to use some of these tips in my job with Kemper Insurance.

The negotiation skills have already paid off in the purchase of a new car just last week.

Not to mention the immediate value in my current job, listing my completion of your course on my resumé should prove to be a real attention-getter. Your work has been held in such high regard in the industry.

Actually, your presentation shed new light on our glibly accepted industry standards. You've motivated me to do more reading on the subject.

MENTION ANY REFERRAL YOU INTEND TO GIVE OR ANY COMMENDATION YOU PLAN TO PASS ON, IF APPROPRIATE, TO HIS OR HER SUPERIORS.

I'm sure you'll have no objection to my passing your name on to others needing a first-rate speaker.

Please know that you will be the first person called when we again need someone of your expertise on the topic.

Perhaps you won't object to my tooting your horn from time to time when I hear of similar groups looking for a speaker.

I've taken the liberty of passing on your name and my enthusiastic referral to our national headquarters.

Dear Pat:

You were certainly a vivacious addition to the conference this weekend. Of course, you know I was vitally interested in your topic or I wouldn't have chosen to attend your particular session. But you gave us so much more than the same old theories.

Specifically, I found the tips on proposals quite useful, never having given much thought to how an effective transmittal document could enhance the proposal itself. Then, too, I discovered that I knew little about proposal structure itself. I'm looking for these two tips alone to bring me some otherwise lost contracts. To sum up, I guess you could say your presentation was one of the best "nuts-and-bolts" sessions I've ever attended.

If the occasion arises, you can be sure I'll have your name on the tip of my tongue for other such managerial meetings. Thank you for making the conference so worthwhile for me.

Sincerely,

COMMENDATIONS/For Excellent Service from Outside Staff

STATE YOUR OVERALL COMMENDATION FIRST.

_____

MENTION SPECIFIC DETAILS ABOUT THAT COMMENDABLE SERVICE: WAS IT EXCEPTIONALLY FAST? HOW WAS IT "BEYOND DUTY"? WAS IT PARTICULARLY EFFICIENT? WAS IT PERFORMED WITH A COMMENDABLE ATTITUDE?

_____

The service was dependable and thoughtful.

His attitude in rendering this special service was certainly one of a person who believes in "going the extra mile."

She made a quick, intelligent decision in the matter.

She offered leadership, enthusiasm, and encouragement.

She was particularly astute in picking up on the little details that could have turned the occasion into a disaster, and she averted the problem quite effectively.

John's "people skills" became readily apparent in the situation. Both men walked away from the problem feeling as though their needs had been met.

_____

EXPLAIN WHY YOU ARE IN A POSITION TO RECOGNIZE AND COMPARE SUCH COMMENDABLE SERVICE. IN OTHER WORDS, MAKE YOUR LETTER SOUND LIKE YOU REALLY KNOW EXCEPTIONAL SERVICE WHEN YOU SEE IT. IN SO DOING, YOU ADD CREDIBILITY TO YOUR COMMENTS AND MAKE THEM MORE VALUABLE TO THE READER.

_____

I travel extensively and can assure you that service is not the norm.

As a frequent attendee to such functions, I can truly say that John's service and willing attitude are among the finest I've seen.

Although I have a personal interest in X as a hobby, I recognize expertise of this calibre when I see it.

_____

INCLUDE NAMES. RECOGNIZE THE CONTRIBUTIONS OF SPECIFIC PEOPLE, NOT JUST GROUPS.

Dear Mr. Meadows:

People are always so quick to complain, but I'd like to start your day with a praise report. Two of your service station attendants in Phoenix, Mike Smith and Steve Bragg, gave me such excellent service that I must let you know about their contribution to your company's reputation.

The details are lengthy, but I want you to have a genuine appreciation of the time and thought these two men put into solving my car problem and seeing to it that I didn't get back out on the road and have trouble in the middle of the night--with little cash at that.

On my recent trip through Phoenix my turn signals became inoperative and my power brakes went out. I eased off the road at the next exit and pulled into your station. Mike Smith, one of your mechanics who wasn't even on duty that day but was at the station doing some repairs for himself before a big fishing trip, came over to my car and offered his assistance. He, along with the help of Steve Bragg, immediately diagnosed the problem as alternator trouble, a problem that would cost about $120. Knowing I was low on cash, Mike began to quiz me about the credit cards I had. Sure enough, he found another card that was good at your station.

Then in the process of disconnecting the alternator, they found a loose wire that had shorted out the alternator. Not about to give up, Mike spliced the wires and took another gauge reading to make sure they had thoroughly repaired the car.

I was soon on my way with no need for an overnight stay in a motel to wait for the parts store to open the next day and no need for an expensive part.

These two men knew they were not making a regular customer; I was from out of state. They could have connected the wires and charged me for a new alternator, and I would have never known the difference. Instead, they were as thrilled as I that they could repair the car quickly, safely, and inexpensively. Additionally, Mike Smith willingly gave up his day off to help a stranger. Both were doing their job with care and alertness to notice the difficulty.

Mr. Meadows, as president of this corporation, you are filling an important position. But it is also good men like Mike and Steve, who give of themselves in real service, that make your company great.

Cordially,

91

Dear Ms. Stammers:

I was most pleased to hear that you are planning to do a story on one of our employees, Martha Hartman. I am also glad that our public affairs department could provide your staff writer, Mark Jones, with the assistance he needed. As you are probably very aware, this department gets many requests for information, but the background research Mark had already done on the subject certainly directed our staff in finding applicable statistics quickly.

We also appreciate your generous praise in the initial phone call, and I'm taking the liberty of sharing your comments with those involved.

You and others on your magazine staff such as Mark and photographer Sheryl Kirkpatrick are to be commended for your hard work on this project, a highly informative and inspirational article that I'm sure will speak to a large audience. We here at Dermott will especially be looking forward to the June issue of your outstanding journal.

Sincerely,

Dear Mr. Contee:

Last week while Mrs. Smith and I were staying at your hotel, we received exceptional service from Ms. Tanya Maskoff, your director of housekeeping. We had a last-minute pressing problem that she solved very efficiently and at a very odd hour with a very helpful attitude.

My work takes me around the world quite often, and such a customer-oriented attitude is not at all common. I wanted to let you know that we appreciated Ms. Maskoff's efforts.

Sincerely,

COMMENDATIONS/For Excellent Service, Work, Results from Your Own Staff

GUIDELINES AND ALTERNATE PHRASES

STATE THE PRAISE OR COMMENDABLE RESULTS.

BE SPECIFIC IN YOUR PRAISE.

Although my work involvement with you is now limited, I can honestly say that your comments to us have always been especially timely and constructive.

The technical expertise that you brought to the job was remarkable.

The professional manner in which you conducted yourself at the project meeting with the client had a very positive influence on a job that was in deep trouble from the outset.

Your response time was incredible.

The excellent quality of the work you did is unlike anything I've encountered here at International.

You have made an excellent contribution over the year to business growth, leadership, and customer satisfaction. Unsolicited favorable responses about our services have doubled.

Your efficient performance of all the tasks we outlined with the client is the primary reason we won this contract.

You have offered superb support every step of the way.

Your explanation and diagnosis were the best I've ever heard on the subject.

Without your help in Phase 2, we would have never met our deadline.

You have been instrumental in establishing the necessary credibility with the client.

We have achieved several wins specifically because you are on our team.

INCLUDE NAMES. PEOPLE, NOT DEPARTMENTS, DO WORK. THEY LIKE TO KNOW THAT YOU

RECOGNIZE THEIR INDIVIDUAL ACHIEVEMENTS AND CONTRIBUTIONS. IF YOU HAVE MANY PEOPLE TO BE COMMENDED, AT LEAST INCLUDE THEIR NAMES IN A DISTRIBUTION LIST.

AVOID NEGATIVE COMMENTS THAT DETRACT FROM THE OVERALL EXCELLENT RESULTS.

LET YOUR GENERAL TONE BE TO CONGRATULATE, NOT SIMPLY TO MOTIVATE TO GREATER ACHIEVEMENT—ALTHOUGH COMMENDATIONS DO OFTEN MOTIVATE.

KEEP YOURSELF OUT OF THE PICTURE. THE TONE SHOULD NOT BE ONE OF "THIS IS WHAT I LED YOU TO DO."

With or without me around, you always seem to do an exceptional job.

You are the kind of employee who enables me to leave the office for a few days worry free.

You contributed just the expertise needed to make the project successful.

FOCUS ON ANY INDIVIDUAL BENEFITS FROM THE ACCOMPLISHMENT RATHER THAN SOLELY ON ORGANIZATIONAL BENEFITS.

Obviously, your move to our division was the right one for you, too.

I hope the work has been as exciting and as challenging for you personally as it has been for the company.

As I hear it, you are making quite a name for yourself around here. Thank you.

I hope other opportunities will surface in the near future that will allow you to gain even more visibility for your efforts.

We will make every effort to let others in the division know that you were the driving force behind the project.

Dear Monty:

Thank you for your invaluable help on the communications committee this past year. Through your hard work and commitment, we have gained increased readership for our publications, on-time delivery, and greater advertising support.

I'm sincerely grateful for your contribution of time and talent. Many of us were aware of the three or four long weekends you devoted to the project, not to mention your expertise in interviewing. And I hope you gained added visibility for your own consulting business. That is always a side benefit of hard work like yours well done.

Best wishes,

Al,

Please accept these two Astros tickets as a personal token of my appreciation of the fine job you did on the Markwardt work request for the 1012 building brace removal. Your solution was inexpensive, timely, and, best of all, exactly what the customer needed.

Performance like this is what the operating departments see as proper support of their business needs, and I commend you for your effort. Thank you for making me look good.

Regards,

To All the Accounting Crew:

Marvin informed me this morning that through your efforts we have set a new record for cash-posting timeliness in April . . . 100% in three days. Even more impressive was the fact that 94% were posted on the first day. These are outstanding results and you should take pride in them!

As you know, our objective around here is to make Varvaughn the best water-purifying company in the world. It is with individuals such as you that we will make this happen.

You've set the standard for everyone else to follow!

Thanks,

GUIDELINES AND ALTERNATE PHRASES

STATE THE PROBLEM.

MENTION THE REASON FOR OR BENEFIT FROM RESOLVING THE MATTER RATHER THAN DWELLING ON THE PROBLEM ITSELF.

This change should make us all more productive.

This action should save us immeasurable time, effort, and money.

Such clear-cut directives, I hope, will make things easier for all of us.

Let me know if you don't find this system much easier for you.

While this procedure may be slightly more time-consuming, I think you'll agree that it will make your efforts more productive over the long haul.

Anything we can do to make this project a success is worth our every effort.

FOCUS ON THE RESOLUTION OF THE PROBLEM RATHER THAN ON WHO IS TO BLAME.

While the reason for these errors is irrelevant at this point, I'm sure that this new procedure should eliminate them in the future.

Regardless of who was ultimately responsible for the situation, please join me in this corrective action.

The solution, not the cause, is my primary concern now.

USE A POSITIVE TONE RATHER THAN A SARCASTIC OR OVERBEARING ONE.

Let's make every effort to make the next one a success.

With such careful attention to these details, I'm sure we'll see improvement to make us all proud.

Thank you for helping me correct this situation.

I sincerely appreciate your attention to this problem and have every confidence that you can turn the situation around.

I'm looking forward to your very best efforts next time and know you won't let me down.

I certainly appreciate the can-do attitude I find every time we discover a situation that needs improving.

May I count on your full cooperation?

Would you help me correct this situation?

Dear Staffers,

Phony "Going Out of Business," Closing Doors," "Liquidation," "Must Vacate Today," "Make Us an Offer" advertising is contrary to our standards here in Hillsboro. If deceptive, these ads are totally unacceptable.

If you have questions about any advertising you are asked to run, please clear the ad copy with me first. Let's keep the reputation of our newspaper beyond reproach by screening ourselves rather than having our readers embarrass us by discovering less-than-honest deals advertised in our pages.

I also suggest that you keep this notice as a permanent reminder when customers try "to slip one by you."

Thanks,

John,

It has come to my attention that customers have been told we cannot take their service applications over the phone. Please correct this misunderstanding. We should most willingly take the application information over the phone, and then, of course, ask them to complete (or verify) the written information when they come in for the first consultation.

This make-it-easy policy should be good news to our customers and should also increase our clerks' sales records. In other words, they can "sign up the live ones" before they change their minds or simply neglect to come in personally by our weekly deadlines.

I appreciate your help in clarifying this policy to all involved.

Sincerely,

Dear Barbara,

As we agreed on the phone, the ad for the medical transcriptionist that appeared in the <u>Globe</u> yesterday gave Ms. Holly Merritta's name and phone number. However, the arrangement of the ad is very confusing, and, as a result, Ms. Merritta has received numerous misdirected inquiries regarding pathology and radiology positions.

Also, the primary reason for the ad was specifically to mention the new pay plan--$5 per 1000 words--at all our branch clinics. (I fear that transcription applicants assumed we were still using the old pay plan and remembered the previous erroneous ad.) Future ads should emphasize our new pay schedule and generate leads for the best-qualified applicants in the field.

Therefore, would you please prepare another ad draft for the July 6 paper, announcing six open positions. The ad should include Ms. Merritta's name and phone number and, specifically, the exact pay rate of the plan. I will review this new ad and will give you approval on it before any newspaper deadlines. Also, I want to approve all transcription ads for all clinics before they are submitted to the media.

Thank you for helping me make sure our advertising gives the message and image we want to present to the public.

Sincerely,

GUIDELINES AND ALTERNATE PHRASES

VIEW YOUR LETTER AS A REQUEST FOR ACTION OR COOPERATION RATHER THAN A COMPLAINT. FIND POSITIVE MOTIVATORS, IF POSSIBLE, SUCH AS SMOOTHER OPERATIONS, SAFETY, SAVINGS IN TIME AND DOLLARS, GOODWILL FROM OUTSIDERS.

———

Because we are all so very busy, it is easy to forget the seemingly minor details that make our equipment operate efficiently. Would you give special attention to the following matters so that we can all save our maintenance dollars?

Bill, can you help me save us all a little time?

I know you're looking forward to the commissions that can be generated from such a deal—if we are successful in finding a way to solve the customer's current problem.

STATE THE PROBLEM WITH ADEQUATE DETAIL SO THAT THE READER CAN THOROUGHLY UNDERSTAND THE CORRECTIVE ACTION SUGGESTED.

———

SUGGEST, WHEN YOU CAN'T COMMAND, THE SPECIFIC ACTION YOU WANT YOUR READER TO TAKE TO RESOLVE THE MATTER; DO NOT COUCH THE SOLUTION IN VAGUE GENERALITIES. IF YOU HAVE NO SOLUTIONS TO THE PROBLEM YOURSELF, THEN SAY SO. SUCH HUMBLENESS GIVES A MORE CONCILIATORY TONE.

———

I must admit I don't have any solutions at this point. But I do know we need to discuss this seriously.

Would you send two additional copies of each month's report?

Will you give me your answer by May 2?

I suggest that your representative make another sales call on the client to explain this policy.

———

ADOPT A MOTIVATIONAL TONE OF MUTUAL EFFORT. INCLUDE COURTESY WORDS SUCH AS *PLEASE, THANK YOU,* AND *WE WOULD APPRECIATE* . . . .

———

USE PASSIVE VOICE WHEN DESCRIBING SOMEONE'S ERROR; THIS CONSTRUCTION PREVENTS AN ACCUSING TONE. "THE ENTRIES IN STEP 2 WERE MISCALCULATED." NOT: "YOU MISCALCULATED THE ENTRIES IN STEP 2."

———

END ON A BUSINESS-AS-USUAL NOTE; REESTABLISH RAPPORT.

———

If I can help you further in solving the problem, let me know.

Please join me in our efforts to make this discouraging situation an ultimate success.

I hope that the next time we correspond it can be under less difficult circumstances.

I hope we have this situation all cleared up by the next time our paths cross.

Give my regards to your staff and thank them for the extra effort this resolution will require.

Although we were caught in a somewhat uncomfortable situation, things should improve drastically and soon.

Millard,

We have spoken on the phone twice about the circuit outages in our building. I have decided that it might be helpful to you if I supplied the attached list of sites with reference numbers. Should I expect the job to be completed by Monday?

If not, please let me know by Friday because I will have to readjust the weekly work schedules of all our people to accommodate the delay.

We will certainly appreciate all you can do to keep us "up and running" over here.

Buford

Dear Ken:

During the past four months, my customer has requested help from us on four different BT2 problems. He also asked for on-site assistance April 6-7, which was rejected.
The four BT2 problems brought his complete system down nine times; twice I had to
help him completely rebuild his database.

I have absolutely no expertise in solving the problem and am at your mercy in letting
him know if we can come up with an answer. The customer has come to the conclusion that we do not appreciate or value his business at all. And I know you are as
concerned about retaining this $200,000 contract as I am.

Would you please call me Thursday afternoon to discuss your ideas and projected deadlines for this overdue help we owe our customer.

Sincerely,

Dear Meg:

Because no one from your division attended last week's status meeting, I had to report on the developments from your area, a report that may not have been totally accurate and up to date.

Representation at the meeting by all areas is the best way I know to ensure a forum for timely discussion of information and alterations in the project plans--alterations that may affect more than one area.

Will someone from your group attend the July 8 meeting at 2:00 in N10?

Sincerely,

GUIDELINES AND ALTERNATE PHRASES

STATE THE PROBLEM BRIEFLY AS IT RELATES TO COMPANY PROFITS AND EFFICIENCY, IF POSSIBLE, RATHER THAN TO YOUR OWN PERSONAL PREFERENCE.

These mistakes have cost us $2300 in the past year.

This problem creates quite an embarrassment for our sales reps when they call on clients.

We could save approximatley $20,000 over the next two years if we actively sought a new vendor.

As I see it, we are wasting proven expertise and excessive dollars, as well as risking the safety of our employees.

OFFER SOLUTIONS FROM YOUR PREVIOUS INVESTIGATION, EVEN THOUGH YOU MAY NOT HAVE AUTHORITY TO MAKE CORRECTIVE CHANGES.

INCLUDE ALL THE DETAILS THE READER NEEDS TO TAKE THE CORRECTIVE ACTION.

ACKNOWLEDGE THE DIFFICULTY OF THE PROBLEM TO BE HANDLED, IF APPROPRIATE.

While a solution will not be easy, there is one that will be effective.

Although this is a difficult situation, I feel certain that my proposal will begin a turnaround for us.

Although you may not have been aware of some of the most recent developments, I can assure you that this will alleviate at least two of the problems that are obvious from my end of the tunnel.

Certainly, I can't promise that this action will solve all the associated problems with this project, but it will take care of the most immediate.

Although a solution is not readily apparent, I think you will agree that some progress toward resolution is urgent.

ASK FOR A RESPONSE. SHOW CONFIDENCE THAT YOU WILL RECEIVE A FAVORABLE RESPONSE AND DON'T LET YOUR READER ASSUME THAT YOU JUST WROTE "TO GET IT OFF YOUR CHEST" OR "TO GET IT OUT IN THE OPEN."

May I have your approval on this?

Would you please phone me with your answer?

If you agree, please sign the attached memo.

If I can gather any more pertinent facts to help you make this decision, please call on me.

Dear Mr. Murphy:

The absence of controls on the production of JXT is creating security breaches and data integrity problems that could cost us two months' lead time on the competition.

Would you please implement a plan of strict controls against these production entries? The requirement of your signature on all new production entries in all upcoming phases would provide a quick and simple resolution to the security problem and also increase user confidence in our final product.

I'm eager to make this our finest product yet. Would you please phone me if I can help draft such a plan for ensuring the security of our system.

Sincerely,

Vivian,

We seem to be having continual problems in our fourth-floor conference-room scheduling. Misunderstandings and overlapping schedules can create an hour or more of lost time for all would-be meeting attendees. More importantly, such conflicts are a company embarrassment when clients are involved. Although there will always be some difficulty with last-minute needs, I think most interruptions and miscommunications can be minimized.

Therefore, I've taken the liberty of drafting some specific policies for use of the conference room. Would you please review my attached draft and sign it if you think these procedures are appropriate?

If you agree that these procedures will enable all of us to plan and use our meeting time more productively, I'll distribute the policy statement to all involved.

Carol

Dear Harvey,

Barry Groden tells me that he is still using the two propane fork trucks without head-lights. To avoid getting OSHA involved in this matter, can you help me resolve this situation and see that we get lights on the trucks before Friday?

The original delay resulted from the fact that this special headlight was out of stock and had to be shipped from the manufacturer. I understand now, however, that the headlights have arrived but that Maintenance can't spare the time to send someone out to our site to install them. I can imagine that Maintenance hears people crying "Wolf" much too often, but this repair falls into another category altogether--danger.

Would you please make a call to Bud Adams at ext. 4500 to see if they can accommo-date us on this problem before Friday?

Thank you,

GUIDELINES AND ALTERNATE PHRASES

INCLUDE ALL INFORMATION BASIC TO THE PROBLEM OR RESOLUTION SUCH AS COMPLETE NAMES, ADDRESSES, PHONE NUMBERS, FULL DESCRIPTION OF THE PRODUCT OR SERVICE, DATES, PLACES, AMOUNTS, METHODS OF PAYMENT, PREVIOUS CORRESPONDENCE, FILE NUMBERS.

STATE THE FACTS OF YOUR COMPLAINT IN AN ORGANIZED, EASY-TO-FOLLOW FORMAT. A BULLETED LIST IS AN EFFECTIVE WAY TO GIVE SPECIFICS. DO NOT CLUTTER WITH IRRELEVANT DETAILS.

DECIDE WHAT SPECIFIC ACTION YOU WANT AND FIRMLY STICK WITH IT. DON'T SOUND WISHY-WASHY IN WHAT YOU WILL ACCEPT AS RESTITUTION.

Please remove the $48 charge from my account.

Please send a replacement tray by overnight mail.

I will appreciate receiving an explanation and an apology from the service representative.

BE FIRM ABOUT ANY AGREED-UPON DEADLINE WITH REGARD TO ANY DELAYED RESPONSE YOU HAVE BEEN PROMISED.

I'll expect to hear from you by Friday.

As you confirmed, I will be looking for the replacement shipment within ten days.

As you suggested, I will wait to hear from Mr. Cox on August 15 about what adjustments he will make on the price.

SOUND FACTUAL, NOT EMOTIONAL.

My calls have not been returned. (Not: The return calls have never materialized.)

As you know, we have a $200,000 investment in this equipment, and we must have it operate dependably 24 hours a day. (Not: We have a $200,000 investment in this equipment; we would like to have it work occasionally.)

INCLUDE COPIES OF ALL NECESSARY DOCUMENTS SUCH AS RECEIPTS, FORMS, CONTRACTS, OR PREVIOUS CORRESPONDENCE.

BE CONFIDENT AND POLITE IN TONE, NOT SARCASTIC OR OFFENSIVE. ASSUME THAT THE READER WILL GIVE YOU A FAIR DEAL UNTIL HE OR SHE PROVES OTHERWISE.

I know that you will want to correct the situation immediately.

I was sure that if I pointed out the difficulties to you personally, you would make every effort to solve the problem.

I hope you can restore our confidence in your product and service.

You have given us excellent service in past years, and we want to continue to depend on you for our data processing needs.

ASSUME A STRONGER TONE IN THE NEXT ACTION YOU REQUEST IF FOLLOW-UP LETTERS BECOME NECESSARY TO GAIN THE READER'S COOPERATION.

If we don't hear from you by August 6, we will be turning the problem over to our legal department.

We will be forced to cancel our account with your firm if we do not have a suitable resolution by August 6.

RE: IRA account #12345678 and IRA account #910111213

Dear Mr. Fulbright:

Today I received my account statement from your office for the period ending 3/31/19-- and found that my instructions for rolling over stock into my IRA had not been carried out. I face severe tax consequences if this account cannot be corrected to indicate a rollover of my company stock into another qualified retirement plan within the next 14 days.

Needless to say, I am disappointed that these instructions have not been followed and am inconvenienced by having to write this second letter of instruction. (Ms. Debra White, the account executive assigned to me, says she lost my January 16 letter. Another copy is enclosed.)

Please take the following actions to correct my account:

1. Roll over 406 shares of Allbright Company common stock into my qualified IRA account #12345678.
2. Roll over 150 shares of TRZZ common stock into my qualified IRA account #910111213.
3. Make the effective date of both transactions February 1 because the delay in the rollover was due to mishandling of my previous instructions.

I know that you wish to maintain the good reputation of your brokerage firm, and I am counting on you to take care of these transactions immediately.

Yours truly,

Dear Mr. Lopez:

This letter will acknowledge receipt of your phone call today to say that you have finished the brochures. As we explained to you on the phone March 19 and again in our meeting at your place of business on March 25, the brochures that you erroneously printed in black ink rather than the brown ink we specified are not acceptable for the following reasons:

- All the inserts to be added to the brochures are in brown ink.
- All the cover letters to go with the brochures are in brown ink.
- The business cards and letterhead to accompany the brochures are in brown ink.
- The brochure's brown cover does not look aesthetically pleasing next to the black ink, a real problem because we use this brochure as a sales tool in soliciting brochure/editorial/layout/design business.
- We have used brown ink on all mailouts, brochures, business cards, and letterhead to establish product and material recognition in the marketplace.
- Finally, our acceptance of your printing bid was contingent on a due date of March 24 (as can be attested by the typesetter, the photographer, the photo-processing lab, and the printer for the accompanying brochure inserts). Your delivery date on the brochures is 21 days past due.

With no work-order paper ever shown us about your record of our oral directions to you, you assumed black ink, never verifying job specifications with us in any written form.

Our original agreement was that you print 2,000 copies of our brochure at a total cost of $4140 by our March 24 deadline. We regret the fact that you chose, after you got a deposit, not to go through with your agreement to reprint the brochures in the brown ink we had specified.

While we in no way find the black-ink printing job acceptable, in light of your reversal of your decision to reprint as agreed upon in our telephone conversation of March 19, we are willing to try to salvage the situation by settling for a full payment of $3,110 for the brochures. In exchange for the $3,110, we will take the 2,000 black-ink brochures, all printing plates, and the return of our photos.

We had hoped to move our own brochure-printing business, as well as the printing jobs for our clients, to this part of the city, a much more convenient location for us. And, of course, we will, in the future, continue to take our large printing jobs to the two printing firms across town, which have served us well over the last seven years.

If we do not have a response from you within ten days from the date of this letter about our offer to settle this matter, we will pursue all legal avenues open to us to recover our total $2,070 deposit and all legal costs.

Yours truly,

Dear Mr. Mossy:

On your flight #344 from Dallas to Tulsa on August 6, my bags were lost. Not only were they three days late in arriving, but also one arrived damaged. During the entire ordeal, your representatives continued to display a don't-tell-me-your-troubles attitude in solving the problem.

To elaborate on the details:

- Upon arrival when I discovered my bags did not make it with me to Tulsa, I filed a claim with baggage service. The agent assured me the bags would arrive on the next flight at approximately 7:00 p.m. She took my name and hotel address and said the bags would be delivered there about 8:00. The bags never arrived.
- I called your Tulsa office again and spoke with Felicia Smith. She could tell me nothing and suggested I call the Dallas office again. I made four long-distance calls trying to reach the appropriate party. No one could tell me where the bags were. They suggested I "just wait." I spent $10 on overnight toiletries.
- The second day I phoned your Tulsa office again and Mike Hertz told me that the bags had indeed arrived on the previous evening's flight; he didn't know why they were not delivered to me as promised. I explained that I was traveling on to Norman, and he took my hotel address there and assured me my bags would arrive there by 6:00 p.m. the second day. I worked the second day in the same clothes.
- When I arrived at my Norman hotel that second evening, the bags had still not arrived. When I called the Tulsa office again, Suzanne Swartz told me she was "busy" and suggested I call her back collect in an hour. I asked to speak to her supervisor. She put me on hold for five minutes. When I hung up and called back, no one answered the phone.
- My bags (one with a broken handle and twisted rollers) were finally delivered at 4:00 p.m. on Thursday--four days after my Monday-evening flight. No apology or explanation was ever given me about the delay or difficulty.

I request full payment for the damaged bag in the amount of $198. Also, I think it only appropriate that you reimburse me $10 for the toiletries and $19.86 for the four long-distance calls made to your airline offices.

Attached you will find

   --a repair estimate for the bag and a brochure listing the price of a comparable re-
    placement bag
   --my baggage claim receipt
   --the hotel listing of telephone charges
   --a receipt for the toiletries
   --boarding passes and a copy of the baggage claim check

My staff and I travel in excess of 60 percent of the year to all 50 states, and we schedule at least 2,000 flight segments on your airline. Needless to say, the quality of service
that I recently received has left a lasting impression. I hope that you will want to correct that impression.

Yours truly,

GUIDELINES AND ALTERNATE PHRASES

MENTION THE DEATH BUT AVOID GOING INTO SPECIFIC DETAILS OF THE TRAGEDY OR ILLNESS.

We would like to extend our deepest sympathy in the loss of your mother.

Everyone in the department has asked me to try to express to you our sincerest regrets about your son's car accident.

I can't say how shocked and saddened I was to hear of your husband's illness and sudden death. Please know that my thoughts are with you during this time.

Although Mildred's illness was a lengthy one and her death not unexpected, that does not lessen the grief we all feel at her passing away.

Please accept my deepest sympathy in the death of your mother, of whom you spoke so affectionately and so often.

Frank, my prayers are with you in this tragedy. Although words are of little comfort at a time like this, please know that we are thinking of you daily.

My thoughts have been with you almost continually since I heard the news of your wife's death. I am so sorry.

OFFER SOME SPECIFIC PRAISE OF THE DECEASED. IF YOU DIDN'T KNOW THE PERSON WELL, PASS ON COMPLIMENTARY REMARKS FROM OTHERS (EVEN THE RECIPIENT OF THE LETTER).

Although I didn't have the privilege of knowing her personally, those in the office who did work with her have frequently commented on her delightful sense of humor.

Though somehow our paths never seemed to cross through the years, I heard of her achievements from numerous sources.

From all those who have mentioned the shocking news around our office this week, I gather that their admiration for Frank ran deep.

Although I didn't know your wife personally, I can recall so many times when you mentioned her supportive attitude about your travel assignments and what part she played in your overall career success. I know you must feel an immeasurable loss.

Even though I didn't know your father personally, I don't have to go far to hear others speak of him so fondly. Evidently, so many, many people valued their association with him through the years.

BE SPECIFIC IN ANY OFFER OF HELP.

If you feel the need to get away for a quiet rest during the coming months, please phone me; we have a house on Lake Livingston that we'd be glad for you to use.

If you'd like me to notify specific clients and colleagues that you'll be away from the office for a while, I'd be more than happy to help in that small way.

Let me know if there is any major project on your desk that can't wait for your return, and I'll be happy to cover for you. My home number is 234-5678.

MENTION ANY MEMORIAL YOU ARE MAKING ON BEHALF OF THE DECEASED SUCH AS FLOWERS, A BOOK, OR MONETARY DONATIONS.

We have made a donation to the American Cancer Society in Bill's name. In some small way, we want to add to his influence in the world.

We've donated two copies of Peter Drucker's latest book to our library in memory of Joan. Everyone interested in the leadership skills and management philosophies that Joan exemplified will see her name on the book's inside cover.

The flowers that will be arriving shortly are a small symbol of my great esteem for Jerome.

USE PERSONAL STATIONERY AND WRITE YOUR LETTER IN LONGHAND.

Dear Mrs. Glover:

I was so sorry to hear of Frank's heart attack and sudden death. He was a person who always had a smile on his face and a word of encouragement for those around him. His can-do attitude about anything assigned to our group became contagious in the company. He was always available to us and showed a willingness to help in any way he could. Day in and day out, he showed the kind of motivation and leadership all of us on his staff so much admired.

But even more than that leadership position, I have always valued my close and friendly association with Frank. There is for most people that one special individual who becomes a mentor, offering guidance, introductions, inspiration, encouragement, solace over failure, and, most importantly, an example of success. For me, Frank was that person.

As a memorial to his leadership and friendship, we have had his latest photo (that from the annual report) framed and hung in one of our conference rooms on this floor. We will not forget him.

In deepest sympathy,

Dear Mrs. Marks:

We were distressed to hear from Brian Ellis that Jim had passed away after such a long illness.

We knew Jim to be energetic, enthusiastic, and a highly motivated employee--constantly looking after the company's welfare. He worked as an inspector, a supervisor, and finally general manager, doing a splendid job at anything we assigned him. A company is only as great as the collected employees who represent it and give it purpose and meaning. Jim comes foremost to my mind in being that kind of representative.

I also know with certainty that he was that kind of devoted husband and father. Please express my condolences to your sons.

All of us at Appleby share with you in your loss. Flowers from the office staff should be arriving shortly. Please accept this as a small token of our sympathy and a tribute to Jim and the fond memories he left with us.

Sincerely,

Dear Jerry:

I have heard of your father's death from several sources during the last two days. I am so sorry. Even though your dad retired some time ago, he maintained his friendships with people in the industry he'd known all his working life.

Many people seem to "fade away" after they retire, but that certainly wasn't the case with your father. He had such a pleasant personality that he created an image in peoples' minds that endeared him to them for years. His name frequently comes up in office conversations and "story swaps."

It must be a great comfort to you to know that your father realized your deep affection for him. The newspaper clipping noted that he had 16 grandchildren and four great-grandchildren. Youngsters need heroes and role models today; please tell them from one who knew your father well that their grandfather had the respect and admiration of all who knew him.

In deepest sympathy,

Buren,

Joe Smith called me early this morning to tell me of your father's death. Although I heard of the tragic crash from news reports, I had no idea your father was on the plane.

Often I've heard you speak of the great weekend trips to your father's lake cabin and the enjoyable times you spent together. I know the loss must be overwhelming to you at the moment. Please accept my deepest sympathy.

I've asked Harold Jarvis to take over all unfinished projects on your desk so that you can take all the time you need to handle details at home.

Sincerely,

Dear Mr. Hartford:

We learned of your son's death when one of your customers, Abrams Milo, called on us this morning. Although we have not worked with your son personally, we have heard from many sources that he was so well respected among his colleagues.

And of course his contributions to the community are known by anyone who has lived in the city for any period of time. Our community needs so many more giving individuals like Jack--those who work and don't care who gets the credit for their achievements.

Jack's company has served us well, and we know that excellence stems from his leadership and tenets of management. Our sympathies are with you in the loss.

Sincerely,

GUIDELINES AND ALTERNATE PHRASES

THANK THE PERSON FOR TAKING THE TIME TO WRITE OR SEND A MEMORIAL SUCH AS FLOWERS OR A DONATION.

I appreciated your thoughtful letter so much. Such kind comments, as you know, help me to remember and cherish the years Marvin and I spent together.

Your donation of the book is just the kind of memorial my father would have loved.

The beautiful flowers meant so much to us as a symbol of your caring.

AVOID MAUDLIN STATEMENTS, BUT ADD YOUR OWN PRAISE OF THE DECEASED.

Melba and I shared many of the same personal goals and dreams, and it makes me feel proud to know that she had that same kind of rapport with those in her office.

John was always sensitive to my needs, sometimes even before I expressed them. Your comments about his personal thoughtfulness and his attention to excellence on the job made me feel very proud. Thank you for letting me know of your appreciation for him.

ACCEPT OR DECLINE ANY OFFER OF HELP GRACIOUSLY.

If we do decide to get away for the weekend, we will give you a call so as not to interfere with your own use of the lake cabin. Thank you for such a thoughtful gesture.

I don't think there's anything on the desk that can't wait until I return to Houston. But I will take you up on your offer to notify the overseas Vitton clients that I will be away for a month. Thank you for thinking of such matters.

Dear Sue:

Most of us probably feel that our own mother is the best. For me, my mother was truly the reason for what I've been able to accomplish with my life. I already miss her deeply. But even though she is no longer with me, she is still giving me the strength, courage, and inspiration to continue to live life to its fullest.

Thank you for your letter; your personal recognition of her death honored her. We as a family appreciate your thoughtfulness in writing. God bless you and your family.

Sincerely,

CONFIRMATIONS/Of Phone Conversations or Meetings

GUIDELINES AND ALTERNATE PHRASES

RESTATE ALL THE IMPORTANT FACTS AND DETAILS THAT YOU WANT TO VERIFY. THIS REPETITION AND VERIFICATION IS A PRIMARY REASON FOR PUTTING A CONVERSATION IN WRITING.

This letter will confirm. . . .

We are pleased to confirm. . . .

Thank you for meeting with me about. . . . We are pleased to say that. . . .

As we discussed today in your office, I will be happy to. . . .

As I promised in our May 6 phone conversation, we can offer you. . . .

MENTION THE DATE AND SUBJECT OF ANY INITIAL CONTACT. TO REFERENCE PREVIOUS DISCUSSIONS BY DATE ALONE IS INSUFFICIENT.

GIVE ALL NECESSARY DETAILS FOR THE READER TO CONTACT YOU IN CASE YOUR LETTER REVEALS SOME ERROR OR MISUNDERSTANDING.

Let me reiterate all the specifics: . . .

Let me see if I have all the details as you specified: . . .

Please review all the procedures outlined below; if there are any discrepancies, phone me immediately.

PROVIDE A SIGNATURE LINE FOR THE READER IF YOU WANT THE LETTER TO BECOME A BINDING CONTRACT.

If this meets with your approval, would you please sign below.

If you agree with what I've outlined here, please sign below, copy this letter, and return the original for my files.

Do you agree? If so, I'll appreciate an immediate reply.

Are we in agreement? Would you write to let me know immediately if we need to modify any of the details.

If there is some misunderstanding or some omission, please write Margaret Hatcher immediately.

Dear Mr. Taylor:

This letter will confirm our February 1 conversation regarding the movement of files and furniture from Towers West to the fifth floor of Cincinnati Commerce Tower in United Fuller Plaza on March 2.

As we discussed, this is a large move because of the Town Davids units involved. We will also be moving file cabinets, chairs, and many boxes. The flat-map file, scout card files, standing map cases, and plotter on the sixth floor will all need special attention. Your movers will need two-wheel dollies and other special equipment.

Please load all furniture at the Bammel Street entrance to the building. The ramp on Berryton Street will be the unloading site. We will furnish elevator operators in both the Towers West and the Cincinnati Commerce Tower buildings. On Saturday when the boxes are to be moved, please schedule all equipment and personnel so as to avoid any delay in our normal Monday-to-Friday office work schedule. We have agreed that all movement of furniture and boxes will be complete by 5:00 p.m. on Saturday.

All your personnel must pick up identification badges and log in with our security desk upon arrival at the Towers West location. They must turn in the badges at the end of each shift. Please call our security people at 123-4567 prior to 5:00 p.m. on February 28 to give them the names of your people working each shift.

If we have misunderstood any of your services with regard to this move, please let me know immediately by calling 456-3355. We look forward to a smooth move under your effective guidance.

Sincerely,

Dear Mr. Fuzzirry:

As a follow up to our March 6 phone conversation, we are pleased to authorize you to represent us in seeking to secure a ruling from the Brazilian authorities that the dividend income distributed by Murphy Government Securities Fund, Inc. to shareholders living in The Commonwealth of Pabbleitz is nontaxable.

We understand that you will bill us at your customary rate of $120 an hour for your services. Please include with your monthly bill an itemized statement. We will pay the amount in full within 30 days of receipt of your bill. Also, we request with your bill a brief letter describing the status of the work.

If this is your understanding of our agreement, would you please sign on the line provided below and return one copy of this letter for our files.

Enclosed are all pertinent documents about the ruling: my January 4, 19--, request to the Bureau of Income Tax and four letters from Murphy Government Securities Fund's general counsel concerning recent developments in Texas and Louisiana that may be of interest to you.

Yours truly,

Larry P. Randall
Ardmore and Ardmore, Legal Counsel

_____   _____
Mr. Harold J. Fuzzirry   Date

Myron,

During our recent conversation with Benton, Inc.'s customer, Ardo Chemical, I think I may have left some confusion concerning whether you should call on them in the future. Let me restate my position:

There is no reason for you or any of your representatives to venture into Benton's territory. As we've discussed on several occasions, territory boundaries are sacred. On occasion, of course, two shop managers may agree that, for a specific situation, crossing boundaries is acceptable. But both shops must agree fully in such a situation, and they should limit such contact to only one transaction.

Benton has a plan to straighten out their problem with Ardo Chemical, and we want to give them the right to do just that. I'm sure you would want the same consideration were the situation reversed.

If, however, you do not agree with my position and feel that the situation warrants further review, you may appeal to have a certain territory transferred to your shop. You may direct any such proposal to Marvin Vindler in the Shreveport office.

Keep up the good work you're doing for us.

Sincerely,

GUIDELINES AND ALTERNATE PHRASES

THANK THE READER FOR AGREEING TO SPEAK AT YOUR MEETING.

We are delighted you have agreed to speak on "Communication Trends" at our upcoming national conference, October 1-4, in Anaheim, California.

REPEAT ALL PERTINENT DETAILS ABOUT THE PROGRAM: OVERALL THEME; OTHER SPEAKERS' TOPICS; THE READER'S SPECIFIC TOPIC, LENGTH, DATE; AUDIENCE DESCRIPTION AND EXPECTATIONS; ANY NECESSARY EQUIPMENT, PRINTING, OR PUBLICITY NEEDS.

You are scheduled to speak on Tuesday, May 6, at 10:00 a.m. Your presentation will be preceded by Dr. Max Apple and Barry Goldman, both from Neiman Associates.

We will appreciate it if you can make your own hotel and flight arrangements.

CONFIRM THE LOGISTICS OF THE MEETING— ESCORTS, MEETING SITE, ADDRESS, ROOM NUMBERS, HOTEL ACCOMMODATIONS, MEALS, TRANSPORTATION TO AND FROM THE SITE.

As you stated in your letter, you will not need reimbursement for overnight lodging, but we will be happy to rent any necessary audio or visual equipment.

All meals will be included in your complimentary registration to the conference.

Please fill out the enclosed forms telling us of your lodging and travel preferences, and we will do our best to handle the details to make your travel headache-free.

EXPLAIN HOW TO HANDLE THE EXPENSES: ARE EXPENSES TO BE DIRECT BILLED TO YOU OR WILL THE SPEAKER BE REIMBURSED? HOW DOES HE OR SHE SUBMIT EXPENSES AND FEES?

We will be happy to provide a $200 advance against your expenses. If you prefer to bill us afterward for your expenses, we can reimburse you within five days.

CLOSE BY EXPRESSING CONFIDENCE IN THE SUCCESS OF YOUR SPEAKER.

We are eager to hear you.

We know you will be a big success with our audience.

Your selection reflects the committee's high interest in your topic and confidence in your ability as a speaker.

Our members have expressed great excitement in having you come.

We're expecting many excellent management tips from your vast experience.

IF THE SPEAKER IS COMING WITHOUT FEE IN HOPES OF REFERRALS OR PUBLICITY FOR HIS OR HER OWN LATER BUSINESS, EXPRESS YOUR INTENTION TO HELP OR YOUR BEST WISHES FOR THOSE POSSIBILITIES.

As we have discussed, our members should be quite eager to make purchases of your audio for further self-study.

We hope you will agree that the time spent in your preparation for our program will be a great investment in future business.

Most of our attendees will be small-business owners and, therefore, primary prospective buyers of your accounting services. We plan to point out in our pre-meeting publicity that you are, in fact, accepting new clients.

Dear Al,

We are so pleased that you have agreed to speak to our Houston Credit Association membership on July 8. Your topic is one that has been bounced around for months as a "wish" until someone gave us your name as a true expert on the subject of collections.

The setting of our meeting is very informal. After cocktails at 6:30 and dinner at 7:30, you will be introduced at 8:30. After your 30-minute presentation, we will allow about 15 minutes for questions and answers. We expect about 120 people to attend, and we hope this question-answer time will allow our members to ask what's on their minds. You should undoubtedly be prepared for questions on how the normal collection letters and schedules can be handled in such a sour economy and with bankruptcies at a peak.

We will have an overhead projector and lapel microphone ready for you and understand that you will be bringing your own handouts. Also, as we discussed, you are free to bring copies of your book for sale; we can furnish a volunteer to sit at the book table to make sales if that would be helpful to you.

Janet Jones, who will be wearing a name badge, will meet you in the United Belasco Tower, first-floor foyer, and lead you through the "maze" to our banquet room. If you need to make any other last-minute requests or arrangements, please phone her at 123-4444.

The program committee is genuinely excited about the information you can provide our credit people; we hope you too are looking forward to meeting potential clients. We plan to publicize your speaking date widely and feel certain that you will attract those most interested in your own professional services.

Cordially,

GUIDELINES AND ALTERNATE PHRASES

EXPRESS PLEASURE THAT THE INDIVIDUAL WILL BE ATTENDING THE EVENT.

We are so pleased you will be attending the. . . .

We are happy to confirm your attendance at. . . .

This letter is your confirmation for attendance at the . . .; please present it at the registration desk for your name badge and welcoming packet.

STATE OBJECTIVES OF THE EVENT.

ESTABLISH THE CREDIBILITY OF ANY SPEAKERS.

Bill Baker is highly regarded among his colleagues for such presentations.

Bill Baker has been a keynote speaker at major conventions across the nation, including. . . .

As a board member for six major corporations, Bill's firsthand knowledge of the philosophies he espouses will give that practical application we all need.

As "one of us," Bill understands the intricacies of the procedures he will be outlining for us and appreciates the specific adjustments we must make in our local arena.

REPEAT ALL PERTINENT DETAILS FOR VERIFICATION—TIME, PLACE, DRESS, ACCOMMODATIONS, FEES.

Please feel free to dress casually. You'll have plenty of time for golf in this resort setting.

In addition to the registration fee you have already submitted, you will have out-of-pocket expenses for three days' meals and local transportation by cab or bus.

MENTION NECESSARY PRE-EVENT PREPARATION ON THE PART OF THE ATTENDEE, SUCH AS READINGS TO BE COMPLETED OR SPECIAL FILES OR MATERIALS TO BRING.

GIVE THE CONTACT NAME AND NUMBER OF THE MEETING COORDINATOR FOR READERS WITH SPECIAL SITUATIONS AND QUESTIONS.

Call Gretchen Calhoun for any other details I may have failed to make clear here.

If we can help you in any other way to prepare for the conference, we would be happy to do so.

For any special circumstances, please contact Gretchen Calhoun at ext. 123.

If neither Gretchen nor I hear from you to the contrary before August 6, we'll see you in Atlanta.

Dear Mr. Faxton:

We are pleased that you will be able to join us at the two-day Effective Writing Workshop on October 6-7 at the Woodlands Inn Conference Center. We will begin promptly at 8:30 a.m. in the Spanish Republic Room and end promptly at 4:30 p.m. on both days.

As we mentioned in our initial brochure to you, the objectives of the program are to help each participant:

- reduce writing time
- improve clarity
- select appropriate formats for reports
- design effective visuals
- condense document length

We ask that you please read pages 10-38 of the <u>Technical Writing</u> text we are mailing to you separately. The instructor will expect that all attendees have previewed these concepts and will begin her presentation on that assumption.

Dr. Sylvia Battmane will be leading this workshop, as she has done on two previous occasions for us in-house. Dr. Battmane has 18 years' experience in presenting effective writing principles and has received excellent evaluations from audiences within the top corporations around the nation.

The dress is normal business attire. If you have any special concerns about the accommodations or schedule, please phone Gretchen Calhoun in our office, ext. 123. She will be glad to answer questions and help you make this a most worthwhile learning experience.

Plan on a productive two days!

Sincerely,

CONGRATULATIONS

EXPRESS CONGRATULATIONS ON THE OCCASION OR ACHIEVEMENT IMMEDIATELY.

FOCUS YOUR MESSAGE ON THE OTHER PERSON—NOT YOURSELF OR YOUR COMPANY.

You deserve all the recognition coming your way. We're delighted.

You have worked long in gathering the expertise necessary to make this step. We have all noted your personal effort and sacrifice to accomplish these goals.

Thank you for your long hours of work and creative effort in making the company look good. In so doing, you've made quite a favorable impression around all of our branch offices.

BE SPECIFIC IN YOUR PRAISE. EXAGGERATION AND VAGUE GENERALITIES SOUND GUSHY AND INSINCERE. LET THE READER KNOW YOU UNDERSTAND THE TIME, EFFORT, EXPERTISE, PERSISTENCE, CREATIVITY, OR WHATEVER WAS NECESSARY TO ACCOMPLISH THE ACHIEVEMENT.

This award simply recognizes what those of us who work with you have already figured out—you're a born motivator. Where would we be on the Thornton project if you hadn't stepped in? This award just underscores the genuine excitement you show around the office daily.

Each time you bring your children by the office for a brief visit, I'm reminded how well behaved they are. This new baby, I'm sure, will be equally fortunate to grow up in such a home.

The new job is one that I think will allow you to use your talents fully—your leadership abilities, your eye for opportunity and new trends, and the articulate way you express yourself to prospective customers.

Publication in such a prestigious magazine certainly underscores the value of your ideas for all of our industry leaders.

BE INFORMAL AND PERSONAL WITHOUT BEING TOO FAMILIAR (UNLESS YOU KNOW THE READER VERY, VERY WELL). REMEMBER THAT THE RECIPIENT MAY NOT WANT A COUNT OF BIRTHDAYS, REMARRIAGES, OR CHILDREN.

EXPRESS ENTHUSIASM. DON'T MAKE YOUR LETTER SOUND LIKE THE TYPICAL FORM LETTER THAT DUTY DICTATES. PROMPTNESS ITSELF INDICATES AN EAGERNESS TO RECOGNIZE THE OCCASION OR ACHIEVEMENT.

Congratulations on your new position as vice chairman! Nimitz is a great company to work for, and I'm glad to see that they recognize their star players.

STAY AWAY FROM NEGATIVES THAT MAY DETRACT FROM THE OVERALL SUCCESS OF ACHIEVEMENT OR THE HAPPY OCCASION.

Dear Frank:

Mark Hammond has told me of your designation as the outstanding engineering graduate of Tulane University! Congratulations!

I know this kind of recognition must make you feel good, but it is a most worthwhile "thank you" on the part of the designating university for all your accomplishments, not the least of which is building a major company in a tough industry.

Cordially,

Dear Francis:

I just learned of your selection for an award for outstanding research from the International Society for Heart Research and the Journal of Molecular and Cellular Cardiology.

Please accept my warmest wishes on your receiving this high honor from your fellow professionals; recognition of such achievements certainly reflects on your individual drive and commitment to excellence. We at the hospital are particularly thrilled that you have put us in the limelight along with your prestigious work.

Again, congratulations.

Sincerely,

Dear Peter:

I read with great excitement the Holden article about your significant achievement. Please accept my heartiest congrats on the award. I know that you and your family are justly proud, as you should be, to be included in such an exclusive group. Imagine, one of 11 individuals out of the whole Kaiser family of 22,000 employees! My hat's off to you.

I've bragged all over our office here in Dallas that I'm on first-name terms with a company celebrity. (The closest I've ever been to the CEO was five feet in front of my TV!)

You know, I'm really not surprised that the company finally recognized your contribution. I can remember when you spent so much time on the FAX project that it seemed you were out of town more than you were home. I know it was tough on your family being without you so much, and I just hope this honor helps all of you as a family unit.

Give my warmest regards to Mary, and God bless.

Cordially,

Margaret,

Congratulations on a healthy, and I'm sure, beautiful and perfect baby girl. We know this is a very special event for you and your family, and we want you to enjoy every moment of the new event without a worry about the office.

Our best for your guidance in all the joys and "trials" that come with raising a child in this fast-paced, exciting world. For Belinda, we wish health and love for each new year.

Warmest wishes,

Frank,

So the wait is up? You ain't seen nothing yet--the waiting in line for Pampers at the 7-Eleven, the waiting at the dentist's office, the waiting for the PTO's costumed angels to sing their carol, the waiting for a driver's permit, the waiting for the first after-school job.

But all that can wait--CONGRATULATIONS. We know this is one of the greatest joys of life. All our best to that big 8-lb. boy.

Best regards,

Jeff,

I just remembered what the big red circle on your calendar represents--the anniversary of your 29th birthday. Here's to a great day, a great week, a great year, a great lifetime!

Regards,

Marge,

Isn't this a special time of the year for you--your birthday? I couldn't let it pass with-out dropping you a note to say how often I think of you and your contribution to our team. But most importantly, I value your friendship personally. Please accept my heartful of best wishes on your birthday.

Cordially,

Dear Robert,

I was very pleased to learn of your selection as Public Relations Professional for the Year in our state. Certainly no one deserves this distinction more than you do. The skywriting over Frank Towers during the lightning storm has got to be your best coup yet--at least the most memorable.

My best personal regards,

Donald,

I want to congratulate you on your outstanding service to the Ballet, first as its treasurer, then as its vice president, and then as its president for the past four years. Bob Snelling, at our annual meeting ceremonies, certainly detailed a long list of the accomplishments under your leadership. They have been no less than tremendous.

I hope you take a great deal of pleasure in all these contributions to the organization. Of course, it makes me feel good simply to have been involved with you from the sidelines.

We're looking forward to even greater things for the future.

Sincerely,

Dear Donna,

Your participation in the Silver Key Circle throughout the year was most commendable, and I congratulate you on your achievement of having earned a lifetime membership in the Chamber of Commerce.

I want you to know that I personally appreciate all of the extra work and effort you put forth to attend the meetings of the Circle and to secure speakers in order to earn the necessary credits required for this lifetime membership.

This is the kind of activity that keeps our company's name in front of the community and proves to our neighbors that we willingly accept our social and civic responsibilities for the good of all. Thank you.

Sincerely,

Dear Mr. Merrymount:

I was pleased to read in last week's newspapers that you've been elected a director of Hartford National Bancshares, Inc. I extend my congratulations and know that this experience will be mutually beneficial.

Just prior to your actual election last week, an associate and I, representing a subsidiary bank's advertising agency, presented a ten-minute audiovisual overview of the company's new graphic look and advertising approach. Please consider this letter an invitation to telephone me to arrange for a personal presentation to you, should your busy schedule permit.

Congratulations on such a prestigious promotion.

Cordially,

Dear Gwen:

Congratulations again, Gwen, on your position as chief financial officer. Bill Hamitz was certainly complimentary of you in the press release, and I know firsthand that all his comments were absolute, well-founded truths. I remember your timely tax advice on my personal situation a few years ago; my accountant still gives you all the "glory" in forseeing the events that led to that wise move.

When I'm downtown again, I'd like to stop by and see your new corporate headquarters. I'll give you a call and a warning.

Regards,

Dear Harold,

Congratulations on your new position as senior vice president with Armand, Inc. In my estimation you've had the necessary leadership skills since you stepped out of the university setting. The next time I have a new venture to propose I know on whose door I should knock.

Seriously, Mack Snookle is a valued, long-time friend of mine, and it is good to see your affiliation with him and his associates. Both of you will be in good company. Here's to a great start and a long string of successes.

Best wishes,

Dear Benny,

Onward and upward! My congratulations to you on your promotion to regional director and for your continuing success story. Particularly, I've heard good things about the challenges you undertook in turning the Atlanta division into a real profit center. You have indeed deserved all the accolades that have been offered you this past year. Best wishes for your continued success and good health.

Regards,

Dear Anna:

Congratulations on your well-deserved promotion to Advisory Council support. I'm even more excited to have you as one of our reps here in this branch. You've already played a tremendously important role in our office by simply handling the day-to-day activities to make things run smoothly and keep us closely in touch with our customers.

Thank you. I look forward to the next months and years together.

Sincerely,

Dear Michael:

As you have no doubt been told by Bill Lawrence, the Board of Directors last Tuesday appointed you as an officer of the company, effective October 1, 19--. I am pleased with their action and want to offer my personal congratulations.

You now, of course, have the authority to commit the company contractually. And every increase in authority carries with it an even greater increase in responsibility. Personally, I've found that additional authority results in even greater restraint rather than greater freedom to act. I'm confident that you will properly carry this additional authority and restraint to our best benefit.

We are expecting great things from you because you have proved yourself over and over in the past. You have the talent, the dedication, and the will that such a job requires. Congratulations.

Sincerely,

Dear Max:

I certainly enjoyed reading the March 20 "Financial Waves" article on your fast-growing company. Such coverage not only reflects good public relations but an excellent explanation of the company's accomplishments and objectives for future products.

The move to Boston certainly must have involved some inconveniences, but your comments in that respect show wise judgment that, I think, will pay handsome dividends in the next few years.

Please accept my sincere admiration--and don't forget to phone me when you're in town again.

Cordially,

Jack,

I read the May 16 <u>Forbes</u> article with much interest--but little surprise. I'm just glad to see that others recognize your know-how and appreciate your leadership in turning your organization around.

My best,

Dear Willis:

Congratulations on the fine job you're doing at Vertex, Inc. I read with interest the article you published in Global Trends. As you might guess, I read quite a bit on your subject, but you presented your viewpoint in the article in a most striking way--an interesting insight into the customer-service arena.

Your sound, fundamental approach to sales management should have been followed by many of our colleagues who were not so well prepared for the recession perils of the last two years.

Cordially,

Dear Dorothy:

Just a note to let you know how much I enjoyed your spring issue of Rex Marketing Record. I see a number of these in-house newsletters and was, in fact, the editor of one for a short while. Yours is the best such newsletter I have read.

Especially, I was interested in the article on DBT-IO-RO. Recently, Bill Macadoo and I met at an ASTD convention in San Francisco. I hope you'll do more with that concept, and he may be just the person to follow up the action in later issues.

An idea: The expense might be prohibitive, but have you considered sending a copy to every stockholder?

Regards,

Grover,

It was startling to see your steely-blue eyes leering at me from the photo atop your byline and bio in <u>Executive Excellence</u>. To write you every time you get a new honor, publish an article, or make big waves elsewhere would be prohibitively expensive-- especially since postage has just gone up.

But having an article accepted in such a prestigious place I certainly felt was worthy of a note. Fine job. We're proud of you. I hope you have long coattails.

All my best,

Fred,

Long live your press agent--now I <u>really</u> want the name of your suit designer. Wonderful article--makes perfectly good sense to my inquiring mind. Now, if we just had someone like you in public office to take care of the whole country. . . .

Warmest wishes,

Cheryl,

I was delighted to receive "hot off the press" a copy of your new book. The layout and photographs were exquisitely done, and the material is based on strong and effective learning concepts.

Cheryl, you are, undoubtedly, one of the most productive people I've met in years.

Best regards,

Dear Jeremy:

I'm pleased to have the opportunity to help you mark your retirement from the company and move into a life of well-deserved leisure and travel. Thank you so much for the excellent sales assistance you've given me numerous times in the past 25 years. Specifically, I'm remembering just last year--without you, I could have kissed the Joverson deal goodbye.

Doesn't the time go fast? But being the effective salesperson you are, you've been just as fast in piling up awards and profit records.

Congratulations on a very successful career--one I hope to emulate.

Sincerely,

Dear Willard:

Come Easter week, they tell me the business is losing some of its real flavor. Are you really retiring? Who will be here to tell about real creative selling--like translating butter and eggs into an initial payment?

And who will be able to show us such good times on the job? Like the time at Ruidoso when I watched your knuckles turn white as the helicopter went into a steep bank and we looked straight down through the open door--several thousand feet.

And who will straighten me out when I tell a customer that the 402 model will cost him $2,800/month instead of $800?

As you can see, the things I remember are not only the problems but the fun. I'm very grateful for having worked with a fine guy who still "wears well" with everyone I know.

My sincerest wishes for your future happy years.

Regards,

Dear Mary,

I learned of your recent wedding from Mack McKenzie. Please accept my best wishes on such a joyous occasion. We hope for you years of happiness, personal and business success, good health, and plenty of time to enjoy each other's company.

Sincerely,

John,

We are delighted to learn that you have talked Joanne into marrying "the most eligible bachelor in the city." Seriously, we couldn't be happier for you. Although we haven't had the pleasure of meeting Joanne, we have the highest regard for your tastes and know she must be special to have earned your love. We wish you the very best in your years together.

Our best wishes,

CONGRATULATIONS/Response to Congratulations

EXPRESS APPRECIATION FOR THE WRITER'S THOUGHTFULNESS IN TAKING THE TIME TO CONGRATULATE YOU.

It was thoughtful of you to take the time to write me about the award.

It is rewarding to find out that the things in which you take so much interest are noticed and appreciated by your colleagues.

Thanks for your note about the article on our company. I hope the author knows what he's talking about!

You are always so observant and thoughtful in letting me know when you read something complimentary about our business, and I want you to know that I sincerely appreciate it.

Thank you for your thoughtful letter on my promotion. Needless to say, I'm pleased, but I think the timing may leave something to be desired. Anyway, thanks for your vote of confidence.

I was pleasantly surprised to hear from you. Thank you for your kind comments.

BE MODEST—DON'T RECOUNT ALL YOUR ACHIEVEMENTS AGAIN IN YOUR RESPONSE.

EXTEND SOME INVITATION TO HOSPITALITY OR FURTHER CONTACT, IF APPROPRIATE.

Dear Rex,

It is always a pleasure to have friends such as you take note of special occasions in my life. Thank you for your recent note,and best wishes.

Sincerely,

Dear Betty:

Awards are always more meaningful when shared with friends. Thank you for your letter of encouragement and display of confidence. I assure you the feeling is mutual.

Can we perhaps get together for dinner at the ASPA New York show in December? I'll phone closer to that date.

Sincerely,

Dear Mr. Hightower:

Thank you for the kind comments in your recent letter about my new responsibilities at Sitco, Inc. There have always been giants in the industry such as you who have led the way for the inroads the rest of us are now making.

Thank you for your thoughtfulness in writing. Perhaps you'll let me call on you again for advice in this new position.

Sincerely,

GUIDELINES AND ALTERNATE PHRASES

ASSURE THE READER THAT YOU INTEND TO PAY THE ACCOUNT BUT UNDER ALTERED TERMS.

We are asking that you work with us in our payment of the account balance.

We do have every intention of paying our bill from your firm; we simply need to restructure our payment schedule in light of some current cash-flow problems.

Your letter arrived yesterday, asking about our outstanding balance of $4,589. We are making arrangements at the current time to consolidate our bills and want to discuss how we might work with you in restructuring our payback schedule.

ENCLOSE SOME SMALL CHECK, IF AT ALL POSSIBLE, TO SHOW GOOD FAITH IN A DELAYED PAYMENT ARRANGEMENT.

Please consider the enclosed check for $500 as partial payment on the account until we can make further arrangements suitable to both of us.

I've enclosed a check for $2,000; with this check, we ask that you understand we fully intend to pay the entire amount within the next 60 days.

OFFER EXPLANATION ABOUT YOUR NONPAYMENT AND CURRENT BUSINESS DIFFICULTIES.

As you know, our industry has been on the skids for the past year. Our firm particularly has felt the downturn because. . . .

One of the owners of our small business, Harold Rathboth, passed away recently, and we have had some legal difficulties and delays in a buy-out plan we are now negotiating.

We have recently acquired three new insurance agencies and have run into cash-flow difficulties in the process of consolidating all our operations.

Our initial marketing effort on the product was delayed by 90 days, and we simply find that we are running 90 days behind our revenue projections.

REMIND THE READER OF YOUR PAST BUSINESS AND REFER TO A CONTINUED RELATIONSHIP IN THE FUTURE.

We have appreciated your willingness to do business during the past decade and hope to continue that relationship.

You were more than cooperative when we ran into difficulties four years ago, and we need to ask that same kind of patience in this current temporary situation. Believe me, we will remember that loyalty in years to come.

Thank you for your farsightedness in this credit matter.

Four months from now, we plan to be current with our account and continue ordering from you at our past volumes.

Dear Mr. Hargrove:

We have received your last statement and letter asking for payment. I regret to tell you that we cannot pay the full $2,400.50 any time within the next three months, but we would appreciate the opportunity to work with you in a different payment structure.

With this letter, I've enclosed a check for $300 toward the balance on that account. We would like to make an additional payment of approximately $300 each month until the balance is paid in full.

As you know the economic downturn in the community has drastically affected our business, too. Most organizations consider their printing needs such as product or service brochures as "nice to have, but unnecessary" in bad times. Therefore, we have seen our long-standing accounts trim their print advertising repeatedly in the last few months.

We have been good customers of yours over the last three years, and we hope to continue the relationship when times improve. In the interim, we hope you will consider our future business worthy of your patience and work with us in paying our account with you in full.

Sincerely,

Dear Ms. Grape:

We are embarrassed. We need to ask for an extension of 30 days to pay our outstanding balance of $1,200.

Two rather large clients' checks to us have been delayed, and that money had been designated to pay our account with you.

We're sorry for the inconvenience to you but know that you will understand our lateness this time. Thank you for the excellent service you have provided us over the past few years.

Sincerely,

Dear Ms. Susanzon:

The reason we have not paid the outstanding balance of $230 shown on your records is that we have discovered an error in your records. In March we wrote to you (copy attached) to point out that the expedited-shipment charges of $72 should not have been added to the account due to your shipping agent's mistake.

We will gladly pay the bill in full whenever we receive a corrected statement with the $72 deducted.

Sincerely,

GUIDELINES AND ALTERNATE PHRASES

ASK FOR THE CREDIT INFORMATION IMMEDIATELY. IF YOU ARE WRITING TO A THIRD PARTY, STATE THAT THE CREDIT APPLICANT HAS GIVEN THE READER AS A REFERENCE.

We are gathering financial information about Garth-Heath and Associates, and the company has referred us to you.

We will appreciate any financial information you can supply us about Mr. John Brown, who has applied for a loan with us and has given your name as a reference.

Would you please supply us with any information about the financial responsibilities of Georgette Adams to help us decide on the amount of credit to extend to her? She has given us your name as a reference.

STATE SPECIFICALLY WHAT INFORMATION YOU WANT.

The loan she is requesting amounts to $28,000. What is your opinion about her ability to repay this amount?

We would appreciate a copy of her last year's account with your company.

We need a profit and loss statement and a signed Note of Agreement form from you to help us determine the company's current financial situation.

Can you tell us the length of time Ms. Brown has had an account with your bank? What is the average balance? Are there outstanding loans? If so, what is the nature of her collateral?

MAKE RESPONSE EASY. SUPPLY A FORM, IF POSSIBLE, AND A RETURN ENVELOPE.

The enclosed form is for your convenience in providing us this information.

We have enclosed a questionnaire that we hope will help you in your reply.

A checklist is enclosed for your response to our questions about Ms. Krueger's credit record.

PROMISE CONFIDENTIALITY.

We will, of course, keep the information in-house and strictly confidential. We appreciate your help.

Such information is for our own use and will not leave my office. Thank you for your cooperation.

Perhaps you might find it more convenient simply to put us on a mailing list for future financial statements your CPA prepares. Then you won't be bothered at inappropriate times for our annual updates.

Gentlemen or Ladies:

Garth-Heath and Associates, located at 22233 Riverside Drive, has asked to open an account with us, and the company has given your name as a reference.

Their first order of supplies will amount to approximately $2,300. Can you give us any financial information concerning this company's reputation for prompt payment of credit accounts? What are the credit terms and lending limits this company has with you? We have enclosed a form for your convenience in reply.

We will, of course, keep the information you provide strictly confidential.

Thank you for your help in this matter.

Sincerely,

Dear Mr. Smith:

We are pleased that you have decided to purchase our telephone equipment. To work out the credit terms you have requested, we need some additional information from you. Would you please forward to us:

- last quarter's profit and loss statement
- certificate of ownership of the business
- the completed, enclosed Form 234 listing business credit references and the financial institutions with which you do business

We will be eager to expedite your order as soon as we have the above information on hand. And, of course, the information you provide will remain confidential.

Thank you for your interest in our products, and we look forward to doing business with you.

Sincerely,

Dear Jack:

In reviewing my confidential work file on your account in anticipation of our visit next week, I noticed that the most recent financial statements for you and your company are over a year old. In accordance with our lending policy requiring that all unsecured credit facilities be supported by financial statements less than a year old, I will appreciate your providing me with updated statements.

As in the past, these financial statements will be retained in my confidential work file and will not be routed to the general credit files of the bank.

To assist you in the preparation of the documents, I have enclosed copies of the most recent information in my possession. Given the bank's increased emphasis on cash flow, I need any information you can provide me concerning the revenues and expenses associated with the assets reflected on the statements.

Jack, Drummond Bank is very appreciative of the business we have done together over the years; personally, I can't think of a relationship I have enjoyed more. Please let me know if there is anything I can do to assist you in your banking needs.

Cordially,

GUIDELINES AND ALTERNATE PHRASES

STATE THAT YOU ARE GRANTING CREDIT.

We have received replies from all your credit references and are pleased to find them all very satisfactory.

Thank you for permitting us to check your credit references. As you are well aware, we find that you have an excellent credit history. We are eager to grant you the credit terms you applied for.

Your credit references were most satisfactory. We are happy to extend credit to you on a net-30-days basis.

MENTION ANY RESTRICTIONS ABOUT THE CREDIT TERMS OR CONCERNS YOU HAVE ABOUT THE REFERENCE CHECK.

Should any transaction exceed $6,000, we will need to reinvestigate your financial position at that time.

Because of our policy not to invoice customers more than once for any transaction, we will require that you supply additional information and submit to a further credit check if any payment arrives in our office later than 30 days after our billing date.

In our reference check, we did discover one question that we need you to clear up for us. Would you provide us with further explanation about. . . . This information may allow us to extend our credit limits on your account.

LOOK FORWARD TO A MUTUALLY BENEFICIAL BUSINESS RELATIONSHIP.

Thank you for providing us with this financial information. We look forward to doing business with you.

We are pleased to welcome you as a customer.

Thank you for your cooperation with our investigation, and we are eager to work with you in meeting your printing needs.

Perhaps you'd like to put us on a mailing list for any future financial statements you prepare. That way, we won't have to trouble you for updates through the months and years ahead.

We pledge to you our best service in the years to come.

Dear Mr. Hartford:

We have contacted the references you gave us, and they all gave you the highest recommendations about your prompt payments in dealing with them.

We are pleased, therefore, to grant credit terms to you and set up your account for monthly billing.

Thank you for giving us your business. We appreciate the opportunity to serve you.

Cordially,

GUIDELINES AND ALTERNATE PHRASES

THANK THE APPLICANT FOR HIS OR HER DESIRE TO DO BUSINESS WITH YOUR COMPANY.

Thank you for taking the time to fill out a credit application with our company.

We appreciate your interest in doing business with our company.

Thank you for dropping by to discuss credit possibilities with our organization.

GIVE THE "NO" ANSWER IN A POSITIVE WAY.

Considering the information gathered in our recent investigation, we do not feel that we can grant credit at this time.

Our credit policies are very tight now in our depressed economy, and we are sorry to say that we are unable to open a credit account for this purchase.

We hope you understand that with the information our credit check has verified we cannot extend credit in this situation.

We have discovered in our investigation that your monthly credit payments are very near your monthly income amounts. Therefore, we fear putting you under such a heavy financial burden with further credit purchases. We hope that you will reconsider your request and understand our position.

We feel it is in both of our best interests to defer credit privileges at this time.

Of course, we would like nothing better than to set up an account for you, but like any other company, we must pay attention to the credit information we receive.

STATE UNDER WHAT CONDITIONS, IF ANY, YOU WILL REEVALUATE YOUR DECISION.

Let's review the situation again perhaps next year and see if we can work out something then.

If you can provide us with additional information you feel we may have overlooked, please contact us again.

We realize, of course, that your financial situation may be only temporary, so please contact us again when you think the facts have changed.

The information we've received isn't entirely sufficient for us to open an account. Perhaps at a later time we can review the situation and open an account such as the one you requested.

If you think we have not gathered all the appropriate facts, please let us know and we will review the situation once again.

We will reevaluate this decision if your financial picture changes in the future.

Perhaps our situation will improve in the future and we can relax our credit policies to some extent.

SUGGEST DOING BUSINESS ON A CASH BASIS.

If you can make prepayment, we'd be eager to ship the merchandise immediately.

We appreciate your interest in our products, and we hope we can do some business with you on a cash basis until the credit situation improves.

We're sorry to have to give you disappointing news, but know that you understand our position. If we can serve you another way, let us know. We are proud of our products and hope you'll find they meet your specific needs.

May we ship your order C.O.D.?

We hope to hear that you've been able to make other arrangements to enable you to make the purchase from us. We think you'll find the equipment to be the best on the market. Let us know what you decide.

Dear Ms. Jennrette:

We thank you for the credit application recently submitted and your interest in doing business with us. We regret, however, that we are unable, within our guidelines, to approve a monthly billing account for your company based on the information you supplied.

We will be happy to reconsider our decision upon receipt of an updated financial statement for your company prepared by an outside CPA firm.

Please be assured that we will keep all information strictly confidential, using it for our internal purposes only.

Thank you for your understanding.

Sincerely,

Dear Ms. German:

We have recently reviewed the year-end financial statements for Ardco Engineering. Because of the unbalanced financial condition at year end, Ardco does not now meet our stringent guidelines for extending unsecured credit.

So that your company can continue its purchases on an unsecured basis, we need a bank letter of credit to serve as security for the account. In view of your firm's past history of monthly purchases, we recommend that the letter of credit be set up for no less than $125,000.

For your convenience, we have enclosed a copy of our format for the bank's letter so that it includes the essential information we need. We look forward to serving you in the months ahead.

Sincerely,

Dear Mr. George:

We are pleased to learn that you are interested in our products and services. Under the strict terms of our present credit guidelines, however, we regret that we cannot grant the credit you requested on this occasion. If we have somehow overlooked part of your monthly income, please feel free to call that to our attention, and we will update your credit application form here in our office.

If you perhaps can make a larger down payment on the sound system, say $300 or more, we could reconsider your request. Let us know if you decide to do so, and we will be eager to review the purchase arrangements again.

Thank you for your understanding. We hope you will give us another opportunity to do business with you on a cash basis.

Sincerely,

GUIDELINES AND ALTERNATE PHRASES

EXPLAIN THE SITUATION IN A POSITIVE LIGHT.

As you probably know, the balance of your loan has not been retired as we had agreed upon.

Sometimes we find that we have opened the wrong kind of credit account for our customers. Because your outstanding balance has been above the maximum agreed upon on our revolving account, we suggest discussing with you a more suitable purchasing arrangement.

TELL THE CUSTOMER WHAT THE UNPAID BALANCE AND THE PAST-DUE AMOUNT ARE.

LEAVE THE DOOR OPEN FOR THE CUSTOMER TO TELL YOU OF AN ERROR IN YOUR OWN RECORDS.

If we've made a mistake in our review of your account, we'll appreciate your pointing that out to us.

If there is some mistake in our records, please call us.

Please let us know if we have overlooked your payment on this loan.

OFFER ANY POSSIBLE ALTERNATE ARRANGEMENT FOR DOING BUSINESS WITH YOU IN THE FUTURE.

We will, of course, appreciate the opportunity to do business with you on a cash basis.

Please come in at your convenience to discuss how we might help you make these payments on a more suitable schedule.

Let us know when you can come in, and we will be happy to work with you in making more appropriate arrangements.

Dear Mr. Samson:

We note that during the past 12 months your account balance at the end of each billing cycle has remained above the agreed-upon credit terms. To date, your outstanding balance is $1,899. The 60-days past-due amount is $1,200.38.

We suggest, therefore, that we determine some other buying arrangement to alleviate that potentially damaging credit situation. Because we will be forced to cancel the current credit arrangement with this next October billing cycle, we ask that you come in to discuss with us the unpaid balance and permit us to help you work out a more suitable payment schedule.

If our records are in error, of course, please let us know immediately. We will be happy to arrange a meeting at your convenience.

Sincerely,

Dear Ms. Tommes:

We appreciate your continued interest in our products. But as we have reviewed our records, we have discovered that your recent pattern of payment has been rather irregular. In fact, your payment record no longer meets our terms for extending credit.

We realize that a continuing economic downturn has taken its toll on many businesses in the area. Perhaps your industry has experienced such a problem and your situation is only temporary. If that is the case, please let us know and we will be glad to review the situation again next year.

In the meantime, we hope we can continue to do business with you on a cash basis. If not, please consider us again for the future.

Sincerely,

Dear Mr. Smith:

We have reviewed your account and decided, with reluctance, that we can no longer continue our credit terms to you. We wish we could help you through this difficult time, but we simply can't because the health of our own business is at stake.

We hope your situation improves. Please let us know when you can again satisfy our credit requirements.

Thank you for the opportunity to serve you in the past, and we will appreciate your business again if you are able to make some other financing arrangements.

Sincerely,

GUIDELINES AND ALTERNATE PHRASES

STATE YOUR REQUEST FOR PAYMENT OF A SPECIFIC SUM IMMEDIATELY.

We are writing to remind you of an unpaid balance of $245.57 on your account.

The outstanding balance on your revolving credit account with us is $899.55. We ask that you please remit the minimum amount of $89 immediately.

May we have your check for $860 by return mail?

USE A POLITE TONE, GRADUALLY GETTING STRONGER WITH EACH LETTER. FIRST LETTERS SHOULD BE SIMPLE *REMINDERS*. FOLLOW-UP LETTERS SHOULD BE *INQUIRIES* ABOUT THE REASONS AND FACTS BEHIND THE DELAYED PAYMENT. THEN YOU MAY WANT TO *APPEAL* TO THE READER TO TALK THINGS OVER WITH YOU. FINALLY, YOU WILL COME TO *DEMAND* PAYMENT IN LIEU OF FURTHER LEGAL ACTION.

MAKE THE RESPONSE EASY. SUPPLY THE TOTAL AMOUNTS OWED, ENCLOSE AN ENVELOPE, PROVIDE A CONTACT PHONE NUMBER, OR ASK FOR AN EXPLANATION ON THE BACK OR BOTTOM OF YOUR LETTER OR STATEMENT.

Won't you phone Susan Deckendorf at 345-5590 and explain why we haven't received your payment?

Please take a moment to jot us a note on the bottom of the enclosed invoice, explaining your situation.

We have provided a stamped envelope and a checklist for your explanation about this outstanding account. Please let us hear from you as to how we might work out a payment schedule suitable to your needs.

PUT THE BURDEN OF COMMUNICATION AND EXPLANATION ON THE READER.

You have not called us to let us know of your specific situation and any difficulties of which we should be aware.

We have not heard from you about the payment.

We have received no response from you to our recent letters asking about payment.

You have not returned our calls to let us know when we can expect payment.

You, I'm sure, will want to protect your credit rating.

If we do not hear from you within the next five days, your silence will force us to. . . .

You have made no effort to settle the matter or even to give us an explanation.

If we do not have your payment within ten days, we will be turning the matter over to the Delmar Collection Agency.

Dear Mr. Steem:

Just a reminder that your account at the Hotel St. Agnes is now due in the amount of $224.33. We would appreciate your attention to this matter, and if your check has crossed this letter in the mail, please accept our thanks.

Sincerely,

Dear Mrs. Shaw:

We are writing to call your attention to a past-due bill you may have overlooked. Your account shows a balance due of $498.22 for dental work done on June 6.

A self-addressed envelope is enclosed for your convenience. We have been happy to serve you.

Sincerely,

Dear Mr. Miller:

We want to call attention to the $245.69 unpaid balance on your account with us. Would you please forward that amount immediately in the enclosed envelope?

Thank you.

Dear Mr. Dennis:

In late January, we wrote you about the shared cost of the refreshments at the Seneca Lakes marketing seminar and reception, jointly sponsored by you and the Marketing Survey Group. Each company's portion of these expenses for the meeting was $248.

To date, we have not received your company's check. We would appreciate your help in covering this expense. Please forward the check to my attention in the enclosed envelope.

Yours truly,

Dear Mr. Jahns:

As we discussed by phone, according to company policy, employees terminating employment prior to their service date must reimburse the company for vacation days taken but not yet earned. Our records reflect your last day of employment was February 1, 19--. Since your service date was November 11, 19--, you will need to reimburse the company for nine vacation days taken in January.

Please remit to my attention in the enclosed envelope $966.44 by sending a personal check payable to Universo Limited. We need your payment by June 5.

Sincerely,

Dear Mr. Asner:

To date, we still have not received your payment for the $468 owed us on your account. Would you please check on the matter immediately and let us know what has happened?

Sincerely,

Dear Mr. Smarmout:

I want to follow up our recent telephone conversation reminding you of our terms of sale and payment due dates. Your account now has an outstanding balance of $2,380, which is 90 days past due.

We have provided you an invoice for each purchase, and that invoice states the date payment is due in our office. Additionally, we send a monthly statement detailing all unpaid items. Your cooperation in remitting payment according to these agreed-upon terms is essential in continuing to do business with us.

It is my understanding that your account is set up on our TIB program whereby you can have the money wired from your bank account to ours. If you are having a problem with the program, please let us know.

We want to continue serving you on a credit basis; however, we need your cooperation. Therefore, we strongly urge you to remit payment according to the terms we agreed upon.

Thank you.

Yours truly,

Dear Mr. Barnes:

We are surprised that we have not heard from you about the unpaid $988 on your account with our company. The balance is long overdue, and we have had no explanation from you in response to our earlier letters.

Please let us hear from you immediately about your plans for payment. We have provided a space at the bottom of this letter for your convenience in replying.

Sincerely,

Dear Mr. Whitaker:

We have not had a response from you about the unpaid balance of $2,300 on your company's account with us.

If you cannot put a check for the full amount in the return envelope, won't you please call us to discuss a more suitable arrangement for payment? We are eager to learn the facts of your situation.

Sincerely,

Dear Ms. Smith:

While we can't understand your nonpayment of the overdue account of $1,800.34 for consulting services rendered your company in January, we do once again urge you to let us hear from you. Would you call Bob Metcalf at 123-4567 for an appointment next week?

Perhaps if we talk, we can work out an appropriate payment schedule. We hope you will be so courteous as to phone us by the end of the week.

Sincerely,

Dear Ms. Jones:

We regret that we must again remind you that your account with the Hotel St. Agnes is delinquent in the amount of $2,344.50.

We must insist that you give this matter your immediate attention because we would like to protect your credit rating.

Enclosed is a return envelope for your immediate payment or explanation.

Yours truly,

Dear Mr. Frank:

You purchased a computer and several peripherals from us back in February. We set up credit terms with you as you requested, with your final payment due April 30. Now five months later, your account balance still shows $4,845 outstanding. You have not informed us of any problem with the equipment, and we, therefore, assume that you received delivery and that it is operating satisfactorily.

You have not responded to our earlier five letters about the overdue payment and have not returned my three phone calls to your office (8/4, 8/9, and 9/6). Without any communication or explanation from you, we have no choice but to turn the matter over to our collection agency.

We've hesitated to do this previously because we know--and I'm sure you're aware of--what this can do to a company's standing in the community.

We're hoping that you'll help us avoid such an action by sending us the full payment by September 30. After that date, we will proceed with the further action I've outlined.

Very truly yours,

Dear Ms. Hornsby:

This note is our final request for payment for the overdue balance of $3,223 on your account. Unless we hear from you by May 5, we will turn the account over to our legal department for further action.

Yours truly,

GUIDELINES AND ALTERNATE PHRASES

BE TRUTHFUL, OBJECTIVE, AND CLEAR ABOUT THE REASONS FOR THE LAYOFFS.

We have today taken difficult but necessary steps to achieve substantial cost reductions required by a continuing decline in advertising revenue. We have found it necessary to terminate 22 full-time and 13 part-time positions. Your position is one that has been eliminated.

We have taken steps today to reduce our work force, steps fully consistent with our mission and its requirements. When times are good, it is easy to forge ahead; the test of a solid company is how well it can manage when times are not so good. We are doing our best to continue to provide quality service for our customers.

SHOW CONCERN.

These terminations were made with great reluctance, and only after other economies, such as holding vacancies and an early retirement incentive program, failed to yield sufficient savings.

OFFER ANY HELP AVAILABLE SUCH AS RETIREMENT BENEFITS, OUTPLACEMENT SERVICES, REFERRALS, USE OF SPARE TELEPHONE AND OFFICE IN A JOB SEARCH.

Please be assured that we can give you the highest recommendations for jobs you may choose to pursue.

To help you in finding another job as soon as possible, we are maintaining three vacant offices (C100-103) for those affected by this layoff to use in telephoning prospective employers, typing resumés, and making copies for mass mailings.

GIVE DETAILS ABOUT CONTINUATION OR CESSATION OF BENEFITS SUCH AS MEDICAL COVERAGE OR USE OF COMPANY VEHICLES.

Dear Bob:

Because of the reorganization of our salaried work force, it has become necessary to eliminate your position. Effective Friday, May 5, you will be placed on a lack-of-work status and laid off with those benefits for which you are eligible.

During the period preceding your last day of work, your primary effort should be in locating a new assignment, either within our company, if openings exist, or outside the company. I will personally help you in your search and will schedule an appointment time for you with Employee Relations for any help they can give.

Attached is an outline of benefits and conversion options available to salaried employees on lack-of-work status.

I regret that business conditions require this action. I sincerely hope that our combined efforts will be successful in finding a rewarding position that fully uses your capabilities and gives you every opportunity for further advancement.

Sincerely,

Dear Ms. Stover:

To lower our operating costs, Bettgo management has made the decision to reduce our operating staff, along with certain other organizational changes and functions. Your position is one of those affected by these changes. Your employment with Bettgo will be terminated under the provisions of a reduction in work force, effective August 14.

You will be paid your salary through the last day worked, including payment for your accrued vacation and two weeks' pay in lieu of notice. Your insurance coverage is scheduled to expire on September 14. You have two options concerning continuation of this coverage; both are outlined on the attached page. When you have made your decision about this coverage and notified us with the attached form, the insurance company will contact you directly for all necessary details and/or payment.

You may also be eligible for state-administered unemployment benefits, and we encourage you to apply to the appropriate state department.

If you are rehired by Bettgo within one year, you may be reinstated with your former service date and all benefits related to that service date.

I'm sure you will have questions concerning this layoff. Please feel free to phone me or Director of Personnel Mark Harkrider at extension 1234.

Sincerely,

Dear Ms. Frazier:

The corporate division has found it necessary to make further consolidations in its operations. These changes will allow us to operate in the most economical and efficient manner possible.

Your present position is being affected by these changes and will be eliminated March 15, 19--. However, we are pleased to say that we have identified another position to make available to you. If you choose to accept this new Secretary-III position, on March 16 you will begin reporting to Howard Peyton, manager of our South American operations.

If you should decide not to accept this position, we regret that you will be laid off under the provisions of the reduction-in-force practices. We must have your decision by March 4 because other employees are involved in these staffing plans.

Please discuss any questions about these changes and new reporting lines with your immediate supervisor. Or perhaps you would prefer to call me at ext. 2588.

Sincerely,

GUIDELINES AND ALTERNATE PHRASES

BE TRUTHFUL, OBJECTIVE, AND CLEAR IN STATING ANY FACTS AND REASONS FOR DISMISSAL. FALSE STATEMENTS, EVEN MEANT TO PROTECT THE EMPLOYEE'S EGO, MAY BE USED AGAINST YOU IF YOUR DECISION IS LATER CHALLENGED. (ALTHOUGH YOU MAY NOT STATE ALL REASONS IN A LETTER ADDRESSED TO THE PERSON BEING DISMISSED, SUCH FULL DOCUMENTATION SHOULD BE IN THE FILES.)

Since you were hired May 4, 19—, as a maintenance technician, your attendance and punctuality records have been unacceptable. We have discussed the problem with you and documented such discussions (both oral and written) in your personnel file.

During the past 120-day probationary period, Mack, we have still noted a backlog of orders in your department. Because we have explained to you the seriousness of these delays in responding to our customers, we feel forced to terminate your employment with Fairton Graphics, effective June 12, 19—.

ASSURE AN EMPLOYEE WHOM YOU ARE DISMISSING THAT YOU WILL NOT BE GIVING A BAD REFERENCE—IF IT IS YOUR COMPANY POLICY TO WITHHOLD BAD REFERENCES.

We, of course, will not be giving the reason for your dismissal to anyone asking for such information. We will verify only. . . .

Our company policy is to mention only your job title, salary, and dates of employment to any prospective employers.

BE MATTER OF FACT IN TONE, NOT HOSTILE.

We wish you success in a new job.

We hope you find other employment that allows you to use your skills and experience adequately.

Dear Ms. Whitespoon:

You have asked us to review the facts surrounding your probationary status with Utco, and we have done so. Extensive conversations with various levels of employees were conducted to gain insight into the situation presented by you in your February 6 memo.

Although separation from a company is never easy, it is often the best possible solution for all persons involved. It is our opinion from the information stated in your memo and from that gathered through our own investigation, that such is the case here.

However, let me assure you that we will strictly adhere to our policy on giving references in such terminations: that is, we will release only the dates of your employment and your job title and will verify your salary with us if the caller has obtained such salary information from you.

We do wish you success in your future work.

Sincerely,

GUIDELINES AND ALTERNATE PHRASES

THANK THE NEW EMPLOYER FOR THE JOB.

Thank you for your confidence.

I sincerely appreciate this opportunity to show you what I can do.

This opportunity is one I've been seeking for quite some time. Thank you.

Thank you for your generous offer; I eagerly accept.

I am pleased to accept your offer of a position as office manager, effective May 1. Thank you for the opportunity to work for a firm with such an outstanding reputation in the city.

I am pleased to learn that you have placed such confidence in me after the many, many interviews you conducted to fill the position.

CONFIRM ANY DETAILS ABOUT FIRST-DAY REPORTING OR MATTERS TO BE SETTLED BEFORE BEGINNING THE JOB.

As you requested, I will be getting my pre-employment physical next week.

As I agreed, I have turned all my consulting clients over to another colleague in the field so that I can devote my full attention to the new job.

I will be looking forward to the 9:00 a.m. orientation in the Wharton training center.

EXPRESS CONFIDENCE IN YOUR ABILITY TO DO THE JOB.

I have every confidence that we will make a great team.

The skills you asked about in my interview are certainly "at your disposal" from day one. I pledge to you my very best effort and have every confidence that we've made a perfect match.

I'm eager to hone my analytical skills on some of the problem situations outlined in our earlier discussions. With care, we should be able to provide resolutions suitable to all concerned.

Dear Bob:

Thank you for your phone call and follow-up letter about my joining you as your rookie salesman. I'm delighted to accept your offer and will be looking forward to the orientation September 1.

As you suggested, I plan to spend my time between now and then studying the specs on the new drilling equipment. I plan to "hit the ground running"; my first effort after September 1 will be to become a shadow to Harry Hines until I learn the equipment and accounts. After that short-term mentoring, I'll be eager to mold my sales experience to such a fine organization.

Thank you for the confidence you've placed in me.

Cordially,

GUIDELINES AND ALTERNATE PHRASES

THANK THE EMPLOYER FOR THE JOB OFFER.

Thank you for the generous offer to join your engineering department.

Frankly, I'm quite honored that you selected me among so many other qualified applicants to fill the job of marketing director.

I received your letter about the job offer and want to thank you for such confidence.

GIVE YOUR REASONS OR CRITERIA FOR THE NEGATIVE RESPONSE.

As you remember, I have teenage children who are quite reluctant to leave their friends and change schools in the middle of their high school "careers." Considering what is best for them, I have decided to stay in Hilldale.

Although the job is certainly an important one to the company, I have in mind to find something with more challenge. Call it a quirk in my personality, but I want to move into a job that offers me a chance to do more than routine administrative tasks.

The compensation package seemed a little low for the kind of skills I wanted to bring to the job.

As you outlined the job to me in your office, I didn't quite see the advancement opportunities that I want to have before me with this next—and I hope final—career move.

I am hoping to find a position that will give me more opportunity to use my selling experience.

STATE YOUR "NO" IN A POSITIVE WAY, LEAVING THE DOOR OPEN FOR FUTURE CONTACTS.

Although the job you offered sounded challenging, I have decided to accept another position with David Hewitt International, a position more in line with my experience.

I don't feel in a position to accept your generous offer at the present time.

I'm afraid, therefore, that for all these reasons, I'll have to decline the opportunity you have presented me.

I regret that my situation is such that I must turn down your job offer at this point.

I wish your job was a little more in line with my personal goals at this point in my life—working for your company would be quite an honor.

I'm afraid that my answer must be "no" under these conditions. I hope you understand my reasoning here and know how much I appreciate your honesty in presenting the job details to me.

REESTABLISH RAPPORT.

I wish you the very best in finding another manager suitable for this position.

Thank you for considering me for this opportunity.

Thank you for taking the time to interview me and share your company goals with me. I plan to stay in touch.

The days my wife and I spent with you were memorable. Thank you for such courtesies in the interviewing process.

May I stay in touch in case your needs or mine change?

During the short two days we spent discussing the job, you and your people made me feel very welcome. I appreciate that tremendously.

Please keep me on your list of interested engineers, and if you have anything else that you think we could work together on, let me know.

If another opening develops along the lines I described to you, please consider me again. I'd love to work with you in another capacity.

I wish you and your firm every success.

Dear Foy:

Thank you for your kind offer to join Harvester Associates. Since our lunch in Phoenix, I've spent many hours analyzing the pros and cons of making the move. The decision was particularly important at this stage in my career because I want my next association to be permanent.

With a decision of such importance, a "yes" response should have been strongly evident, and it was not. There was no one overriding factor but rather the cumulative impact of a number of considerations that influenced my decision.

My family has learned to love a particular way of life in this part of the country--the climate and the slower pace.

Additionally, the salary was some consideration. While the compensation package seemed generous for the job you outlined, a change from my present situation would be quite costly. After our tour through the surrounding subdivisions in the area, it appeared that it would be impossible to match our present circumstances at anything like comparable costs.

Neither of the above nor any other one consideration about the job itself was dominant in my decision, but their combination amounted to a "no."

It has been a personal privilege to meet you and your colleagues, and I appreciate your considering me for the position. You, your courtesies, your people, and the position itself have made the offer extremely attractive.

Thank you,

GUIDELINES AND ALTERNATE PHRASES

STATE THE EXPENSE IN QUESTION
SPECIFICALLY.

INCLUDE BOTH OBVIOUS AND NOT-SO-OBVIOUS
REASONS FOR YOUR REQUEST.

Of course, such uncontrolled expenses reflect an attitude of carelessness to those we supervise.

Such extravagance is not the kind of image we want to project to our customers. Our niche has always been the highest quality at the lowest profit margin.

Such expenses may drastically affect our available funds for bonuses and raises at year's end.

As we are all happily aware, sales are going up. But if expenses rise to the same point, or even higher, what have we gained?

GIVE SPECIFIC COSTS—DOLLARS AND CENTS—
NOT VAGUE GENERALITIES.

SUGGEST OTHER WAYS, IF POSSIBLE, TO MEET
THE PERSON'S, DEPARTMENT'S, OR COMPANY'S
NEEDS AT A LOWER COST. OR ASK FOR SUCH
SUGGESTIONS FROM THE READER.

BE ACCURATE IN YOUR PREDICTIONS AND
FIGURES. AVOID SOUNDING LIKE YOU'RE GOING
INTO BANKRUPTCY IF THE POSTAGE METER
ISN'T REPLACED, BUT DO MAKE THE READERS
AWARE OF THE SERIOUSNESS AND SPECIFIC
REPERCUSSIONS OF THE SITUATION.

ESTABLISH YOURSELF AS ONE OF THE TEAM
PLAYERS TO MAKE THE EXPENSE-CUTTING
EFFORT.

I have every confidence that you as directors can pull us out of this unpleasant predicament.

I'll appreciate any suggestions you can give me on how you plan to cut expenses in your division during the next quarter.

I know you won't let me down.

Come on, we can do it. Keep one hand on the wheel and the other on your wallet.

Dear Ms. Myres:

In developing my portion of next year's budget, I came across an alarming situation--our increase in long-distance telephone expenses. The increase for all three buildings in this past year has been more than $6,000 monthly. It seems that we have totally lost control! We have no way to allocate long-distance costs to any one area, and we have no management reports whatever to aid us in gaining the control we now need or to plan for the future.

Here is a brief outline of the problems as I see them:

- Telephone company increases in long-distance charges
- No method to allocate cost of calls to individuals or departments
- No monthly reports to managers
- The possibility that we've outgrown the present system

Can you put in some time on this situation and get back to me in a month with your recommendations for lowering these telephone expenses? My priorities are rather straight-forward--excellent service that allows for company growth with the lowest possible costs. Within those guidelines, I'm open to just about anything you can suggest.

Thanks,

G U I D E L I N E S   A N D   A L T E R N A T E   P H R A S E S

COMMENT ON THE VALUE OF THE RELATIONSHIP TO YOU OR TO THE COMPANY.

You have been a tremendous influence in my career.

I can hardly believe we are having to say goodbye to someone who has singlehandedly been responsible for so much of the company's success.

If you ask me, the years have been too short. We're not ready to see you go.

Your association with Hubco, Inc. has been more than a long one—it has been a valuable one.

Your friendship has meant more to me than I can express in this short note.

Thank you for your contributions to my own well-being and to my personal as well as career goals.

My working association with you has been invaluable. Under your leadership, I have grown tremendously in my knowledge of the industry and. . . .

As they say, it's not the job—it's the people. Never was that truer than in my case. It has been absolutely great to work with you. I'm trying not to think about how much we'll miss you around here.

I really hate to write this letter, Ed. Your leaving means goodbye to one of the most rewarding associations I've had through the years.

MENTION EITHER PLEASANT PERSONALITY TRAITS, SPECIFIC TALENTS, CAREER ACHIEVEMENTS, OR FUTURE PLANS OF THE INDIVIDUAL.

Your witticisms and humor have brought us all through some pretty difficult times.

You are a super salesperson—exceptions, none.

When we're all in a dither around here trying to decide whom to call when and where, may we call you? For the last 20 years, you're the one person who always had, or who knew where to find, the answers.

Your creativity has been what has brought this department through time and time again.

Your fairness and your consistency in applying policies have created much respect for you.

Your organizational skills and your analytical thinking have directly contributed time and again to the bottom line.

Your attendance record, your thoroughness, your attention to detail—all of these have been the necessary ingredients that made working with you so easy.

Your even temper, your easy-going supervisory style, and your sometimes off-the-wall suggestions have been just the tension relievers we have needed through some past difficulties.

BE WARM, SPECIFIC, AND PERSONAL IN YOUR COMMENTS, BUT BE CAUTIOUS ABOUT REMARKS THAT MAY UPSET AN EMPLOYEE WHO IS LEAVING THE COMPANY UNDER ADVERSE CONDITIONS.

We wish you the best in the years ahead.

Thank you for all your efforts here.

Enjoy those travel, job, or leisure plans that you've been meaning to get around to for the last few years.

We will miss you.

Please call me from time to time to keep me informed of your whereabouts and your new achievements.

I'm planning to stay in touch with you. I'm sure I'm going to continue to need your expertise that has been so readily at my disposal over the years.

Dear Phillip:

Is it really possible that you are leaving Hilton?

Over the years it has always given us a secure feeling to know that we had such an efficient and dedicated spokesperson in the Northeast. Your role in dealing with the Bayer government people has greatly aided us in retaining the good reputation we've had in the region.

Since your coming to work here, many events have changed our nation and the entire globe, and you have always remained receptive to growth in your vision, your responsibilities, and your interests on Hilton's behalf.

I even remember your assignment to Peru to supervise the major repair jobs there-- spending so much time away from your family during that year. No less important were the design projects in Australia three years ago--designs that put us so far ahead of the competition we haven't looked back.

It will be impossible to replace your unique qualities and talents, but I'm pleased you now have the opportunity to enjoy a well-deserved rest.

Hilton is a much better company because of your efforts.

Cordially,

Myra,

I've been traveling so much these past six months that I didn't want to express my goodbyes to you until I had time to reflect on our long association and what it has meant to me.

Although we haven't always agreed, I'm sure we've always respected each other's opinions and talents. Certainly, I can say without any reservation that I've always been proud of what we've been able to accomplish together.

As you take over the new job, I know you will go on to achieve even more personal career objectives. It will greatly please me to hear and read of your accomplishments in the years to come. Perhaps another project sometime will bring us together again.

With best personal regards,

Sid,

A brief note to apologize to you for not being able to say goodbye in person. But I didn't want to miss this opportunity to thank you for your contribution to my career. You and Phil Stockton have been my models, inspiration, and motivators through so many difficult times.

Remember Graphton? How about the interview with Jackson out in Phoenix? Not to mention my "hibernation" after the difficulties between Myrna and me.

My best wishes for your success with the new company. I'll always be around to brag that "I knew you when. . . ."

Keep in touch,

G U I D E L I N E S   A N D   A L T E R N A T E   P H R A S E S

INFORM THE READER IN A POSITIVE, UPBEAT MANNER THAT YOU ARE LEAVING YOUR PRESENT POSITION.

I'm writing to let you know of my good news. I have recently had an opportunity to. . . .

On August 6, I will be transferring to the Atlanta service center, an exciting new challenge for my abilities.

Jack, next week I'll be a beginner again—I've accepted a position with. . . .

MENTION WHO WILL BE REPLACING YOU IF THE RELATIONSHIP WILL BE AN ONGOING ONE FOR THE READER.

Tom Posten will be joining the company to assume my duties and I'm sure he will be in touch with you shortly. As I understand it, Tom has been in mechanical engineering for ten years and I'm sure will be more than qualified to handle all your needs.

Your new company contact will be Sarah Hughes. Sarah has heard me speak of you often and is very eager to meet you and find out more about how you can work together.

RECALL ANY SPECIFIC BENEFIT OR SATISFACTION FROM THE ASSOCIATION AND ASSUME THAT THE COMPANY RELATIONSHIP WILL BE AN ONGOING ONE.

I can't think of a client relationship I've enjoyed more. Your investments are with a sound company, and I pledge to leave you in good hands.

The stimulating chats we've had in your office have been very helpful to me in formulating my own management philosophies. I count myself very lucky to have been associated with you and your staff.

The trips on which I accompanied you to our annual conventions have been some of my most memorable times at Hightower. Thank you for your guidance and friendship.

(See "Sales and Marketing/Introduction of New Sales Representative" for sales reps' farewells to clients and customers.)

Dear Ms. Fincher:

I will be leaving Betmax Limited on June 12 to pursue my own consulting work in the area of financial systems.

The central employee relations functions now coordinated by my department are being decentralized into divisional activities. The names of your new contacts within the divisions are provided on the attached sheet.

I've enjoyed working with you in the HR support function and think that we together have recruited and trained some very talented employees. I look forward to other, similar professional relationships in the future.

If I can help you in any way after June 12, please call my old number and Sharon Alexander there will be able to provide you with a new number where I can be reached.

Cordially,

To All the Staff:

The rumor is true; they have finally kicked me upstairs so that you people here can get some real work done. Seriously, although I'm excited to be assuming the position of Director of Nursing, I am reluctant to leave all of you who have made me look so good during the past four years.

As you may have also heard, Margaret Ellman will be capably taking over my job here, and I know that you will very soon come to appreciate her expertise, dedication, and pleasant disposition.

Once again, thank you so much for your support during these past years. You have given the best care possible to our patients, and I have experienced your compassion firsthand, observing time and again how much emotional and physical strength such commitment requires. Thank each of you for inspiring me on such occasions to do my very best behind the scenes.

Cordially,

Dear Margaret:

I am pleased to tell you that I am moving on to a new assignment and will supervise our branch system in Queens County and Nassau County. The new position will be a real challenge, but I'm excited about the opportunities and new learning experiences.

I regret, however, that I'll be unable personally to introduce you to Kelley McFee, who will be succeeding me as the officer in charge of the 40 Wall Street branch. I've asked her to stop by and introduce herself at your convenience sometime in the coming weeks.

Although I look forward to my new duties, I do want to say how much I've enjoyed working with you and your associates during the last few years. Specifically, I always appreciated your taking the time to receive my calls and provide any account information I've needed.

I hope that everything continues well for you and that I have occasion to work with you or visit socially in the near future.

Sincerely,

GUIDELINES AND ALTERNATE PHRASES

CONFIRM RECEIPT OF THE RESUME AND/OR LETTER.

We have received your letter expressing an interest in working for HardGlow. Although we have very few openings at the present time, we are enclosing an application for you to complete. After we receive your completed application, we will contact you again if we have an appropriate opening.

We have reviewed your resumé along with those of other applicants, and have selected for further consideration an applicant whose background more closely matches the job requirements.

Thank you for forwarding your resumé. We will review it carefully, and should we have any suitable openings, we will phone you to schedule an interview.

Thank you for your well-written letter outlining your qualifications and your interest in a job with Metbar.

We have received your resumé and your credentials are impressive.

TELL THEM WHAT YOU PLAN TO DO WITH THE RESUME—FILE IT, REVIEW IT, PASS IT ON TO OTHER MANAGERS FOR FOLLOW-UP.

Our plan is to spend the next two weeks reviewing the resumés from the many, many qualified respondents to our ad. If you have not heard from us by March 1, you can assume we have filled the position.

We have a number of applicants to consider and will be in touch with you if the situation warrants.

We will circulate your resumé to any managers who have openings where your experience is appropriate. They will contact you directly for an interview if they would like to discuss specific possibilities with you.

We will be reviewing your resumé along with those of several other candidates in the next few weeks. If we find a suitable match between qualifications and job, we will call you to talk further.

We have taken the liberty of forwarding a copy of your application and resumé to our other subsidiaries. Representatives from those companies will contact you if it appears your credentials are what they need.

CLOSE WITH A GENERAL GOODWILL STATEMENT.

We appreciate your desire to become affiliated with Metbar.

Thank you for giving us an opportunity to review your information.

Thank you for taking the time to contact us.

Best wishes in your job search.

216

Dear Ms. North:

Thank you for submitting your resumé to ATW in response to our advertisement about the sales representative position.

We have carefully reviewed the information you provided. Although your experience and qualifications are outstanding, there is not a close enough match with our current job opening.

Your resumé will be kept on file for 12 months. Should a suitable position become available in that time, we will contact you again.

Thank you for your interest in ATW.

Sincerely,

Dear Ms. Hargroves:

Your resumé has been received in response to the recent ad about sales representatives. All resumés are currently being reviewed to find the appropriate matches in skills, experience, and interest level.

We will contact you again in 30 days if there is a further desire to discuss employment possibilities.

Thank you for your fast response to our ad and for your interest in working at Metbar.

Sincerely,

Dear Mr. Herrington:

We have received your resumé for the consulting assignment in South Africa. As our plan now stands, we will be forwarding resumés of all those who have expressed interest in the project to our Boston office, where they will select those they wish to interview.

If there is further interest from them, Martin Cardwell from that office will contact you directly. Thank you for taking the time to prepare a resumé for us.

Sincerely,

GUIDELINES AND ALTERNATE PHRASES

CONFIRM THE JOB OFFER, INCLUDING POSITION TITLE, SALARY, AND EFFECTIVE DATE.

This letter will confirm your acceptance of our employment offer as an accountant in our audit division at $28,000 annually. Your first day on the job will be October 6.

CONFIRM KEY JOB RESPONSIBILITIES FOR MANAGEMENT EMPLOYEES.

ASK FOR A DECISION BY A SPECIFIC DATE IF THE OFFER HAS NOT BEEN ACCEPTED BY PHONE OR IN PERSON.

INCLUDE DETAILS ABOUT WHERE TO REPORT FOR ANY EMPLOYEE ORIENTATION OR FORMS PROCESSING.

Please call Sharon Peyton at 123-4567 to arrange for a pre-employment physical prior to your beginning date.

We have planned for you to spend your first two days in an orientation meeting designed to introduce our eight new reps to the company's key executives, our major product lines, and our management philosophies.

END WITH A WELCOME TO THE COMPANY.

We look forward to your contributions to the company.

We are pleased that you have accepted our offer.

We are excited about your coming to work with us.

We have every confidence that this assignment will be just the career opportunity you are seeking.

Welcome to the team.

Dear Sarah:

This letter will confirm our offer of employment to you as our new divisional office manager, effective September 1. Your starting salary will be $35,000.

As we discussed, your primary responsibilities will be to:

- Supervise 28 clerical employees
- Maintain equipment and inventory
- Coordinate shipping and payment schedules with all suppliers
- Develop improved community relations by participation in local civic affairs

On your first day, please report directly to our HRD office (lower level, room 155) at 9:00 a.m. for a general orientation on job benefits and forms processing.

We're sure you will find exciting challenges and opportunities here, and we look forward to a mutually rewarding relationship. Welcome to Metbar!

Cordially,

Dear Mr. Foster:

You certainly made a fine impression during your visit with us last week, and we are pleased to confirm an offer to join our staff as regional sales manager, effective August 5. Your starting salary will be $54,000. I've enclosed some information on our benefits program.

We appreciate the fact that you gave us an opportunity to show you our facilities and to expose you to our people and their ideas. We're ready to have you jump aboard in August for our biggest advertising campaign ever!

Cordially,

Dear Doug:

Thank you for visiting with us last week. We are confident that you can make an important contribution to Herrington International and would like for you to join us as senior vice president with all financial responsibilities.

If you do, your base salary will start at $65,000 and will be reviewed annually. In addition, you will be on the executive incentive-bonus list. Those on this list receive an incentive bonus based on both corporate and individual performance. Last year the bonuses at your proposed level averaged about 28 percent.

You will also receive a company car and an Avvar Club membership.

We will also immediately grant you an option in the amount of 5,000 shares. I believe you have read this year's proxy statement outlining our new stock grant program for key executives. You will be eligible to participate in this program when the next grants are made in January.

I've enclosed information about the company's benefit programs and our relocation policy.

I'll appreciate your making a decision as soon as possible, and, of course, we will defer to your timetable if our suggested beginning date will not allow sufficient time for your move.

We look forward to your long and successful career with us.

Cordially,

GUIDELINES AND ALTERNATE PHRASES

OPEN WITH A NEUTRAL OR POSITIVE STATEMENT THANKING THE APPLICANT FOR HIS OR HER INTEREST IN THE POSITION AND ANY TIME AND EFFORT SPENT IN THE INTERVIEWING PROCESS.

We were quite impressed with your achievements and enjoyed our opportunity to talk with you about job possibilities here.

Thank you for giving us an opportunity to consider your experience in filling the plant manager position. We especially appreciate your time in making the special trip to Dallas for the interview.

We appreciate yesterday's follow-up call from you regarding the position for which you interviewed on May 5.

Thank you for taking the time to visit with me while I was on campus recently.

GIVE THE REASON(S) YOU WILL NOT BE MAKING A JOB OFFER.

We have no positions that match your qualifications.

Because of the downturn in the economy, we have all vacancies in a "hold" position.

After careful review, we have decided that this position requires quite broad experience in the personnel compensation area.

We have chosen another person for the position, one who had the specific graduate degree we felt necessary for the job.

After more careful thought to our conversation and the job requirements, we have determined that the currently available job would not effectively use your background and skills.

After serious deliberations, we have concluded that we cannot offer you a position appropriate to your experience. Our decision was not an easy one—especially in view of the fact that we interviewed more than 200 qualified candidates, such as you.

We apologize for taking so long to determine if we had jobs to fill after our recent reorganization. That planning is now complete, however, and we regret to tell you that we are not contemplating adding anyone to our staff during the next few months.

TELL THE APPLICANT WHAT THE STATUS OF HIS OR HER APPLICATION IS. WILL YOU KEEP IT ON FILE? DO YOU EXPECT TO HAVE SUITABLE POSITIONS OPEN IN THE NEAR FUTURE?

We will have another opening in the graphics area within the next 60 days. I'll forward your resumé to the appropriate manager, and should he wish to schedule an interview, he will contact you directly.

Please contact us again in about six months to a year; perhaps our situation will have changed.

I'm sorry to have disappointing news; your resumé shows just the kind of experience we need—if we had any appropriate openings. When there is an upturn in the industry, we will contact you again to see if you still have any interest in a position with us.

CLOSE WITH A GOODWILL STATEMENT ABOUT THE APPLICANT'S JOB SEARCH.

Thank you for your interest in our company.

Best wishes in finding just the right job.

Thank you for the chance to review your fine credentials. We wish you the best.

Your resumé shows valuable experience, and I wish you the best in finding an appropriate "fit."

We wish you success in finding a position that suits your needs and expectations.

With your achievements and specific academic credentials, we know you will find a position that challenges you and offers the appropriate advancement and rewards.

Dear John:

Thank you for discussing employment possibilities with EZEE-Grow. I sincerely appreciate the time you spent with me in the interview and regret to tell you that we were unable to find the funds to meet your salary requirements.

We will keep the information you provided us in our active file for six months. In the event we have an opening at the level for which you want to be considered, we will contact you again to determine your interest.

I wish you the best in finding a rewarding position where your talents can be fully used.

Cordially,

Dear Skip:

I want to thank you for coming by our offices and interviewing with us last week. I enjoyed visiting with you and discussing job opportunities that might be available.

While you certainly have accumulated fine qualifications, we have decided that we do not currently have a position appropriate to your interests.

Please stay in touch and let us know what you decide to pursue.

Regards,

Dear Melinda:

I want to thank you for taking the time to come by for the two recent interviews for the plant manager position.

We have now interviewed all four of the remaining candidates, and we have chosen someone who does have six years of experience in the financial areas we discussed. These financial responsibilities are of utmost importance in this critical branch office, and we simply had to let that part of the job overshadow the rest at this time.

We appreciate your interest in our company and wish you every success for a rewarding future.

Sincerely,

HOLIDAY GREETINGS

GUIDELINES AND ALTERNATE PHRASES

FOCUS ON INDIVIDUALS, MENTIONING SPECIFIC TEAM ACHIEVEMENTS, SOLUTIONS TO PROBLEMS, OR INSIDE-THE-COMPANY ANECDOTES.

As we approach this season, I want to express my gratitude for your efforts to turn around the Hitton project. You've all done an outstanding job in sharing the marketing load.

The figures speak for themselves. This past year has been tremendous. What a way to spread the news.

Here it is almost Christmas, and we're putting on the finishing touches—no, not on the tree, on the Silverton proposal. Oh, well, we landed three big ones this year anyway.

GIVE DETAILS ABOUT ANY PLANS TO GET TOGETHER FOR A CELEBRATION AS A GROUP.

I'm looking forward to our dinner at the Hyatt on December 10. Each employee is welcome to bring a spouse or friend.

We will close the office at 4:00 p.m. on the 23rd so that we can exchange greetings personally. Please join us in the Burgundy Center at that time for light refreshments.

MENTION ANY ACCOMPANYING GIFT IN A MODEST WAY.

I'm mailing separately a calendar that I think will bring a laugh or two.

I hope you can use another one of those fruit baskets, ubiquitous around the Christmas season. But mine will be special because it comes with much heartfelt appreciation for the help you've given me this past year.

EXPRESS WARM WISHES FOR THE SEASON. AVOID MAKING THE NOTE SOUND LIKE A "DUTY." BE WARM, CREATIVE, AND SINCERE.

Have a happy holiday.

Cheers.

The very best to each of you for the coming year.

One of the best parts of ushering in the new year is remembering the good times of the past year. Thank you for the productive, fun-filled, collaborative projects.

I wish you a safe, happy holiday.

Best wishes for the happiest of holidays.

May this holiday be everything you wish for your family and friends.

Have a blessed holiday.

You deserve the best during this holiday season.

May the joy of the season make your holiday especially nice.

Enjoy every minute with your family and friends. I wish you a wonderful holiday season.

Dear Francis:

There is no more appropriate time than the beginning of a new year to wish you and Arvillo International every success and to express our appreciation for past assignments.

We hope that in the coming year you will consider us as an extension of your own team for both organizational counsel and executive recruiting.

We wish you the best in the new year.

Cordially,

Greetings To Our Salespeople:

It's December again--almost before we have our heads out of the Bilton-Sinclare compensation-package proposal. Let's get together for lunch on December 21 and throw it in neutral for a few hours.

Yes, I do appreciate your dedication--the long hours you've put in, the anxiety attacks over client acceptances, and the hustle for short deadlines.

But, no, I don't want you to miss out on a well-deserved rest and holiday! We'll meet for lunch in the Westin lobby at noon. (It's dutch, sorry.)

I hope the new year is the very best for you.

Regards,

A Note to Everyone in the Field:

It takes a great deal of both individual and collective energy to have a successful year in an organization like ours. As the year comes to a close, I want to thank all of you for your contributions on behalf of the support staff.

We're looking forward to another year of excitement, change, and opportunities. Thank you for your help and best wishes for a happy, prosperous, and healthy new year.

Sincerely,

Dear Jim,

It sure has been a prosperous and successful year for us at the Cleaning Technology Clinic, and we owe a big part of that success to you.

During this past year, we have had the pleasure of seeing professionalism and growth in numerous companies in the industry, but none as expansive as yours. The enthusiasm generated by you and your staff has led to mutual respect among several in the industry.

This coming year presents a real challenge for us, and we hope to continue our good working relationship with you.

On behalf of all the staff here, we want to thank you for the most generous services you have provided in the past year. We wish you a most refreshing holiday, and we look forward to expanding our mutually beneficial relationship in the new year.

Sincerely,

Dear Bob:

As the year closes, we want you to know how much your business and your friendship mean to us. As a small token of our appreciation for your help in the development of our compensation packages, we have enclosed a desk calendar that we hope will help keep you on schedule in 19--.

Once again, thanks. Have a wonderful holiday season and a successful new year.

Regards,

Dear Martha:

As the holiday draws near, Sybil and I want to thank you for the many kindnesses you have extended to us in our travels during this past year. I can assure you that our pleasant business association has been the source of much less travel anxiety than before our paths crossed.

We've sent a little gift to say thank you--a subscription to Forbes for the coming year. We hope that you will enjoy reading it throughout the months ahead as much as we enjoy sending it.

With warmest regards,

Dear Fellow Staffers:

I want to take this opportunity to let you know that I have appreciated your efforts over the past 12 months. Our growth--particularly of the software line--can be traced directly to your support services to the customers.

To each of you, may the holidays bring a relaxing, meaningful time with family and friends. Best wishes.

Sincerely,

G U I D E L I N E S   A N D   A L T E R N A T E   P H R A S E S

GIVE ALL PERTINENT BACKGROUND INFORMATION ABOUT YOUR CAUSE OR GROUP IF IT IS NOT WELL KNOWN.

STATE CLEARLY WHAT WILL BE INVOLVED IN THE USE OF THE NAME, AND INFORM THE READER WHAT PERSONAL EFFORT WILL BE EXPECTED.

We can assure you that your name will be more than adequate to support our effort, and, of course, we expect nothing further than your reputation.

There'll be no meetings, phone calls, or dollars requested from you. Your best wishes and name will add all the prestige necessary to make our project a total success.

BE PERSUASIVE ABOUT WHY THE READER SHOULD LEND HIS OR HER NAME TO THE CAUSE.

MAKE IT EASY FOR THE READER TO REPLY POSITIVELY.

Simply sign the enclosed letter granting us permission to use your name in the way we've outlined.

We'll be eager to receive your phone call (345-8233) permitting us to name you as our honorary leader.

Would you write us with your "yes" so that we can go to work making Dallas a better place to live and do business?

Dear Mr. Lomax:

As chairman of the St. Agnes Foundation, I am writing to ask your help--a friend has suggested that you might be willing to let us use your name as honorary chairman of our upcoming fund drive.

Our foundation, a Texas nonprofit corporation, was founded in April 19-- for the advancement of health care in Dallas, and particularly, at St. Agnes Hospital. Management of the foundation is entirely separate from that of the hospital. Since its beginning, the foundation has become one of Dallas' most respected charitable organizations.

In order to maintain this status, we must continue to ask individuals like you for help. Your name will lend us the influence and prestige we need to call once again on corporations for their help in maintaining adequate (and the only major) health-care service in the central city area.

We sincerely hope you will honor us and your friends by granting this request. The extent of your involvement will simply be your name on printed letters of fund solicitation. I've enclosed drafts of three letters we plan to use in our efforts.

Leo Harseton will phone you in a few days to see if you can help us out in this way. With kindest regards, we look forward to your acceptance of this honorary position.

Cordially,

Dear Ms. Grafton:

Do you belong to a college or university advisory board? A mutual friend of ours, Hugh Shaffer, recommended that I extend an invitation to you to join our Harris College advisory board in an honorary capacity. Perhaps you know of some others in Colorado who have agreed to serve--Dr. Carolyn Fullerton, Mr. Matt Johnson, and Dr. Bruce Wellenberg.

Until recently our advisory board has been small, but if we are going to continue to grow we need to add people of your stature to help us.

I'm sure by now you are wondering what will be expected of you. Therefore, I want to assure you that as an advisory board member you will be required to give very little of your time. All of our board business will be conducted by mail, unless you want to attend some of the college's functions. About every three or four months I will write you and your fellow board members with a couple of questions about various issues here at the college. We will be most grateful if you can either write or phone us with your opinions.

Also from time to time, we will be sending out brochures about the college and would like to be able to list your name as a member of our advisory board. If we have your permission to do that, would you please let me know by signing the attached form.

Because your name is so well known in the state, I am aware that you have lived here for a number of years and are familiar with our school. But should there be any specific questions I can answer about our success record, expansion plans, or anything at all, feel free to call on me.

May I tell our trustees that you have agreed to lend your name to our efforts to educate tomorrow's work force?

Sincerely,

Dear Mr. Meadows:

Together with my co-chairman, Mayor Henike, may I invite you to join an honorary committee being formed to assist the Governor's Club of San Diego in the celebration of its 30th anniversary.

Founded in 1958 to advance the economic, civic, and social well-being of the people of San Diego, the Governor's Club through the years has been closely identified with the city's successes in these areas. Therefore, we want to make the 30th anniversary a memorable tribute to San Diego and to those who have served our city with devotion and zeal.

The celebration will be held on Thursday evening, March 4, in the Grand Ballroom of the Hilton. On this occasion, the Governor's Club will pay special tribute to a selected group of Californians and the institutions and achievements they represent.

Proceeds will benefit the Governor's Club of San Diego to strengthen their efforts to secure permanent good government for the city and for the state.

I assure you that no obligations of your time or money will be involved. The mayor and I hope that you will join our honorary committee because your name will ensure the success of our anniversary tribute. Would you please write or phone us (123/456-7899) with your answer?

Sincerely,

HONORARY USE OF NAME, TESTIMONIAL, OR CHAIR POSITION/Accepting

GUIDELINES AND ALTERNATE PHRASES

ACCEPT THE INVITATION GRACIOUSLY.

I am delighted that you have asked me to serve.

I sincerely appreciate the confidence you've shown in choosing me for this honorary position.

I am always pleased to help out the community in small ways such as lending my name to an excellent cause.

Thank you for expressing such trust in my endorsement of your cause. I'm very pleased to accept your invitation.

VERIFY THAT YOUR PERSONAL INVOLVEMENT IS UNNECESSARY.

I understand that no time or travel on my part will be involved.

Because my schedule is already so full, I'm counting on your assurance that no time will be required of me in this effort.

As I understand from your letter, no personal appearances or telephone meetings will be expected of me. It all sounds easy enough to me; the real contribution to the community will be made by you and your staff. On their behalf I thank you.

STATE ANY PERSONAL OR BUSINESS GOALS YOU MAY HAVE IN THE OUTCOME OF THE ORGANIZATION'S EFFORTS.

Yours is a worthwhile, respected organization, and I'm proud to be associated in this small way.

Our company has reaped tremendous rewards because of your past help to our employees. We know that our people can continue to look forward to improved schools in their neighborhoods because of your efforts in fighting drug abuse.

WISH THE ORGANIZATION SUCCESS IN ITS EFFORTS.

I wish you great success.

Best wishes to you in this effort.

Your organization deserves all the help that may come its way during the days ahead.

We hope your fund-raising effort is hugely successful.

240

Dear Howard:

Thank you for the invitation to become the honorary chairman of the CISC. Also, I appreciate the invitation to join you and Bill Jamieson for lunch.

I will be delighted for you to use my name in promoting your organization. One of the main thoughts contributing to my decision is my understanding that your headquarters will eventually be relocated to our city.

Bob Shearers, my assistant, will be in touch with you about the details. I understand from your letter that all you need from me is a recent photo and a facsimile of my signature.

All of our staff wish you great success with the 19-- plans for community involvement.

Sincerely,

HONORARY USE OF NAME, TESTIMONIAL, OR CHAIR POSITION/Declining

GUIDELINES AND ALTERNATE PHRASES

GIVE THE REASON YOU CANNOT ACCEPT THE INVITATION.

While I understand your dedication to the cause, I hold totally opposite views on the issues involved.

My family members have very strong feelings about the related issues, and, therefore, out of concern for their feelings, I'm afraid I can't accept your invitation.

I've always been the sort of person who brings great enthusiasm to her interests; I'll have to be honest enough to say that I just do not feel that strongly about the illiteracy matter. I suggest, therefore, that you can probably find others who would have much more success for you.

Thank you for your confidence, but I simply do not feel that I have the broad appeal such an issue deserves.

I'm sorry to say that I cannot lend my name to such a project unless I can actively participate in it. And such active participation is out of the question for me at this time because of health problems.

In other instances, as you may be aware, I have permitted my name to be used. Unfortunately, some groups made decisions and used advertising methods of which I did not approve. Because of those situations, I simply have decided that I must refrain from such use. I hope you understand.

I've already permitted two other groups this year to use my name in their efforts. Therefore, I fear "overkill" for the public. Please forgive me for not agreeing this time.

EXPRESS APPRECIATION FOR THE HONOR SHOWN BY THE REQUEST.

Thank you for the invitation, and I hope you understand my concern.

I appreciate your thinking of me, and I'm sorry I cannot help in this instance.

Your request is a compliment, and I appreciate your thoughtfulness in contacting me.

Receiving your request has been an honor that I appreciate. I know others will be eager to help you in this way.

Thank you for the confidence you have shown by this request. I'm flattered.

EXTEND BEST WISHES FOR THE SUCCESS OF THE PROJECT IF YOU CAN DO SO SINCERELY.

I wish you overwhelming success in your efforts.

May you have the best of success in this matter.

I commend you on your enthusiasm and efforts.

HONORARY USE OF NAME, TESTIMONIAL, OR CHAIR POSITION/Declining

Dear Ms. Jones:

I appreciate very much your extending to me the invitation to participate in the President's Tutorial Program. My associates and I think this would be a marvelous opportunity for a young person in today's business world. In fact, when I look back on the matter, I would like to have had the opportunity myself in my earlier career.

Unfortunately, however, we have decided that we simply cannot grant the use of our name to your organization. In the past three years, we have allowed various groups to use our name as endorsement for their services and have been highly offended at some of their solicitation tactics. Therefore, we have established a policy against such use.

We hope you understand our position, and we appreciate the recognition your request implies. Best wishes for every success with the student program.

Sincerely,

GUIDELINES AND ALTERNATE PHRASES

REQUEST THE INFORMATION YOU NEED IMMEDIATELY.

BE SPECIFIC ABOUT WHAT YOU NEED, INCLUDING DATES, AMOUNTS, NAMES, APPROVAL SIGNATURES, OR APPROPRIATE FORMAT OF THE INFORMATION.

I specifically wanted information about the two books that dealt with pets, advertised in the May issue of your magazine.

I've enclosed a letter from Ms. White authorizing release of the documents to me.

Please send me the product pamphlet pictured on page 22 of your general catalog dated September 19—.

EXPLAIN HOW YOU PLAN TO USE THE INFORMATION IF THE READER MAY BE HESITANT TO RESPOND TO YOUR REQUEST.

Our investment club in my local subdivision is compiling research on companies within your industry to guide us in future stock purchases.

This information will in no way jeopardize our current orders with your company. We simply want to know what new items you plan to offer next quarter.

This information is strictly for our own internal use.

STATE ANY DEADLINES AS SPECIFICALLY AS YOU CAN, BUT AVOID A DEMANDING TONE IF THE READER'S RESPONSE IS OPTIONAL.

Could you have the updated summary to us by May 6?

Would you let us have your reply as soon as possible?

Thank you for any information you can forward to us immediately.

We'll appreciate your helping us meet our July 7 deadline if at all possible.

We plan to make our decision the first week of October. We hope to have your information by that date.

SUPPLY ANY FURTHER FORMS, INFORMATION, RETURN ENVELOPES, CONTACT NAMES AND NUMBERS, OR APPROVALS/RELEASES SO THAT THE READER CAN RESPOND QUICKLY AND EASILY.

If it's more convenient for you, please feel free to call me collect at (713) 955-9525.

We've provided all the necessary forms to make your response more convenient.

If you have questions about the information we need, call 123-3455 and ask for Jack Smith, who has a list of our project requirements.

I've included all the necessary release papers and permission forms ready for your signature.

THANK THE READER.

Dear Bill:

The homeowner's policy #34998HT45 we are servicing for you is due for renewal. In order for us to provide proper coverage, we need your help in completing and returning to us the enclosed questionnaire. (A stamped return envelope is provided.)

We need to have your questionnaire returned by May 5.

This information will enable us to "custom fit" your policy to your specific home and needs. Thanks for your help.

Sincerely,

Dear Mr. Lietke:

I visited your site on March 2 and again on March 8, but I've been unable to determine where your gas meter is to be located.

Would you please send me a site plan with the gas meter location marked. If the location is to be at the property line, there will be no charge for this installation. Once the location is established, it will take us about three weeks to complete the service-line installation—subject to weather conditions, of course.

Also, please provide me with a list of the gas-burning equipment (cooking, hot water, and heating) and the BTU input for each so that we can determine the correct meter size.

We'll be happy to provide this service for you as soon as we receive the site plan and your list of equipment.

Sincerely,

Dear Mr. Shotwell:

Thank you for your inquiry about your current bill. Before we can answer your questions, we need further information from you. We have enclosed a postcard listing the appropriate information we'll need to verify that our records are correct.

Your cooperation in completing the card and dropping it back in the mail will help us answer your inquiry as quickly as possible. Thank you for your time in responding.

Sincerely,

Dear John:

We will need this basic information before we can submit your bond request to Universal General:

- Completed "Contractor's Questionnaire"
- Financial statement on A-1 Horizonal Drilling
- Descriptions of your operations, equipment, and personnel

Thank you for allowing us to serve you.

Yours truly,

Dear Mr. Matthews:

I would appreciate your sending me more information about the ABGF Institute seminar scheduled about March 1 in the Chicago area. Specifically, I need to know the registration procedures and the cost of tuition.

We received your mail-out announcing the seminar two weeks ago and are very much interested in sending several members of our sales staff.

It certainly appears that you have lined up a most impressive program and an outstanding group of speakers.

Thank you for the above information; we'll look forward to participating in this program.

Sincerely,

Dear Mr. Hightower:

We are in the process of reviewing and evaluating all of our outstanding agreements with vendors and their representatives. Would you please give us the following information by April 6?

1. A list of the manufacturer representative agreements in your territory
2. Actual sales credited
3. Actual commission paid to each representative

We hope this request won't be perceived as just "more paperwork." Please keep in mind that this is a necessary step in being able to control all our B&P costs and report them accurately.

Thank you for helping us.

Sincerely,

Gentlemen and Ladies:

Please mail one copy of the report entitled "The Economic Value of Ocean Resources" to me at the following address:

Herman Sweetwater
12345 Riverside Blvd.
Houston, TX 77070

Enclosed is a check for $1.50 to cover the cost of duplication as mentioned in your letter of June 5.

Yours truly,

Dear Mr. Lamear:

May I ask a favor? Can you give me the name of an individual to whom I should write about contract rights to construct residential housing for the Navy?

From other sources, my understanding is that I should contact:

    Commanding Officer
    Northern Division
    Navy Facilities Engineering Command
    Philadelphia, PA 19112

However, I would much prefer writing to a specific individual who could take us out of the general paper shuffle.

Thank you for any help you can offer.

Sincerely,

Dear Mr. Drujon:

The staff of Briton Magazine is currently involved in preparing its Annual Directory Issue to be published in October. This survey presents vital information on nearly 2,000 major companies in the U.S. and abroad.

We, therefore, need some information from you. Our annual always includes a special feature that lists remuneration, age, years of service, and education of the chief executives of these companies. Would you please verify the information we have on you by completing (anonymously, of course) the enclosed questionnaire and returning it to us by July 1?

We greatly appreciate the cooperation your company has given us in the past. We think these statistics are vital to all of us who are financial planners. Thank you for your assistance.

Sincerely,

INFORMATION/Providing

THANK THE READER FOR THE INQUIRY.

We are glad to learn of your interest in our products.

Thank you for letting us know of your specific needs. We are happy, of course, to supply you with the information you need.

Thank you for your interest in our bidding procedures.

We are pleased to receive your letter asking for information about local distributors.

MENTION IMMEDIATELY THE INFORMATION YOU ARE PROVIDING.

We are pleased to enclose. . . .

We are mailing you separately. . . .

Shortly, you will be receiving. . . .

Today I have mailed. . . .

MENTION ANYTHING THAT YOU CAN'T SEND AND EXPLAIN WHY.

Such information is confidential, and, therefore, not available for distribution.

We regret that we cannot also include the list of stockholders participating in this venture, but the information is quite confidential, as you might understand.

We regret that we simply do not have the available staff to research the kind of information you need.

Although we would like to provide this information to all our vendors, the cost is quite prohibitive.

The other information, I'm afraid, is simply not available to me. I'm sorry.

OFFER TO HELP THE REQUESTER IN SOME OTHER WAY. WHAT INFORMATION CAN YOU PROVIDE? CAN YOU REFER THE REQUESTER TO SOMEONE ELSE WHO MAY BE ABLE TO HELP?

I'm forwarding your request to Joe Bitten, hoping that he may be able to answer your last two questions.

In an attempt to give you at least a partial answer, I've enclosed. . . .

EXPRESS APPRECIATION AND INVITE FURTHER INQUIRIES IF THAT IS APPROPRIATE.

Let us know if this doesn't answer your questions fully. Thank you for asking.

Thank you for giving us the opportunity to provide the information upon which you can make a decision. We hope to hear from you again soon.

I hope this helps. Thank you for your letter and feel free to write again.

Gentlemen or Ladies:

Thank you for your response to our recent Trends newsletter. As you requested on our response card, we are enclosing your free copy of "Hot Tips for Cold Investors."

We noted your answers to the other card queries about your specific investment interests. As new offerings are made, we'll contact you again with items in those areas.

We appreciate the opportunity to assist you in your financial decisions and hope you'll contact any of our staff again when you need further information.

Sincerely,

Dear Mr. Whitmeyer:

I have attached copies of the certificates requested by the Port of Houston Authority:

- Insured endorsements
- OCP policy with $500,000 limits
- Notices of cancellation

The job will last approximately 90 days and will involve earthwork and some underground storm work to provide proper sloping and drainage of the site. The site is approximately 3,500 feet from the ship channel and involves no in-water or on-water exposure.

We have a very limited time (until May 1) to get the approved bonds and certificates to the Port Authority; therefore, I will appreciate your help in delivering them as soon as possible. We have come to expect your fine servicing of our accounts.

Thank you,

Dear Ms. Jones:

Some of the materials you recently requested had to be retrieved from our archives, and if you could see our archives, you'd know that's no easy task!

We are pleased to enclose the old product pricing policies you needed. However, we have been unable to locate the specifications on the AW-1893 engine. I've noted your request on my calendar and will ask my assistant when she returns from vacation if she can give me further clues as to where we might locate that information. If you don't hear from me again, you'll please understand that that information is simply too old to be still in our possession.

Best wishes with your research. Let us know if we can help in other ways.

Sincerely,

GUIDELINES AND ALTERNATE PHRASES

BEGIN ON A NEUTRAL OR POSITIVE NOTE.

We received your letter asking about the nature of our bidding process.

Thank you for your letter inquiring about our legal difficulties with Norman Raymond International.

EXPLAIN WHY YOU CANNOT SEND THE REQUESTED INFORMATION.

The information has not been compiled at this time.

The information is not in a readily accessible form that would be appropriate for mailing outside the organization.

Because some of the information is rather sensitive to our clients, we do not want to jeopardize client relationships by sending these documents outside our firm.

We used to provide these maps to our customers, but the cost of mailing over 150,000 copies annually has become prohibitive. We hope you understand.

DECLINE TO PROVIDE THE INFORMATION IN A COURTEOUS, POSITIVE TONE.

OFFER TO MEET THE REQUESTER'S NEEDS IN ANOTHER WAY.

Please write us again if we can help you in another way.

Perhaps we can help you the next time.

Thank you for writing. Let us know if we can provide anything further in the way of specification sheets.

Let us know if we have overlooked another piece of information that may help you with your study.

Is there some other way we can assist you?

Dear Ms. Warren:

I have received your November 1 letter requesting financial statements for Zeeler Company; we especially appreciate your complimentary remarks about the future of our new Dallas division.

Because Zeeler Company is a wholly-owned subsidiary of Buford Manufacturing Corporation, Zeeler does not publish financial information outside the company. Cash requirements for Zeeler are supplied by the parent company. I am, therefore, enclosing a copy of Buford Manufacturing Corporation's Annual Report for 19--, which I hope will be of some help to you.

Please call me at 666-9983 if you need any additional information on the other two companies you are researching.

Sincerely,

Dear Mr. Wharton:

We're so pleased to hear from you after your having read the Wall Street Journal story on BYMED. The staff writer did such a fine job in extolling our virtues and growth pattern that we were caught unprepared for such a response from its readership.

I'm sorry to say that we do not have completed brochures containing all the appropriate information on our radiators and heaters for the automotive market. As the *WSJ* story detailed, our total sales have increased 82% in the past six months, and current projections are that sales will indeed continue that growth pattern and profitability.

In lieu of a slick sales brochure, I have enclosed a specifications sheet, which I hope will answer some of your questions. We hope, too, that after reviewing the enclosed information you will agree that BYMED represents an excellent investment opportunity.

Cordially,

Dear Mr. Martin:

Your March 2 letter to Mr. John Trudeau has been referred to me because of the sensitivity of the Marietta issues.

Unfortunately, we don't agree with your interpretation of the Section 6 clause of our November 10 contract. We do not think that we are required by law to furnish you with the proposal information developed over a period of time at a great expense to Vitco Inc. After careful consideration, you will, I'm sure, understand our position.

If you have other questions to which we may be able to provide answers, please write again.

Sincerely,

INTRODUCTION/Of a New Employee

GUIDELINES AND ALTERNATE PHRASES

STATE THE NEW EMPLOYEE'S NAME, POSITION, EFFECTIVE DATE OF EMPLOYMENT, AND, IF APPROPRIATE, THE REPORTING LINE.

With great eagerness, I introduce to you Sarah MacIntire, who on August 1 will become our general counsel handling real estate loans. She will report directly to Bill Bledsoe.

Jim Fuller will join our organization as Controller, reporting directly to me.

GIVE DETAILS OF THE PERSON'S EXPERIENCE— EDUCATION, EXPERTISE, PAST EMPLOYERS, MAJOR CLIENTS, OR SPECIAL PROJECTS HANDLED.

Sarah is a graduate of Mississippi State University and received her law degree from Baylor University in 19—, the year she became

associated with the San Francisco law firm of Belco & Blevins.

Jim is an expert in the areas of business/real estate/energy and has a broad range of knowledge in banking and corporate law as well.

ASK THE READERS TO WELCOME THE EMPLOYEE.

We extend our heartiest welcome to you, Sarah.

I will appreciate your help in making Jim feel welcome.

Please show Jim the ropes around here.

Help me welcome Jim to our team.

(Note: For introduction of your own company or service to prospective clients, see "Sales and Marketing.")

Dear Joan,

The "help" I've spoken to you about has finally arrived! My associate Michael James expects to be in Dallas from February 2-10 (staying at the Wyndam Gardens). I would very much like for you to meet him because I'm sure that, from time to time, he will be gathering information for me on some of the projects that you and I regularly coordinate.

Michael is one of the senior people in our corporate finance area and will be regularly traveling to Dallas and other Texas cities for me.

I've suggested that he give you a call when he arrives. If you are unable to see him during this time, could you perhaps refer him to Martin O'Hara for a tour of your operations there? The more he knows about how my job and your job dovetail, the more he'll become a vital link on which we can depend.

Thank you. Michael is looking forward to meeting you. By the way, you two should have some stories to swap--he's an Aggie also.

Sincerely,

INTRODUCTION/Of an Outside Person

INTRODUCE THE PERSON AND GIVE THE REASON FOR THE INTRODUCTION.

After our recent lunch, I gave more thought to your question about overseas contracts and am writing to suggest that you might want to meet Bill Wydermer.

Joan Littlejohn has worked with me on numerous projects, and I have the highest regard for her opinions. Therefore, I have suggested that she phone you so that you can get together for a brief visit. I think she'll have valuable ideas for you on the. . . .

PRESENT DETAILS OF THE PERSON'S BACKGROUND.

MAKE IT EASY FOR THE READER TO MAKE CONTACT.

I hope you'll be able to talk to Art. He'll phone your office.

I've enclosed a vita on him with home and work numbers.

If you prefer, I can make arrangements for us to get together for lunch this next week.

If you think a meeting would be helpful, let me know and I'll handle all the details.

EXPRESS APPRECIATION FOR ANY COURTESY SHOWN TO THE PERSON BEING INTRODUCED.

Thank you for any help you can give Randy.

I'll appreciate your introducing him to the business community there in Seattle.

If I can ever return the favor, let me know.

Harvey is one of my closest friends and associates; I'll take it as a personal favor for you to take him under your wing as you have me from time to time.

Dear Bert:

The man I mentioned to you as a possible consultant for the Arizona BARK Commission is James E. Tinsleberger. He formerly was executive director of the Appox Foundation and left with John Capon's blessing. He is now practicing as an independent financial and management consultant.

James, 36 years old, has recently completed his work at Harvard Graduate School of Business Administration. He is a CPA and has not only had extensive experience in state government financial matters but is also an expert in international commodity trading. The attached newspaper clipping will give you a more detailed background.

I personally spoke with him about the BARK Commission assignment, and he indicated considerable interest. My associate Karl Marietta asked him to have an outline of his plans to propose to you and the remuneration he would expect. If you're interested in pursuing the matter with him, he will have all the details worked out.

You can reach him at 12250 Jones Road, Houston, Texas 77070. I have alerted him that he might be considered for the assignment; therefore, if you decide not to contact him, please let me know and I'll inform him that you've made other arrangements.

Sincerely,

Dear Sid:

During our discussion of the difficulty in finding staff for your new Pilton designs, I spoke to you about a young man, Harold Richards. He has just graduated from Texas A&M School of Architecture, carrying 140 semester hours with a 3.8 average. He is going to call you on June 2 to see if you are interested in interviewing him.

I'd appreciate your talking with him and think you'll be quite impressed.

Best regards,

Dear Max:

Sidney Wahmon, partner in the management consulting firm of Bolinger International, is returning to Dallas to head the firm's local office. He is a good friend of mine and a leader in the business and industry networks. You may have met Sidney a few years ago when he was associated here with Clayton and Pool & Company.

I do want you to meet or renew your acquaintance with Sidney and hope you can join me and a few friends for an informal reception on Thursday, May 4, at the Tonondo Club, 4th floor, Bank of the Southwest, from 6:00 until 8:00 p.m.

Will you be able to join us?

Sincerely,

GUIDELINES AND ALTERNATE PHRASES

INTRODUCE THE SERVICE OR COMPANY IN TERMS OF THE READER'S INTEREST.

You mentioned to me recently your interest in investigating the Australia market. Therefore, I have suggested that Harold Martin of RedMar Inc. contact you about. . . .

Your CFO wrote me in the spring about your decision to add temporary PR staff when the new computer product line was in full swing. I've found a personnel agency specializing in placement of the sort of temporary employees you mentioned.

GIVE BACKGROUND INFORMATION FROM YOUR PERSONAL EXPERIENCE ABOUT THE SERVICE, PRODUCT, OR COMPANY.

They enjoy a fine reputation with our own company.

Their services have been invaluable to us during our recent problem with. . . .

Although we have had no specific need of their professional services while I've been associated with Universal Corporation, I do know the company reputation here in Jackson is outstanding. Mr. Smith has served with me on numerous Chamber of Commerce committees, and I continue to hear nothing but compliments about his firm.

INDICATE ANY REFERRAL INFORMATION YOU'VE GIVEN, BUT AVOID OBLIGATING THE READER.

I did give their representative your name, thinking you would appreciate his input if you can find the time to chat a few minutes on the phone.

If you're not in a position to use the kind of service they provide, perhaps you can refer Bill Wamock to other prospective clients. I'll thank you for any consideration you may be able to give him.

Dear Margaret,

With this letter, I want to introduce you to a very well-known French company, Constructions Metalliques de Provence (CMP) with which we have been doing business for quite some time. We have joint ventures concerning the fabrication and erection of all kinds of tanks, pressure vessels, and refinery columns--all ventures that you, too, might be interested in pursuing.

CMP is opening an office in your area. Mr. T. S. Goulette, who is to be in charge of that location, is a good friend of ours, very personable, and extremely knowledgeable about our industry. You'll also find him very articulate, with a perfect command of the English language.

To give you a better idea of CMP's activities, I'm enclosing a recently prepared brochure.

When Mr. Goulette contacts you, I'll appreciate any cooperation you can give him. I do think you'll find several common business interests to pursue.

Sincerely,

G U I D E L I N E S   A N D   A L T E R N A T E   P H R A S E S

INVITE THE PERSON TO SPEAK AT A SPECIFIC EVENT, GIVING THE TIME, PLACE, AND PURPOSE OF THE EVENT.

Your presentation will kick off the "roast" we have planned for Hank Marshall, who will be retiring January 14.

On August 28 at a regional managers' meeting, we'd like you to give an hour's overview of the new InfoMart concept and marketing campaign. If you can help us out, your presentation will begin at 4:00 p.m.

GIVE DETAILS ABOUT THE AUDIENCE AND ENTIRE PROGRAM SO THE SPEAKER CAN MAKE HIS OR HER COMMENTS APPROPRIATE TO THE GROUP: ARE THERE OTHER SPEAKERS COVERING SIMILAR TOPICS? WILL THERE BE A QUESTION-ANSWER PERIOD? CAN YOU DUPLICATE THE SPEAKER'S HANDOUT MATERIALS? WHAT IS THE TIME LIMIT?

You will be one of six speakers covering the following aspects of a good marketing campaign.

In past years, we have had speakers to cover. . . . This year, we are wanting a complete change of pace. We'd like you to address the issues relating to. . . .

The audience is basically looking for practical how-tos rather than theory.

We expect a large audience of around 200, so small-group interaction might be difficult.

Please provide a handout covering your key points as back-on-the-job reference material for our supervisors. May we also suggest a biography from you? We'll be happy to duplicate any materials for you.

BE CLEAR ABOUT ANY HONORARIUM, FEE, OR TRAVEL EXPENSES INVOLVED. IF YOU OFFER NO PAYMENT, POINT OUT ANY OTHER BENEFITS THE SPEAKER MAY VALUE: PUBLICITY, FOLLOW-UP BUSINESS CONTACTS, OR AN OPPORTUNITY TO SELL PRODUCTS SUCH AS BOOKS OR AUDIOCASSETTES.

Because our organization is a nonprofit group, we have no budget for an honorarium. We will, however, be happy to reimburse you for all of your travel expenses.

We encourage you to bring along any books or audiocassettes that our attendees may want to purchase. We'll be happy to have a table set up for that purpose and someone to help with the sales of such items.

Although we wish we could offer a fee for your presentation, we simply cannot. We are hoping, however, that you will find sufficient interest among the attendees for follow-up business and that the meeting will be well worth your time.

We can offer you an honorarium of $500 for the evening's talk.

REQUEST A REPLY BY A CERTAIN DATE.

We will appreciate your response by May 4.

If you must disappoint us by not accepting our invitation, we will need your answer by January 4 in order to make alternate plans.

Would you please let us have your answer by January 4?

EXPRESS EAGER ANTICIPATION OF THE READER'S ACCEPTANCE.

We are hoping you can work us into your busy schedule.

We will look forward to hearing from you.

Our audience will be so delighted to know that you can accept the invitation.

We've heard what a dynamic speaker you are and are eagerly waiting for your "yes."

Please let us know whether we can count on you to make this our most successful program to date.

Dear Mr. Hartz:

We are hoping you can help make our upcoming June 6 International Community Dinner a great success. We'd like to ask you to address our distinguished group, including well-known political figures in both state and federal government and high-ranking executives from major corporations around the state.

Specifically, we want you to address the international monetary situation, zeroing in on the roles that politics and economics play. We will have one other speaker, Vernon Allen, founder and chairman of American Surety Corporation. Mr. Allen epitomizes, just as you do, the ideals of business success and public responsibility on which our annual service award has been based.

In short, we want the evening to be both enlightening and enjoyable. Your speech, I'm sure, will accomplish both purposes.

We expect about 90 guests to join us for a cocktail reception at 6:30 p.m. in the Princess Room of the Republic Hotel. Dinner will be served at 7:30. Your speech will begin at 8:30. Mr. Allen will speak at 9:15. Then we will ask that you both make yourselves available for a brief question-answer session with the audience. We hope to conclude the evening by 10:30.

Because of the international business importance of the meeting, we hope your own company can underwrite the cost of your time and travel to the meeting. If that is not possible, please let us know.

If you need any special room arrangement or equipment for your presentation, we will be happy to take care of those details for you.

We will be delighted if you can give us an answer by March 31.

We know our audience will be eager to hear your views and hope that you--and any of your associates who wish to join you for the evening--can take away important ideas for your own future business efforts.

Sincerely,

Sharon,

Just a brief note to ask if you would consider presenting a one-hour workshop on "How to Get Your Ideas Published" at our October 12 management meeting. Max Smith heard you speak at the University of Houston's Southwest Writers Conference and said you gave at least two days' worth of valuable information in your 30-minute slot.

Our audience, however, will be quite different from those attending that conference; they will be PR professionals who routinely publish trade journal articles. They're hoping you can give them help in placing articles in popular magazines.

As always, we have a whopping big budget of $75. Would you give us a cheap thrill anyway? We need an answer by September 1. If you can't accommodate us, we'll have to go for second best. Thanks. I'll be eager for a "yes."

Regards,

Dear Ms. Sweeten:

Your name has come to us as one who has extensive experience in managing accounts for retirement investment. We would like to invite you to address our monthly meeting of senior citizens at Bondale Resort Center on April 5. The topic will be "Investing Opportunities without the Trouble."

We'll serve lunch sharply at noon and then ask you to speak from 1:00 to 1:30, followed by a 15-minute question-answer session.

The audience will be people with diverse past work experience and financial management know-how. As you can imagine, some have sizable assets to invest; others do not. But we do think it will be worth your time in future "prospecting" to have these senior citizens become acquainted with you and your firm. I also suggest that you bring business cards for those who will want to pass on your name to family members taking care of their finances.

If you can accept our invitation, please let us hear from you by the week of February 6. Should you like to speak to our group but simply find the date inconvenient, let us know that also so that we can arrange to schedule your talk at a later monthly meeting. We will be delighted to receive a "yes."

Sincerely,

GUIDELINES AND ALTERNATE PHRASES

EXPRESS APPRECIATION FOR THE INVITATION AND PLEASURE AT BEING ABLE TO ACCEPT.

CONFIRM DATE, TIME, PLACE, AND SUBJECT. MENTION YOUR NEED OF ANY SPECIAL EQUIPMENT, MATERIALS, OR ROOM ARRANGEMENT.

ASK ANY SPECIAL QUESTIONS ABOUT THE AUDIENCE.

Has this subject ever been addressed before your audience?

Do you have in mind a how-to approach or a theory-based presentation?

Will the audience be willing to participate in small-group critique exercises?

What is the range of investment experience of those in your group?

What is the educational background of those who will be attending the session?

Do you think the topic will be of more personal or business interest to your attendees?

CONFIRM TRAVEL ARRANGEMENTS.

Dear Steve:

Thank you for your invitation to share the "Tapping Your Investment" program with the other divisions at their August 3 dinner at the Hilton. I eagerly accept.

I understand that the dinner begins at 7:00, but I plan to arrive about 6:30 to take care of any last-minute details.

I've enclosed my biography; please feel free to condense it or select any of the details you may want to use in your pre-program publicity.

Can you provide the following equipment?

- 3/4" VHS video player
- television monitor and stand
- 2 flip charts and markers
- overhead projector and table

If I understand you correctly, the audience will be primarily senior executives looking for retirement investments. As soon as I finish updating my program materials for your specific audience, I'll forward my handout originals on to you for duplication.

As you suggested, I have made my own airline reservations. I look forward to addressing your group.

Cordially,

GUIDELINES AND ALTERNATE PHRASES

EXPRESS APPRECIATION FOR THE INVITATION.

Thank you so much for thinking of me in choosing a speaker for your upcoming May 2 luncheon.

I was delighted to get your invitation to address the group on May 2.

Your invitation to speak to the ECCO Council on May 2 was a flattering surprise. Your programs are always so outstanding that I've taken the invitation as quite a compliment.

I was pleased to receive your letter asking me to address the ECCO Council on May 2.

Thank you for your confidence in asking me to address your group on May 2.

EXPRESS REGRET THAT YOU MUST DECLINE. YOUR REGRET SOUNDS MORE SINCERE IF YOU CAN GIVE A SPECIFIC EXPLANATION OF WHAT PREVENTS YOUR ACCEPTANCE.

Although I'd love the opportunity to speak to your group, I don't feel adequately knowledgeable on the subject you have in mind. My previous experience has been limited to . . . .

Unfortunately, I have a meeting in London that day and because so many people are involved, I simply cannot change it.

I have had an out-of-town seminar scheduled for quite some time and will be traveling on the day of your dinner meeting.

Unfortunately, I have a previous commitment with a client on that day and simply cannot rearrange my schedule at this time.

REFER THEM TO ANOTHER EXPERT IF YOU THINK THAT IS APPROPRIATE.

If you have no one else in mind to address that topic, give me a call and perhaps I'll be able to suggest a colleague who could speak knowledgeably on the subject.

I suggest that you call Harry Smith, whom I've heard on several occasions. He is a dynamic speaker who can tackle even the toughest questions from your most experienced attendees.

WISH SUCCESS FOR THE EVENT.

You have my very best wishes for a successful meeting.

Best of luck to you in finalizing your program.

I know the program will be outstanding.

I'll be eager to hear from those who have the opportunity to attend. The programs seem to get better every year.

I hope the dinner meets all your expectations.

With such attention to detail, I'm sure you'll have a fine program.

My best wishes in lining up the additional speakers for the regional meeting.

Dear Mr. Shotwell:

Your invitation for me to address the Economic Development Council was very flattering. I would very much like to speak to the group; unfortunately, however, I am program chairman for a CPA professional association meeting that is to be held in Nashville the night of May 5. I've checked that meeting and my travel schedule, and there's simply no way I can make it back to Denver by noon on May 6.

I have another suggestion that you may want to consider. Fred Hanke, our senior vice president, could make an excellent presentation on the same subject; you can reach him at 123-3456. If you have other alternatives in mind, I don't mean to be presumptuous with this suggestion, only helpful.

Thank you again for the invitation. Best wishes for an informative meeting.

Sincerely,

GUIDELINES AND ALTERNATE PHRASES

EXTEND THE INVITATION, GIVING THE DATE, TIME, AND PLACE, AND MENTIONING OTHER ATTENDEES.

We hope you can join E. Patrick Smith and a number of Austin's business leaders for a networking breakfast at 7:00 a.m., June 6. We want to exchange views on the new economic turns in the oil and gas industry.

Will you join us and your other area insurance agents for an informal cocktail hour and dinner on July 7?

Will you please be my guest for lunch at noon Monday, May 5, at the Frazier Club at 12556 Madison Avenue? I've also invited. . . .

We are reserving a seat for you at our upcoming dinner, May 15, 7:00 p.m., at the Radison Square.

We are pleased to invite you to join us. . . .

We ask that you be our guest on May 5 for a luncheon honoring. . . .

TELL WHY THE EVENT IS TAKING PLACE: TO INTRODUCE SOME PERSON, PRODUCT, OR SERVICE; TO HONOR SOMEONE ON A SPECIFIC OCCASION; TO CELEBRATE A SPECIAL ANNIVERSARY DATE; TO PROVIDE NETWORK OPPORTUNITIES.

The principal purpose of this reception is to introduce the services we now offer.

It will be an informal cocktail buffet honoring our city officials and a special group of supporters of the Houston Symphony.

This informal get-together will give you an opportunity to hear Bob Maxwell's comments on the legislative climate for issues such as the domestic program, the federal budget, and welfare reform.

Please be assured that there is no fund raising hidden in the agenda for this meeting. The purpose is simply to express appreciation to the business leaders who have supported us this year.

MENTION WHETHER A GIFT IS EXPECTED AT ANNIVERSARIES, RETIREMENT DINNERS, OR FAREWELL GALAS.

This is a very informal get-together. No gifts are expected.

STATE THE APPROPRIATE DRESS IF THAT ISN'T APPARENT BY THE REST OF THE INVITATION.

Please note that this is a black-tie event.

Please dress comfortably; our speaker will be asking us to participate in stress-reducing exercises that may require moving around a bit.

STATE WHETHER YOU WANT TO EXTEND THE INVITATION TO A COLLEAGUE OR SPOUSE IF THE READER IS UNABLE TO ATTEND.

Because we hope that you personally will attend, we ask that you not send a representative.

We are hoping that you yourself can attend, but if you are unable to do so, feel free to send another associate who you think will be able to bring back ideas to your company.

Spouses or guests are cordially invited.

If you are unable to accept, an alternate officer will be most welcome.

MENTION ANY FEE FOR THE EVENT.

If you can accept, the $20 fee is due by August 4.

Of course, there is no charge for this event.

We welcome you to be our guest for the evening.

ASK FOR A RESPONSE BY A CERTAIN DATE.

BE AS FORMAL OR INFORMAL AS YOUR RELATIONSHIP TO THE READER DICTATES.

Dear Mr. Tunnel:

You are cordially invited to be our guest at a luncheon on April 2 to meet His Excellency Ambassador Michael Wo from Taiwan. The Ambassador's first visit to the country is being cosponsored by the international division of the Pullman Club and by Mitchell Associates.

The Ambassador has asked me to arrange a luncheon at which he could meet you and a dozen other leading Miami business people. In addition to meeting the business leaders and seeing the city firsthand, the Ambassador's purpose is to explain the economic situation in Taiwan and to discuss possible areas of foreign investment.

We are confident the Ambassador will leave Miami favorably impressed. As Taiwan is becoming increasingly important to our community, I hope that you will be present or will be represented by another senior member of your organization.

We'll appreciate your reply by March 2. Because I will be out of town for most of the next month, please direct any questions you may have to Vice President Howard Hunt (123-4567). We would also be happy to relay any suggestions you may have for the Ambassador to include in his discussions.

Sincerely,

Dear Fellow Club Member:

Three senior editors from <u>Herald Business Journal</u> will serve on a panel at a special luncheon, November 12, at noon in the Georgia Room of the Westin Oaks. We'd like you to join us.

These editors will be giving their informed views on the post-election economy, the business outlook, the fate of wage-price controls, and tax reform.

The price of the luncheon for members is $16; guests, $20. I'll look forward to seeing you there.

Sincerely,

Dear Jack:

In March, Harold Wilson will be retiring from the bank. Would you believe that at his own retirement dinner, February 22, we are asking him to give us his views on the new directions in banking?

Sylvia and I have reserved a table for the occasion and will be very pleased if you and Marge can join us and our other guests that evening. We'll meet in the building lobby at 6:00 p.m. for cocktails before we go next door to attend the dinner at Shephard's.

If you can be with us, please write or phone by February 3. We're looking forward to visiting with you again.

Sincerely,

GUIDELINES AND ALTERNATE PHRASES

EXPRESS APPRECIATION FOR THE INVITATION AND PLEASURE AT BEING ABLE TO ACCEPT.

I'm delighted to be able to accept your invitation for dinner on May 4 at the Anatole at 8:00 p.m.

Thank you for the invitation for cocktails on May 4; I'll be happy to meet you at 6:00 at the club.

Yes, I'm free on May 4 for Harry's retirement party; I've already marked it on my calendar.

We're pleased to tell you that we most certainly will be able to attend the May 4 dinner at the Averton House. We're so anxious to have an opportunity to talk with all of you again.

CONFIRM THE DATE, TIME, AND PLACE.

CONFIRM ANY TRAVEL ARRANGEMENTS.

I'll be arriving the evening before and staying at the Fairmont. I can be reached there if you have any change of plans.

I'll be leaving my office for London two weeks prior to the dinner date; therefore, if you need to contact me again, please phone Ms. Smith. She will know where to reach me.

EXPRESS YOUR EXPECTATIONS FOR THE EVENT.

We are very excited about seeing you again.

We'll look forward to the evening.

It sounds like an informative and enjoyable evening. We'll be eager to attend.

Thank you for thinking of us on this occasion. We'll look forward to hearing Bob speak.

We'll appreciate this last opportunity to exchange ideas with the group before moving.

Dear Fred:

I was delighted to get your phone message and invitation to the Hawkins-Flacat breakfast on May 4, and of course I'll plan to attend. Since the commuter flight schedule is
so dependable and convenient, I'll plan to fly in that morning and will meet you at the
Hyatt at 8:00 a.m.

The breakfast and later meeting should give us both the opportunity we need to make
final plans on the campaign. Thank you for your time and trouble in arranging the
details for us; I'm very eager to move forward with this project.

Regards,

Dear Mr. Holland:

I accept with pleasure your kind invitation to attend the dinner honoring Jack Demont, senior vice president of Occidenton, on February 3 at the Fairmont.

I will be looking forward to receiving further information from you as the dinner plans progress.

Sincerely,

Dear Mr. Raymond:

In your recent letter you asked about the possibility of meeting Harold Coffman for lunch some time when I'm in Tulsa. Luncheons are often difficult for me to attend, but may I suggest that we meet perhaps for a cocktail at the Fairfax Club at 6:30 p.m. on March 6?

If you can arrange to meet on the 6th, let me know and I'll see whether Harold is available.

Best wishes,

GUIDELINES AND ALTERNATE PHRASES

EXPRESS APPRECIATION FOR THE INVITATION.

I was pleased and honored to be invited to the ground-breaking ceremony for the George R. Brown Convention Center on March 1.

While I would be delighted to participate in the gala honoring Charles Laufton as Poet of the Year, I will not be in the city on March 1.

Thank you for including me on your guest list for the upcoming dinner with Bob Mattock.

I'm flattered that you have asked me to attend the luncheon with you and your distinguished guests.

EXPRESS REGRET THAT YOU MUST DECLINE. YOUR REGRET SOUNDS MORE SINCERE IF YOU CAN GIVE A SPECIFIC EXPLANATION OF WHAT PREVENTS YOUR ACCEPTANCE.

Unfortunately, the mail delayed my invitation and it did not arrive until two days ago. There is no possible way I can rearrange my schedule at this time. I'm very sorry I'll have to miss the meeting.

I regret that I'll be out of the city, meeting with a client on March 6.

March 6 is my wedding anniversary, and we have made special plans to go away for a long weekend. Please accept our regrets this time.

I've just now dug to the bottom of my stack of mail and found your invitation for the reception. As you know I spend a great deal of my time on the road, and March 8 is the day I return from my next jaunt. Will you please forgive me for getting so far behind as to have to miss this luncheon?

I am sorry to find that I have a meeting of my professional organization on March 8, one at which I have consented to introduce the keynote speaker. Please accept my apologies for having to miss your luncheon.

Due to both scheduling and budgetary constraints, we will not be able to attend the SHARE meeting this year. We're sorry.

Your invitation reached me here in Houston. We have moved our headquarters from New York and are no longer in the city.

WISH SUCCESS FOR THE EVENT.

My best regards for the dinner and discussions.

I do hope the meeting turns out to be profitable for all concerned.

Thank you for thinking of me and best wishes for an enjoyable and successful evening.

Let us know how the evening turns out.

We hope to be able to attend next time. Best wishes on this one.

I know the event will be both informative and fun.

I know the other attendees will find this to be a very worthwhile conference.

Dear Mr. Henry:

I deeply regret that I will be in New York on August 8, and, therefore, will be unable to accept your kind invitation to meet you and your associate for the reception honoring William Tow.

If it is possible I would like to have Faye Forsythe, senior vice president, represent me at this reception.

I also hope that you will invite me again for another get-together. Mr. Art Mace has asked me to welcome you to the city and to extend the use of our facilities to your entire organization. Just let me know how we can be of further service.

Best wishes with the reception.

Sincerely,

Dear Max:

It is disappointing for me to check the regrets box on your invitation to the Foxbotha dinner, but I am committed to be in Europe on a client matter for the week of August 9. Having sampled your hospitality on other occasions, I know that the dinner will be an event to be remembered.

Please accept my best wishes for such profitable operations that you will have to throw another party.

Sincerely,

Dear Mr. Harkrider:

Thank you very much for inviting Mrs. Ledbetter and me to attend the Union-Houghton dinner on August 8. We would like very much to be your guests, but unfortunately we have already made plans with other associates. Shall we make it another time?

I know we'll hear from several sources what an enjoyable evening we have missed. Thank you for thinking of us.

Sincerely,

Dear Ms. Golightly:

Thank you for the recent invitation. I'm sorry that I will not be able to attend the reception honoring your board of directors in your new office building. I have another meeting in Canton, which has been scheduled for several weeks; and because so many people are involved, I cannot change it now.

I have watched your building go up almost from the start and hope you will give me another opportunity in the future to visit with you and get a closer look.

Sincerely,

Dear Margaret,

Thank you for your telephone invitation about the Houghton Grand Ball on March 8. I apologize for taking so long to respond; I've been trying to work out my schedule. But unfortunately as it's turning out, there is simply no way I can be in Washington at that time.

I hope you'll give me another opportunity to join you in the coming year.

Best personal regards,

G U I D E L I N E S   A N D   A L T E R N A T E   P H R A S E S

ACKNOWLEDGE THE SITUATION AND EXPLAIN THE ACTIONS YOU HAVE TAKEN TO MANAGE THE CRISIS.

———————————

In light of further studies on the cause of the recent biking mishap, we have redesigned the rear guard for our bike wheels.

Until further studies are complete and conclusive, we have asked our distributors to remove our dairy products from their shelves.

We have investigated all possible causes for our AMRCO bath oil's association with the flu-related symptoms and find absolutely no connection between this product and the reported symptoms. We have presented our evidence to the media and have requested continued review of the case from the Food and Drug Administration.

———————————

EXPRESS YOUR CONCERN FOR EMPLOYEES, STOCKHOLDERS, AND THE GENERAL PUBLIC WHO MAY BE AFFECTED BY THE SITUATION.

———————————

More than the immediate profitability of our product line, we are concerned with the long-term effects on our employees.

We know of no stronger action to take in this situation. We are expecting a full reversal of the decision and feel that our stand is in the best interest of our stockholders, employees, and the general public.

We feel that you will agree we have made a responsible decision in light of the facts discovered to date. We have the utmost regard for the sentiments of our managerial staff in the field operations handling this service to our customers. It is their consensus that we relocate our manufacturing plant.

———————————

ASSURE EMPLOYEES AND THE PUBLIC THAT YOU WILL CONTINUE TO KEEP THEM INFORMED OF FURTHER DETAILS, CHANGES, OR ACTIONS.

———————————

As soon as other details become available, we will pass them on to you.

We will keep you informed every step of the way until this situation is resolved.

Please direct your questions to my office. We want you to have all the facts as soon as they become available.

We plan to provide you with daily bulletins over the coming weeks to summarize court proceedings and our further research of the facts.

September 24, 1980

To the Procter & Gamble Organization:

The Company has taken an unprecedented step in voluntarily suspending the manufacture and sale of Rely Tampons. Though you have received our press releases of the last ten days, we believe you are entitled to more information than such releases can carry.

In order that you better understand what has happened, we attach for your information and any discussion you may wish to have with your associates, your families, the Company's customers and suppliers a statement tracing developments surrounding Rely. This statement was prepared by the group in management who handled the problem and recommended to this office the suspension action which was taken on September 22.

It is my sincere hope that after studying this material, you will understand the course we have followed and agree that the Company has behaved responsibly and in the long-term interest of the public, our stockholders, and our organization.

I am personally proud of the way our people in all concerned departments have behaved under the pressure of real concern for human life and often misleading publicity.

Very truly yours,

GUIDELINES AND ALTERNATE PHRASES

IDENTIFY YOUR EFFECTIVENESS BY DESCRIBING YOURSELF AS A VOTER, TAXPAYER, CAMPAIGN CONTRIBUTOR, SENIOR EXECUTIVE OF A LARGE COMPANY, WRITER, OR AN INDIVIDUAL WITH OTHER CONNECTIONS TO MAKE YOUR VOICE HEARD.

As the president of Melton Inc., I am concerned for the well-being of our 40,000 employees.

As you may have read in my recent interview with the *Boston Globe,* I am opposed to. . . .

We became acquainted with your staff in our recent campaign work in Texas last fall.

ADDRESS ONLY ONE SUBJECT OR ISSUE IN THE LETTER.

IDENTIFY THE LEGISLATION BY A BILL NUMBER UNLESS IT HAS BEEN WIDELY PUBLICIZED BY A PARTICULAR NAME.

DESCRIBE THE ACTION YOU WANT AND WHY.

I encourage you to support this issue with your upcoming vote and in your campaign speeches. Passage of this bill will only lead to a. . . .

We would like to see you sponsor such a bill in order to. . . .

I urge you to vote for the proposed delay.

ADD WEIGHT—LET THE READER KNOW YOU ARE IN A POSITION TO INFLUENCE OTHER VOTERS. EXPLAIN YOUR EXPERTISE.

I would like to include your comments in an upcoming speech I will be making to the Gippart Club on September 5.

Our 28,000 employees and their families all over the U.S. are extremely concerned about the added burden this will place on their children's financial future.

As a personnel director who is well aware of various compensation packages offered by major corporations across the nation, I have seen the direct effects these incentives have on employees.

My associates and I will be conducting a door-to-door campaign in the next two weeks informing our neighbors and friends about the upcoming legislation and the various positions their representatives hold. We want to include statements regarding your position. Will you clarify to us whether you are opposed to this bill?

ASK FOR A REPLY IF YOU WANT ONE.

I'll appreciate a response about your position on this important legislation.

Would you let me know what you are doing to combat this waste of public funds?

Will you clarify your position on this issue?

How do you plan to vote on this bill?

On the bottom of this letter, would you add your reply about how you plan to vote on this bill?

GIVE PRAISE, IF DUE, FOR PAST ACTION.

I appreciate the support you have given to similar legislation, such as S123456.

Thank you for your willingness to be vocal about the harmful effects of such chemical spills.

Thank you for bringing this out of committee in a most timely way. If I can be of further help in getting it through the House, let me know.

Thank you for your help. You can count on my support in your upcoming bid for reelection.

Dear Senator Long:

Only July 2 Senator Charles E. Beasley introduced S1234 known as the Conservation Reform Act of 19--. This bill makes reform in the Residential Conservation Service program and repeals the Commercial and Apartment Conservation Service program.

I ask that you give consideration to cosponsoring this bill. Your support will be of great benefit to your constituents back home and particularly to the employees of my company.

Implementation of the RCS program has not accomplished the original intent, and the enormous expenses utility companies have incurred gearing up for the program are being paid by users of electricity.

I have enclosed a copy of a letter to the editor, published in the Barton Gazette, expressing these same views. Thank you for the help and leadership you can give those many of us concerned with this vital issue.

Respectfully yours,

Dear Mayor Russell:

As a voter and taxpayer in Chelsea, I ask that you support the much-publicized effort to make all elementary schools in our city bilingual. Specifically, I would like to hear your endorsement of the Garris-Truney legislation now before the House.

We have always been a state and city with compassion for the underprivileged. To give our preschoolers and elementary-age children any less opportunity than to learn the basics in their own language is to deprive them of an equal start in our country.

As a member of the program committee for Horton Civic Association, I urge you to let the public know where you stand on this issue so that we can decide about continuing our support of your mayoral campaign. We thank you for your past remarks about the contributions of our Hispanic citizens in the community, and we urge you to put "feet" to those earlier campaign words--either through a regularly scheduled press conference or by a special release to the local newspapers.

Would you let us hear from you on the vital issue of bilingual education?

Sincerely,

Dear Representative Lindsey:

As a taxpayer and campaign supporter, I urge you to please consider, before casting your vote, the dangerous balance of power that the Labor Reform Act of 19-- (H.R. 3545) will give to the labor leaders. Short election periods and contractors blacklisted from government projects are not in our state's best interest or the nation's best interest. I urge you to vote against this legislation.

Your vote is important to 7,500 employees of the Louisiana-based PetroLenor Company. Would you please give us your position on this issue?

Yours truly,

GUIDELINES AND ALTERNATE PHRASES

GENERATE ENOUGH EXCITEMENT TO CATCH THE READER'S ATTENTION.

STATE EXACTLY WHAT YOU ARE ENCOURAGING THE EMPLOYEE/COLLEAGUE TO DO OR NOT TO DO.

We encourage you to contact your representative today and urge a "no" vote on this bill.

Please consider it your personal responsibility to attend the reception.

PERSUADE THE READER TO COOPERATE BY GIVING PERSONAL REASONS, IF POSSIBLE.

This action will affect each person's pocketbook by an estimated $22.56 a month.

We know you are as concerned as we are about the image this building would create for the businesses in our area and the employees who work here.

We think you will value this kind of security in your retirement years.

This fund-raising drive is the kind of effort in which we can all be proud to have had a part. Literally thousands of handicapped workers all across the nation must have this access to public buildings.

Your career advancement depends on decisions such as this, and on our participation in community activities to promote a better quality of life for our school children.

CLOSE WITH AN URGENT CALL TO ACTION.

Please vote.

Please call us today with your answer.

Don't miss this opportunity to purchase your flag.

Inform your field staff immediately about the dangers of such delays.

Reconsider your investment and, if changes are in order, drop the enclosed form in the mail to us.

Dear Investor:

As an investor in insured certificates of deposit (CDs), you should know that there is a proposed government ruling that would effectively prevent you from participating in the insured CD market currently available to you through Hargrove Investment.

This proposal, known as the "Doggett Rule," has been initiated by the Federal Deposit Insurance Corporation (FDIC) and the Federal Home Loan Bank Board (FHLBB) to address certain problems in the financial marketplace. Unfortunately, the rule as it is currently written is far too broad.

We encourage you to take the time to write, call, or telegram your congressional representatives today to let them know of your opposition to this rule. The enclosed directory lists their names and mailing addresses.

The enclosed fact sheet will explain the problems this proposed ruling was intended to address and why we believe it penalizes you unfairly. It is important that you read this fact sheet carefully because you can do something about the "Doggett Rule." There is a comment period during which your senators and representatives can work to see that this ruling does not take effect.

Don't allow your rights as an individual investor to be curbed. We urge you to communicate with your congressional representatives today.

Sincerely,

Dear Fellow Houstonian:

The arts in Houston are bustling with excitement. Houston Proud and the Cultural Arts Council of Houston invite you to join our campaign to Celebrate the Arts.

With the opening of the Wortham Theater Center and the Menil Collection in May and June, Houstonians will have a special opportunity to enjoy the benefits of Houston's cultural diversity. Here's how you can participate:

- Attend Performances and Exhibitions
  Reward your employees and customers with a Celebrate the Arts sampler kit or buy one for yourself. The sampler enables you to see some of Houston's best performances and exhibitions at a fraction of the regular cost. The kit includes coupons which may be exchanged for five performing arts tickets and five visual arts admissions. The cost is $40 with a total value of more than $250. Call 524-ARTS to order. See enclosure for details.
- Promote Awareness of the Arts
  Combine the Celebrate the Arts theme with any of your regular advertising to promote the arts. When you use the Celebrate the Arts logo or advertise in an arts section of the Houston Chronicle, the Chronicle will give you a special discount. See enclosure for more information.
- Create Your Own Celebration
  Consider our list of suggestions or use your imagination. Respond by completing the enclosure or call the Celebrate the Arts Hotline, 524-ARTS.

In just a few weeks, Houston will be the focus of international attention. Houston Proud, the Cultural Arts Council and you can demonstrate to Houstonians and people around the world that Houston is a world-class city. Be a part of the excitement. Join the Celebration!

Sincerely,

Dear Fellow Employees:

With the November 3 general election less than 60 days away, it is time to consider voter registration and continued eligibility.

In cooperation with the League of Women Voters, we at Barton, Inc. will sponsor a voter registration drive to be held in the third-floor lobby on September 15-16 from 7:00 to 10:00 a.m. We believe that the most meaningful way to participate in the election process is through the power of the vote.

We hope you will use this opportunity to register to vote, if you have not already done so, or to make any necessary changes in your current registration such as name and address.

Representatives will be available during the registration periods to answer questions about any special problems you may have.

Remember that you must be registered no later than October 3 to be eligible to vote in the upcoming election.

Cordially,

MEDIA NOTICES/Press Releases

INCLUDE A RELEASE DATE AT THE TOP OF THE PAGE.

PROVIDE A CONTACT NAME AND PHONE NUMBER FOR FURTHER QUESTIONS.

USE A HEADLINE IF YOU WISH, BUT THE EDITOR WILL PROBABLY CHOOSE HIS OR HER OWN.

TYPE THE WORD "MORE" AT THE END OF EACH PAGE AND "-0-" OR "-30-" AT THE END OF THE RELEASE.

SUMMARIZE YOUR STORY IN THE FIRST PARAGRAPH—WHO, WHAT, WHY, WHERE, WHEN, AND HOW.

ELABORATE ON THE DETAILS, INCLUDING QUOTES FROM IMPORTANT SOURCES, AND OTHER NEWSWORTHY TIE-INS.

RAISE OTHER INTRIGUING QUESTIONS OR SUGGEST SPECIFIC TOPICS OF INTEREST IF YOU ARE HOPING TO GENERATE A FEATURE STORY OR PERSONAL RADIO OR TV INTERVIEW. IN OTHER WORDS, MAKE IT EASY FOR THE JOURNALIST TO GET YOU IN PRINT.

SUGGEST, IN A COVERING "PITCH" LETTER, AN INTERVIEW WITH THE PRINCIPAL PERSON OR ORGANIZATION INVOLVED (SUCH AS A BOOK AUTHOR OR THE CHAIRPERSON FOR A FUND-RAISING EFFORT).

The author, Mel Jones, will be in Philadelphia March 2–3 and will be available for interviews during those days.

Because the organization's headquarters are located locally in Chicago, we can provide several people to answer questions you may have about the campaign and the amount of donations received to date.

Ms. Eisenhower has some fascinating stories to tell about the opening of this way station in Peru. If you'd like to talk with her further, we will be happy to arrange an interview for you.

For Immediate Release
Wednesday, July 1, 1987

Contact: Doug Nicoll
(313) 956-1909

HIGHLAND PARK, July 1--Chrysler Corporation Chairman Lee Iacocca, saying "a simple apology is not enough," today announced that Chrysler was taking immediate steps to assure continuing public trust in the company and consumer confidence in its products.

"The only law we broke was the law of common sense," Iacocca told a press conference at the company's Highland Park headquarters. "We made mistakes that we will never make again. Period."

Iacocca said charges that the company had violated the law and press reports about those charges are causing some customers to question their confidence in the company's products.

Since October 1986, the company tests vehicles with their odometers connected and places a notice in the vehicles informing dealers and purchasers of the test mileage.

For vehicles tested before October 1986 with their odometers not connected, which can be identified from company records, Chrysler as a goodwill gesture is voluntarily extending its warranty coverage to 7 Years or 70,000 Miles. Most of the affected vehicles are already covered by the company's 5 Year or 50,000 Mile Warranty, the best warranty in the industry at the time the vehicles were built.

In addition, the company is extending warranty coverage on those vehicles to include additional major systems such as brakes, suspension, electrical, steering and air conditioning. And third, Iacocca said the company will ask owners of the affected vehicles to bring their cars to their dealers for a free inspection under the new warranty. "If we find any product deficiency, we'll fix it free of charge," he said.

Iacocca said owners of affected vehicles will be notified by mail. "We are trying to show our good faith to our customers and to reassure them of the quality of their vehicles, so we're going to back them even better and longer."

Iacocca said the company also would offer to replace--"no questions asked"--40 vehicles that were damaged in the overnight testing program, even though these vehicles met all the company's standards for quality and customer satisfaction at the time of shipment. "The owners will get a brand new car or truck if they want one," he said.

(more)

"We're going a little overboard maybe," Iacocca said, "because when people trust you and you give them reason to question that trust, a simple apology isn't enough."

The company will begin mailing letters today to owners of affected vehicles and hopes to complete the mailing by early next week.

The overnight quality test-drive program utilizes a small number of vehicles selected at random at each of Chrysler's assembly plants, driven by qualified and authorized personnel. If any problems were found, the problems were corrected prior to the vehicle being shipped to the customer. If a common problem was found among the test vehicles, the entire day's production was inspected and any required corrections were performed prior to the vehicles being shipped to the customer.

Chrysler said that the quality test-drive program was one of the contributing factors to Chrysler having the best safety recall record of the domestic auto industry for the past five model years.

--30--

Release date: July 1, 19--

For more information:
James Wells--(605) 345-6789

MARSELL-DONMELSON OPENS OFFICES IN HONG KONG AND SINGAPORE

Marsell-Donmelson, a leading financial and accounting firm, has announced the formation of Marsell-Donmelson (Asia) Ltd. with offices in Hong Kong and Singapore.

Each office will have an initial staff of 40 people. The staffs will include English, Australian, American, Chinese, Malaysian, and Singaporean nationals.

A third office will be opened in Tokyo this year, the firm announced.

Ronald Lofton, London-based president of Marsell-Donmelson who supervised formation of the new companies, said: "Hong Kong is perhaps the fastest-growing financial center in the Far East. Many companies, including present clients, have established regional headquarters there. From this office we will have access to the increasingly significant market areas of Malaysia and Indonesia. This Asian capability, added to the six offices we have in Europe and North America, will allow us to offer complete financial service to the world's three most important business areas," he said.

Donald Matthews, a leading financial spokesman in Singapore for the past two years, will be executive vice president in charge of Marsell-Donmelson Asian operations. A CPA by background, Matthews also managed a public relations consultancy in New Zealand.

The Singapore office will be managed by Paul Baker, regional vice president, who previously managed a public relations firm in Singapore for three years.

Both Mr. Matthews and Mr. Baker will be on the board of the Asian company.

--30--

305

MEDIA NOTICES/Support for a Position

GUIDELINES AND ALTERNATE PHRASES

EXPRESS APPRECIATION TO THE MEDIA FOR ITS POSITION.

We commend you on your strong stand about. . . .

We are pleased to see you respond to the matter of. . . .

Thank you for being so alert to the dangers of. . . .

Sunday's feature story entitled . . . has been long overdue. Thank you so much for the fine research in bringing to light the pitfalls in. . . .

SUMMARIZE WHY YOU AGREE WITH THE POSITION.

THANK THE MEDIA FOR BRINGING THE ISSUE TO THE ATTENTION OF THE PUBLIC.

You have done a valuable service in bringing this to the attention of the community.

Thank you for providing the research necessary to help us make an informed decision.

Our city owes you much for presenting this often unheard side of the issue.

The citizens of Hillsboro owe you a great deal for supporting this cause with your in-depth research and fine article.

I, for one, am grateful that your newspaper has chosen to make the facts known to the citizens of Hillsboro.

Dear Editor:

We at Avalon Incorporated commend your editorial denouncing the trend among major companies in the U.S. to resort to bankruptcy as a means to avoid labor contracts, legal difficulties, and retirement obligations to their employees.

In my graduate school, we were taught that a declaration of bankruptcy was an admission of failure. Now, chief financial officers often urge bankruptcy as a means to reduce labor costs and dump their retirees at the doorstep of profit.

Avalon believes that this is an alarming trend that will undercut the gains made in labor relations for the past 20 years.

We commend you on your farsightedness in presenting these all-too-often hushed reflections among companies that do their very best to treat their long-term, loyal employees as they deserve to be treated--retirement benefits as promised.

You may have raised a few hackles from "bankrupt" corporations, but your editorial has done a service for our local retired and soon-to-be-retired citizens. Thank you.

Sincerely,

GUIDELINES AND ALTERNATE PHRASES

POINT OUT ERRONEOUSLY PRINTED
INFORMATION OR YOUR DISAGREEMENT WITH
A POSITION.

———————————

STATE THE CORRECT INFORMATION AND GIVE
YOUR SOURCES, OR OFFER FACTS AND REASONS
IN SUPPORT OF YOUR OWN POSITION.

———————————

REQUEST A RETRACTION OF ERRONEOUS
INFORMATION.

———————————

We demand a retraction on this evening's
news.

In your next issue, please print a correction of
Mr. Hilburn's current affiliation.

We expect an immediate correction of these
losses and damage awards to be printed in tomorrow's paper.

We demand that you correct this impression
and state clearly that Ms. Tightson is being
paid by the plaintiff for her legal opinions in
this case.

Dear Editor:

The photo accompanying your story "Freedom Fighters" that appeared in the Sunday Chronicle supplement, Zest, was incorrectly identified as "Julius K. Lark, an employee of Hughes Tool Company."

The photo did include one of our former employees--Jerome T. Pickens, not Julius K. Lark. Mr. Lark is a senior executive at our firm but has nothing to do with the freedom fighters portrayed in your story.

We ask that you retract this erroneous identification immediately.

Yours truly,

Dear Editor:

We were quite distressed to read your erroneous reports of our profits here at Mercantile Bank. In your Monday edition you erroneously stated the amount of our third-quarter deposits and indicated the bank's deposits were down from a year earlier.

Here are the correct facts: Our deposits dropped by about $122 million, or 3.3 percent, in the third quarter, but they were up 2.2 percent at the end of September from a year earlier. At the end of September, we had $4,980,345,678 in deposits.

Please make an immediate retraction in your next edition.

Yours truly,

Dear Editor:

Your July 31 article "Seat-Belt Slack: Comfort Device in U.S. Cars Raises Safety Concerns" concerns me, too. At General Motors Corp., we recognize that customers will be most effectively protected by our safety belts when they know the proper way to wear them--without excessive slack. Our owner manuals fully explain how to adjust the belts. When adjusted properly, the comfort feature of the belts is a decided benefit to drivers and passengers. From my own experience I know that women, especially, benefit from the comfort and convenience afforded by this feature.

But to suggest that safety belts do not provide occupant protection is misleading, and may lead readers to the dangerous and mistaken conclusion that they are better off not wearing safety belts.

Belts equipped with the tension-relief mechanism became a standard feature in cars in the mid-1970s as GM sought to respond to customer requests for less tension and pressure from shoulder belts, and to increase public acceptance and use of seat belts. These efforts, along with the passage of belt-use laws, have resulted in more people buckling up, and more lives being saved in auto accidents.

GM safety belts are designed for customer safety and comfort, and our crash-test procedures exceed the federal requirements established by the National Highway Traffic Safety Administration.

Betsy Ancker-Johnson
Vice President
GM Environmental Activities Staff

GUIDELINES AND ALTERNATE PHRASES

GIVE THE MEETING PARTICULARS—WHO, WHERE, WHEN, WHY.

——————————

ASK FOR CONFIRMATION OF ATTENDANCE IF NECESSARY.

——————————

Please phone if you will not be attending.

Please arrange to have an alternate (senior level) attend the meeting if you cannot be there personally.

Let us know if we can count on you.

INCLUDE THE MEETING AGENDA.

——————————

MAKE ANY PRE-MEETING ASSIGNMENTS.

——————————

Please review the enclosed packet of materials.

Please bring a list of your accounts with service problems.

We ask that you read the first two chapters in the enclosed booklet before attending the meeting.

It is essential that you become familiar with the equipment before this meeting.

Will you please return the enclosed presidential ballot before the meeting date.

Dear Bob:

I have scheduled a meeting of the auditors for 1:00-5:00 p.m., June 6, in conference room 286. Please let me know by Friday if you can attend.

The purpose of the meeting is to allow you and Max Applebaum time to discuss the audits conducted last month and to make suggestions for improvements in our procedures. Our focus will be how to help Al's department.

Come ready to present your views--this is your opportunity to elaborate on specific weaknesses you want to see corrected in the next quarter.

Thanks,

Dear ANNT Alumni:

You are cordially invited to attend a meeting of ANNT alumni in the Dallas area. We will meet from 6:00-8:00 p.m., June 27, at Babbit's Restaurant, 3300 Delmar.

The purpose of this meeting is to get acquainted with your fellow alumni and to determine interest in organizing on a formal basis. Also Ms. Marie Wilson, executive director of development, will give us a 30-minute overview of what is now happening in various campus programs and answer your questions about the advisory committees now forming.

As you know, we do not have a formal, local alumni association. However, the University Advancement Office is currently organizing advisory committees in 20 cities across the state. These advisory committees are being organized around seven committees designed to involve alumni with ANNT and to provide research services and other information to our alumni. Attached is a list of the committees with their corresponding functions.

Please return the enclosed card if you can attend this meeting. If you cannot attend but are interested in organizing a local chapter or working on an advisory committee, please phone William Reynolds (214/444-5555).

Come early to the June 27 meeting and get acquainted!

Sincerely,

Dear Marketing Representatives:

Mark Stevens, Ellen Crowe, B.D. Taylor, and Darin Poindexter have scheduled a meeting for their staff members for March 1-2 at the Courtyard Marriott in Executive Park, Atlanta. Please arrange your schedules to attend.

Also, I suggest that you come prepared to ask questions about the new product lines as they apply to your major customers.

Here is the agenda:

March 1, Monday: 1:30-4:00 p.m. Frank Smith will speak on packaging.

March 2, Tuesday: 7:30-9:00 a.m. Gene Holtz will speak on the MUTE reports. Then we will break into small groups around various CRTs set up for us at the surrounding branch offices.

March 2, Tuesday: 10:00 a.m.-12:00 p.m. A question-answer session at the hotel will be moderated by Sarah Bind.

March 2, Tuesday: 1:00-5:00 p.m. The comptroller's group will make presentations on how the MUTE reports relate to them.

There will be a group dinner at the hotel on March 1 at 7:00 p.m. Lunch both days will be on your own.

See you there,

STATE THAT YOU WILL BE ATTENDING THE MEETING.

_____

CONFIRM ALL DETAILS OF TIME, PLACE, AND TRAVEL.

_____

Can you suggest a nearby hotel?

Will someone arrange to have a company car there?

I will be staying at the Hyatt if you need to reach me before noon.

_____

CONFIRM YOUR PLANS TO COMPLETE ANY PRE-MEETING ASSIGNMENT.

_____

I have phoned all committee members asking that they prepare their input to present at the meeting.

The statistics you requested will be ready for printing next week, and I will mail them to you about a week prior to the meeting.

I have reviewed the packet of materials you sent and will be ready with my comments.

_____

SUGGEST ANY ADDITIONAL AGENDA ITEMS.

Dear Marian:

I am pleased to say that I will be able to make the Region IV Roundtable on Thursday, May 5, at the branch office at 12345 Harry Blvd. If the intent of the meeting is as you outlined, the ideas presented should be stimulating as well as profitable.

As you suggested, I will be prepared to make a ten-minute presentation on "unsuccessful" marketing of software. May I also suggest an additional ten-minute question-answer period for the concerns this presentation will raise about one of our major accounts?

Will you please arrange to have an overhead projector and screen available?

Also, I will appreciate it if your secretary can confirm a late arrival on my room at the Sheraton. My flight doesn't arrive until 9:50 p.m. on May 4.

I look forward to meeting your group.

Sincerely,

GUIDELINES AND ALTERNATE PHRASES

DECLINE ATTENDANCE, IDENTIFYING THE SPECIFIC MEETING.

GIVE THE REASON FOR YOUR ABSENCE: DO YOU NOT WANT TO ATTEND? IS THE SCHEDULING A PROBLEM? OTHERS MAY DECIDE TO POSTPONE OR CANCEL THE MEETING ACCORDING TO YOUR RESPONSE.

Under doctor's orders, I must decline to attend the meeting in Atlanta; travel is much too strenuous during my recovery period.

After careful consideration of your proposal, I feel that my attendance at the meeting would be premature.

I don't think I have the proper perspective, and, therefore, I feel that my contributions at the meeting would be invalid. I'd be happy to participate at a later date perhaps.

I'm afraid that with only three weeks' notice I can't alter my schedule to attend. If you decide to change the meeting date, let me know.

MENTION HOW YOU PLAN TO FOLLOW UP THE MEETING RESULTS: BY SENDING A REPRESENTATIVE? BY PHONING AN ATTENDEE? BY REVIEWING THE MEETING MINUTES?

Although I'm involved in another major project right now and can't attend the meeting personally, perhaps one of my staff can sit in for me. Is that acceptable to you?

I will plan to phone the week after your meeting to hear the results of the group's discussions.

John Hayden will be taking good notes for me in the meeting and will report the results to the group.

FORWARD ANY APPROVALS, INFORMATION, OR COMMENTS THAT WILL BE NECESSARY FOR THE MEETING TO BE SUCCESSFUL FOR THE REST OF THE GROUP.

Dear Diedra:

I regret to say that I will be in New York the week your representative will be here (August 5) to discuss how our employees can begin to complete undergraduate business courses and degree requirements while on the job. The special "hook-up" from our company to your campus sounds exciting.

I have asked Garrett Smith, however, to attend the meeting and bring me a summary of the how-tos. He will look forward to meeting you here in our fourth-floor conference room about half an hour before the 3:00 p.m. meeting.

Enclosed are my projections for the number of participants we'd have interested in each degree plan. I hope this will help in your discussions. I'll look forward to hearing your ideas via Garrett.

Sincerely,

GUIDELINES AND ALTERNATE PHRASES

PLACE THE ORDER WITH ALL DETAILS AS TO STOCK NUMBERS, PURCHASE-ORDER NUMBERS, CATALOG OR MODEL NUMBERS, AND DESCRIPTIONS, QUANTITY, SIZE, COLOR, OR TYPE.

GIVE ANY SPECIAL SHIPPING INSTRUCTIONS AND DELIVERY DATES OR ARRANGEMENTS.

Will you please make every effort to ship the equipment by August 1?

We must receive the merchandise by August 1. If it is shipped to arrive after that date, we cannot accept it.

We ask that you arrange back-door delivery because of the bulkiness of the merchandise.

Please ship the books by special UPS two-day air. We will reimburse the extra shipping charges for this quick service.

MENTION METHOD AND DETAILS OF PAYMENT.

Please ship C.O.D.

We've enclosed the required 50% deposit (check #2456 for $866.78) and understand that the net will be due within 30 days after you ship the order.

When invoicing us, please use purchase order #234782 and send the billing directly to Accounts Payable at the following address: . . .

Dear Mr. Stewart:

We would like to order four dark oak desks (catalog #234D) at $698 each. Please ship them with your normal trucking firm in the least expensive way.

The ship-to address is:

Reynolds Paper and Supply
14566 Riverside Drive
Houston, TX 77070

The invoice should be sent to the following address:

Accounts Payable
Hammond Insurance
12444 Elk Drive
Arlington, TX 76015

On your invoice, please refer to our purchase order #349598. Thank you for your prompt service.

Sincerely,

Dear Mr. Hyde:

On May 6 we loaded 19,895.38 barrels (835,605.96 gallons) of natural gasoline on board the Startrack 2000 under tow of the Hughie E. This is the third delivery on our contract #4899994, which now has a remaining balance to be delivered of approximately 10,000 barrels.

Freight for this movement was $6,465.

We have invoiced your account for this product and associated freight. As a matter of record, our next delivery to you is scheduled for August 1.

Thank you for doing business with us.

Sincerely,

Gentlemen or Ladies:

Would you send me a dozen tubes of LIPS ALIVE, the lip balm used before applying lipstick. About six months ago, I bought your excellent product at a local Wal-Mart chain but since that time have been unable to find it again on store shelves anywhere. One store clerk, however, took the time to give me your address and suggested that I order directly from you because she didn't know if the product was still available to their buyer.

The price was $5.99 six months ago; however, since I do not know the appropriate shipping charges or current price, I have not enclosed a check with this order. Please bill me or phone me collect (123/345-5555), and I will mail a check for the correct amount immediately.

Thank you for such a fine product and for handling this individual order for me.

Sincerely,

GUIDELINES AND ALTERNATE PHRASES

TELL THE CUSTOMER THAT YOU CAN OR CANNOT SHIP THE ORDER, REPEATING KEY DETAILS OF DESCRIPTION AND DELIVERY.

EXPLAIN THE CAUSE FOR THE DELAY.

As you know we are a small, family-owned operation and Frank Heath, our owner-president, was killed suddenly in an accident last week. The warehouse has been closed for two weeks during our effort to deal with this tragedy.

As you may have heard, our distributor on this product has declared bankruptcy and can no longer provide us with the quality merchandise we expect. If you can wait, however, until. . . .

SUGGEST REPLACEMENT MERCHANDISE IF YOU CANNOT SHIP WHAT THE CUSTOMER HAS ORDERED, BUT NEVER PRESUME UPON READERS

BY TELLING THEM THEY WILL BE ABSOLUTELY SATISFIED.

Would you consider trying our. . . .

We would like to suggest that you give one of our newer products a trial run. . . .

For the purposes you've outlined in your letter, we think you might be equally pleased with. . . . May we send one to let you see how it works for you?

THANK THE CUSTOMER.

Thank you for your confidence in our products.

Thank you for thinking of us again.

We appreciate your checking with us before deciding on your purchase of this equipment.

Dear Mr. Tanner:

We received your order #556688 (dated April 22) for assorted office supplies but regret to say that we cannot fill it by your requested ship date of May 1.

Unfortunately, fire last week destroyed most of our inventory. Because we have had some delays in our insurance settlement and were in the process of moving into a new warehouse when the fire occurred, we have temporarily closed our office for 30 days to allow time to restock and to relocate our offices and warehouse.

Therefore, we are returning your check with this letter. If you find you can wait for 30 days on this order, please let us know and we will be happy to ship your merchandise at the low prices you've come to expect from us.

We've also enclosed a new catalog that had just been completed and was still sitting in the printer's office the day of the fire. We hope you'll find other supplies you need to order when we reopen.

We appreciate your patience during this difficult time for us. Thank you for your patronage through the years.

Sincerely,

GUIDELINES AND ALTERNATE PHRASES

STATE WHAT YOU ARE DOING ABOUT THE ORDER. WILL IT BE SHIPPED IMMEDIATELY WHEN THE CUSTOMER SENDS FURTHER INFORMATION? ARE YOU RESTOCKING? HAVE YOU DISCOVERED THE ERROR IN SHIPMENT AND HAVE YOU REPLACED THE DAMAGED PRODUCTS?

EXPLAIN BRIEFLY HOW THE MISTAKE HAPPENED.

We had no idea that we would have such an overwhelming response to our sales letter. We find ourselves totally embarrassed by the lack of stock, but we can assure you. . . .

We apologize for such a goof. Evidently the order was filled by some of our part-time summer help while our regulars were on vacation.

The message was not passed on to me about the special ship date, but I should have followed up myself after our last phone call. Please accept my apology for this miscommunication on our part.

REASSURE THE CUSTOMER THAT YOU WILL GET THE ORDER CORRECT.

I have made a note on my calendar to check with the shipping people personally on Friday to see that the order has gone out.

I do have your order on my desk and have made the necessary changes in the information you asked us to imprint on the handle. I'm sending you a copy of your revised order for your files.

Your order has been red-tagged with our code that identifies special-delivery orders. We will be monitoring the work daily.

EXPRESS YOUR APPRECIATION FOR THE BUSINESS AND REESTABLISH RAPPORT IF THE ERROR HAS BEEN YOURS.

We wish you the best in setting up your displays.

Thank you for doing business with us.

We value our customers' goodwill. Thank you for giving us an opportunity to replace the damaged merchandise.

Thank you for your patience.

Thank you for calling the error to our attention.

Thank you for phoning with the additional information; we will revise your order accordingly.

We have revised your order as you instructed today on the phone. The mower should be rerouted by Thursday, and we hope you enjoy using it.

We hope you enjoy the books.

We want to ship you your next order at a 10% discount—just our way of apologizing for this error.

I've enclosed a new catalog for your upcoming season. We'll look forward to your next order so that we can give you the prompt attention you deserve.

Dear Ms. White:

We will be happy to ship your three word processing software packages (your purchase order #45899 dated May 6) as soon as we have the specific package titles and release numbers. Evidently you ordered from an old brochure--one prepared during the time we were distributing only one package, the WriteRight. We have now added four other word processing packages to our product line: WriteOne, Letter Perfect, WordPro, and OnWord.

Please refer to the enclosed brochure and tell us which of the four software packages you need (order numbers are included with the product descriptions). We also assume you want the latest release of whatever package you choose.

Thank you for writing. We'll be happy to ship your software the day we get your further information. If you'd rather phone, please call our Orders Department at 914/345-6789.

Sincerely,

Dear Ms. Brancobar:

We have replaced your shipment of damaged control units (purchase order #245599), and you should have your purchase by the time you receive this letter.

Frankly, we are puzzled about how the units ever left our warehouse without the proper packing insulation. Our only explanation is that someone from either our warehouse or the trucking company mistakenly picked up a unit that had been returned for repair (and improperly packed) and placed it on the truck with the other boxes.

Whatever the case, we apologize for your having to point out our mistake to us. We have cautioned our warehouse personnel about mislaid (even for a few minutes) equipment returned for repair and should have the problem corrected now.

By now you should be "happily installed" and up and running. Best wishes with your other expansion plans.

Sincerely,

Dear Mr. Cracker:

We are holding your printing order in the pending file until we receive your deposit for one-half the order amount, $480. As our brochure explains, our printer must have this guarantee before he will begin the job.

We regret the inconvenience in your having to attend to this order twice. However, as I'm sure you can imagine, customers do sometimes change their minds about their printing needs after placing their orders with us. And, of course, specially printed labels such as yours cannot be resold to another customer. We hope you understand our policy of requiring a deposit on all such custom orders.

We can assure you of the finest quality printing and a speedy turn-around time. Just let us hear from you about how you plan to handle the deposit, and we'll go to work on your labels. We appreciate your business.

Cordially,

GUIDELINES AND ALTERNATE PHRASES

Pave the way for the request by telling who you are and how you plan to use the quoted material.

———————————

Request permission for the specific material to be used. If you are telling an anecdote, supply a copy of how you will word the story and in what context. If you are using printed material, be specific about page, lines, figures, photos, etc.

———————————

Give the exact use of the material: one-time limited use? In all foreign translations? On video? On audio? In all associated product brochures and manuals?

———————————

Suggest a permission line to be used to show copyright, or ask the granter of the rights to do so.

———————————

Reprinted by courtesy of Holdern Corporation.

Courtesy of Tom Mitchell Group, Inc.

Reprinted by permission. From *Banking in America,* by Harold Smith, Harper and Row Publishers, copyright 19—

———————————

Make it easy for the reader to respond: include copies of anything to be reprinted, the context of the reprint, and permission forms or approval-signature space on your letter of request.

———————————

Thank the reader.

———————————

I appreciate your cooperation.

Thank you for your courtesy in allowing this use of your material.

Thank you for granting permission for this limited use.

Such statistics in our handbook will be of great benefit in adding credibility to our own company studies. We appreciate your help.

Dear Mr. Johnson:

I am preparing a speech on corporate ethics to be delivered at the ARP national convention November 6. At a recent Chamber of Commerce meeting, Dave Ferguson used a story about your business and your convictions about not permitting your staff members to enter a competitor's booth during a trade show. I'd like to use that anecdote in the speech if you don't mind.

Dave gave me some statistics and other particulars, but I wanted to check with you for verification. Therefore, I've enclosed a small segment of the speech that relates to you. Would you mind glancing over this portion and verifying, correcting, or adding any other comments you feel further describe your feelings on the ethics of this situation?

Thank you for your help in making this an inspiring speech for our convention audience.

Sincerely,

Public Relations Department:

I am preparing a brochure/catalog for our new line of accounting software packages. In a paragraph about increased productivity, we would like to use the attached comment and statistics taken from a paper by Dr. Howard Hunt entitled "Electronics Syndromes in People" published as part of a collection called Productivity, Power, and People.

The quote will in no way be used to indicate endorsement of our product. (A copy of our brochure text with the quote inserted is enclosed.)

If you will grant permission for this limited use, would you so indicate by signing the bottom of the enclosed manuscript in the blank space provided. We will, of course, include a permission line: Reprinted by courtesy of Holden Foundation.

If for some reason, you do not control this right, I will appreciate your letting me know whom I should contact about getting permission to quote.

Thank you.

Sincerely,

Copyright Department:

As a corporate trainer preparing a leader's guide for one of our leadership courses, I am requesting permission to include the following in our manual:

Author: Jim J. Jones
Title: Leadership and the Western World
Copyright date: 1988
From page 16, line 12, beginning with the words "Nature even reveals . . ."
To page 17, line 2, ending with the words ". . . in our civilization."

Please indicate agreement for this use by signing and returning the enclosed copy of this letter. In signing, you verify that you control the rights granted and that your material does not infringe upon the copyright or other rights of anyone.

If these rights belong to someone else, would you please let me know to whom to forward this request. Thank you for your help in preparing our employee training manual.

Sincerely,

Harvey Highwater

Agreed to and accepted by:

_____

Signature   Title   Date

Credit and/or copyright notice to be printed with the material used:_____

_____

GUIDELINES AND ALTERNATE PHRASES

GRANT PERMISSION TO QUOTE OR REPRINT FOR SPECIFIC USES AND FOR SPECIFIC MATERIAL.

We are pleased to grant you the rights to use Dr. McDonald's statistics as you have outlined in your May 6 letter. We understand that this report will be for internal use in your organization and will not be published or distributed to any other organization.

Yes, we can grant you the rights to reprint the article entitled . . . for your limited use in Hatden Inc.'s marketing guide.

We have received your letter, and you have our permission to use the four paragraphs of Dr. Suzanne Howard's speech originally delivered at the ATMD national conference, June 22.

INDICATE ANY SPECIAL NOTE OR COPYRIGHT LINE THAT YOU WANT TO APPEAR WITH THE MATERIAL USED.

We ask that all quoted material contain the following note: . . .

Please include a notation stating that copyright belongs to us.

Please use the following copyright note on all appearances of the material: . . .

ASK TO SEE THE CONTEXT OF THE MATERIAL IF THE USE GIVES YOU ANY CONCERN.

As you are probably aware, we would not want to endorse any service without being fa-

miliar with it. Therefore, we ask that you send us a copy of your brochure text before we grant permission to quote.

We would like to see the exact nature of the surrounding text before we grant permission to use the information you have outlined.

We are concerned about the use of our materials for profit by any outside organization. Will there be any resell of this material?

MENTION THE REPRINT FEE THAT YOU REQUIRE, IF ANY.

For the limited use you have outlined, we will waive the reprint fee.

For the uses you have detailed in your letter, there will be a reprint fee of $75.

There is, of course, no fee in reprinting our material. We are simply pleased that you can use it to your benefit—as long as you credit us as your source.

REFER THE REQUESTER ELSEWHERE IF YOU DO NOT CONTROL THE RIGHTS TO REPRINT.

The rights you requested do not belong to us. We suggest that you contact the editor of. . . .

We do not control the rights you requested. For reprint, we suggest that you write to. . . .

Dear Ms. Turner:

You may have our permission to reprint the article "Watching Your Tongue" by Sarah Hartford from <u>Comments from the Edge</u> #34/89 as a handout for your listening skills workshops.

We require, however, that you publish the following note prominently on that handout:

> Reprinted by permission of <u>Comments from the Edge</u>, the Fuller Group employee magazine. C 1988.

Please send us a "blue" or the layout of your proposed handout because we are concerned with the design of your final handout package. If you can let us take a look at the context and final package, we would be happy to have you use the article in your workshop.

Thank you for writing us.

Sincerely,

GUIDELINES AND ALTERNATE PHRASES

BEGIN ON A NEUTRAL OR POSITIVE NOTE ABOUT THE SPECIFIC PERMISSION REQUEST.

———————

Thank you for writing us about reprinting the newsletter column by Meg Whittier.

We appreciate your kind comments about Mark Hatter's new book, *Time and Tax*.

We're glad you enjoyed our editorial on creative penalties for drunk drivers.

———————

EXPLAIN YOUR REASONS AND THEN DECLINE TO GIVE PERMISSION.

———————

MENTION ANY CONDITIONS UNDER WHICH YOU WILL RECONSIDER.

———————

If there were no fees involved in your workshops, we would be happy to grant such permission.

If the design is changed in later printings of your brochure, we will be happy to reevaluate your request.

———————

REESTABLISH RAPPORT WITH A GENERAL GOODWILL STATEMENT.

———————

Thank you for writing.

We wish you well in your training project.

Let us know if we can provide assistance in another way.

We appreciate your letting us know of your interest in the material, and we wish we could help.

Dear Jack:

I received your note about using the Hartford story in your upcoming tour. As you know, tales have a way of growing through retelling--particularly, my retelling. To be quite honest, I'm not sure that all the figures I use are exactly correct. Time muddles the memory. And I don't even know how to tell you where I got the numbers so you can verify and update them.

I know Raymond is depending on this media blitz to turn things around. And I believe we know each other's thinking sufficiently well that I am correct in assuming you want every incident to be accurate and verifiable for any press people who pick things apart. For all these reasons, I'd rather you not quote me and not use the story.

My best wishes for your tour efforts.

Sincerely,

Dear Ms. Singer:

We received your request to reprint the material from Joe Davis's article as it appeared in our company magazine. We get such requests frequently and like to think they are a compliment on the informative nature of our articles.

Several years ago, we did try to evaluate each reprint request that came to us as to its use and any possible liabilities relating to the situation. However, we have found this follow-up investigation too prohibitive in both time and cost. Therefore, we have recently established a company policy not to allow any such reprints of articles from our company newsletter. I am sorry.

Perhaps we can help you in another way sometime. If so, please write again. Best wishes with your other research and the final manuscript.

Sincerely,

Dear Mr. Winger:

We are pleased to hear about your new seminar, Managing People Effectively, and to learn of your interest in our annual Memphis Management Institute.

As you may be aware, our trainers have spent over five years assembling the case studies and other handout materials that they use in this management training program. Some of the research and ideas came from our in-house staff; other materials have been purchased from outside sources. Because it would be impossible to trace the sources of all such materials and because of the fear of granting permission to rights that we ourselves do not own, we must decline permission for our course materials to be used outside our own organization.

If we can help you with one specific class exercise, please write us again and we will see if we own the copyright to that specific material. If indeed your selection has been developed by one of our staff trainers and if you can be more specific about your plans and audience, we will be happy to grant limited use.

We are most flattered by your interest and comments on the quality of our management training. Our best wishes as you develop your own seminar sessions.

Sincerely,

POLICY STATEMENTS

GUIDELINES AND ALTERNATE PHRASES

SUMMARIZE THE POLICY AND THE MAJOR BENEFITS TO THE EMPLOYEES.

INCLUDE EFFECTIVE DATES.

POINT OUT ANY MAJOR CHANGES IN EXISTING POLICY.

This is a marked departure from previously existing policy in that. . . .

Notice that this policy differs in. . . .

Primarily, there are two changes to be aware of: . . .

KEEP THE TONE INSTRUCTIVE RATHER THAN RESTRICTIVE.

If I can help in implementing the system or explaining the reasons behind these changes, let me know.

PROVIDE A SOURCE FOR FURTHER DETAILS AND QUESTIONS.

MOTIVATE READERS TO EVEN GREATER SUCCESS BY EXPRESSING APPRECIATION FOR THEIR COOPERATION WITH THESE POLICIES AND THEIR CONTRIBUTIONS TO THE ORGANIZATION.

Thank you for your efforts in making this a successful year for Baxton, Inc.

Without your efforts, we could have never realized the profit we've seen during the last six months.

I want to express my appreciation to each of you for your efforts on behalf of the company and our department.

Let's keep those profits growing.

Thank you for your loyalty and extra efforts.

You have gone above the call of duty, and I thank you.

We think you'll agree that these policies benefit the company as a whole.

We know you'll agree that it is in your best interest to make these changes.

When the company benefits, eventually we all reap the rewards in bonuses, raises, promotions, and additional jobs. Thank you for expending this extra effort to increase our bottom line.

To Our Suppliers and Contractors:

We welcome you as a supplier to Surefire Ltd.

We continually strive to maintain our reputation for setting the highest standards of conduct in all phases of our business activities. One of our policies states that no employee or member of his or her immediate family should accept gifts, entertainment, or favors, other than those of a very nominal value, from individuals or firms with which we do business or may do business.

We ask your support of this policy. Would you please bring this letter to the attention of the people in your organization who have business contacts with our employees. We consider total compliance with this request an essential element of our business relationship. Our own employees review this policy, among others, each year and are fully aware of the importance of these precautions covering conflicts of interest.

Thank you for your fine service to us. We appreciate your cooperation.

Sincerely,

To Operations Managers:

We have a good opportunity to reduce our travel budget expenditures, and your units will benefit to the extent you participate in our new travel-agency plans.

Effective immediately, please have our travel agent in Hudson City use "Flyer Opportunity Certificates" when making your airline reservations. The value of these certificates ranges from $50 to $100, depending on the regular cost of the tickets.

Of course, some restrictions do apply to these discounted tickets, and these restrictions will appear on the tickets and/or the itineraries. If you have specific questions about any limitations, call Rebecca Greenfield at ext. 4446.

Please plan accordingly, and let's save ourselves some money. Thanks.

Sincerely,

To All Employees:

As a result of our excellent earnings, Hayden Inc. has become more newsworthy to financial and trade publication reporters. This increased interest should be good for Hayden if we present our story comprehensively and competently.

However, as most of you know, a few reporters are more interested in sensational reporting than in accurate reporting. Obviously, we must be prepared to prevent this kind of misrepresentation in the press.

With this caution in mind, we have a new policy that requires approval from the third-level manager to handle such media inquiries. This approval policy applies to both foreign and domestic inquiries. Therefore, effective immediately, if you have any media questions, please refer them to our senior vice president, or to my office in her absence.

We have recently experienced an incident in which the media put Hayden in an embarrassing position with possibly serious detrimental effects. We cannot afford a repetition of this kind, and, therefore, we must handle press inquiries more carefully.

Thank you for your cooperation in putting our best side to the cameras and the papers.

Sincerely,

To All Employees:

The Graham Group plans to continue its long-standing support of after-hours recreational activities for its employees. Lasting relationships between employees are often formed, and we view these as just one of the many positive benefits for both the employees and the company.

We have made one change: Effective immediately, the procedure for handling expenses for medical treatment due to injuries suffered while voluntarily participating in a company-sponsored recreational activity should be the same as handling other off-duty injuries. That is, employees should submit expenses for reimbursement through the medical benefit plan just as they would for any other non-work-related illness or injury.

Call Joan Rivers at 444-6788 with any further questions. Thank you.

Cordially,

To All Shop Managers:

The news you have been waiting for is finally here--and it's good: Effective immediately, the Weekly Sales Activity Report is no longer required. We will move to only a monthly reporting system.

We thank you for your past cooperation in supplying the information. We hope it has helped you plan your daily sales calls with specific objectives in mind for each call. In fact, we hope you continue to do such planning even though you're not reporting such activity to us. Planning your calls is the very best way for each of you to stay competitive.

Keep up the good work.

Regards,

To All Employees:

We are pleased to announce that our board of directors has voted a change in the eligibility requirements for participation in the Employee Stock Purchase Plan. Effective January 1, all employees who have completed one year of service with the company will be eligible to join the plan. Previously, employees had to complete two years of service before being eligible to enroll.

The Employee Stock Purchase Plan is an effective savings plan that you may wish to consider joining if you're not already participating. You may be interested to know that there has been a 62% increase in employee participation during the last two years. Currently, 2,466 employees are enrolled in the plan and saving for a secure future.

Enrollment cards are available from Doris Dubui at ext. 2345. Please refer any questions to her.

We're happy to make this plan available to you, and we thank you for making our company a success.

Sincerely,

To All Employees:

No more walking in the rain. On February 1, the new parking garage will be completed and ready for use. All Denver employees will be allowed to park there on the upper five levels without charge.

To enter the garage, you must have a windshield parking sticker or a red temporary parking permit displayed on your vehicle. All the green, restricted permits will expire on February 1.

Both the Hilton and the Rusk entrances will be open during normal work hours (7:00 a.m. to 7:00 p.m.). The exits are activated automatically at any time.

We think you will enjoy the convenience of this new parking facility.

Sincerely,

G U I D E L I N E S   A N D   A L T E R N A T E   P H R A S E S

REQUEST THE PROMOTION OR TRANSFER.

STATE YOUR REASONS, BASING YOUR REQUEST ON YOUR PAST ACCOMPLISHMENTS, QUALIFICATIONS, SKILLS, AND PERSONAL OR COMPANY GOALS.

I have completed my graduate business degree during this past year at night school and now feel I'm ready to put these new ideas into practice for the company.

As you know, my department has shown a steady increase of about 12 percent each quarter for the last two years.

In my present position, I've handled two similar projects—development of the Management Leadership Program and the Strategic Planning for Nonfinancial Managers—both of which required the exact skills this new effort will require. I think I can bring to the job creativity in course design, course facilitation skills, and the contacts necessary to encourage senior management support of the programs.

I've worked with Bob Newman for the past six months, observing his management style and interactive skills, and I think I've gained sufficient depth to take on a department of my own.

My present job has become routine and therefore offers no further challenge for me to develop my skills.

I think I'm ready to contribute to the company's goals in a much bigger role because of my increased exposure to. . . .

FOCUS YOUR REQUEST ON THE COMPANY'S STANDARDS FOR MEASUREMENT. IN OTHER WORDS, WHAT DO THEY VALUE IN AN EMPLOYEE AND DO YOU POSSESS THAT SKILL OR TRAIT?

I have the energy and perseverance such a job requires.

As you may know, I'm single and, thus, travel and long hours will be no problem for me.

I can be tough when the occasion calls for such decisions and can handle the unpleasant tasks this job will require.

ASK FOR AN APPROPRIATE SALARY. THIS FIGURE IS THE BEGINNING FOR NEGOTIATIONS.

Although my present salary is slightly higher than what the new job offers, I'm willing to make that adjustment for an opportunity to advance and to gain skills in this new area.

May I suggest $45,000 as a beginning salary—all of which I should be able to generate myself from increased sales during the next six months.

NAME ANYONE YOU HAVE TRAINED TO REPLACE YOU. OR SUGGEST THAT THE RESPONSIBILITIES OF YOUR PRESENT JOB ARE UP TO DATE AND READY TO BE ASSUMED BY SOMEONE ELSE.

Bob Parkins has become thoroughly familiar with the job and could replace me quite easily.

With perhaps a month's training, Sheila Stowers could assume the responsibilities here.

I've been working with Carole Jackson for the past year in developing the skills my present job requires. I think she is fully capable of taking on this work.

Dear Chip:

I want to let you know that I am very much interested in the negotiations with MLB. Should this contract come through, would you please consider me for that project? I understand that the assignment will require a four-month stay on site at MLB headquarters in New York.

As you know, I've had experience on the System 347 with six other accounts, amounting to annual billings this past year of $2,455,000. Additionally, my department has trained three other reps on this system and has successfully rotated them into the field operation.

One of my personal goals is to gain more general experience in interaction with senior people from our various accounts. And, incidentally, Bob Stewart emphasized this same strategic planning on behalf of the company in making all of our middle management people "generalists" during the next few years.

May I suggest a raise of $3,000 for this promotion, bringing my total salary to $63,000?

Bob Fillimore, who has been working with me here on the six accounts mentioned above, is ready to take the reins here--and he is fully qualified, I might add.

Sincerely,

GUIDELINES AND ALTERNATE PHRASES

THANK THE BOSS FOR THE PROMOTION OR TRANSFER.

EXPRESS CONFIDENCE IN YOUR ABILITY TO DO THE JOB.

I'm looking forward to making a difference in the bottom line.

I already have some ideas I'm eager to discuss with you—ideas that I think can pay off handsomely in the months to come.

My previous jobs have brought me just the experience needed to tackle this new project.

EXPRESS APPRECIATION FOR THE NEW OPPORTUNITY.

Thank you for your confidence.

This new opportunity will be a life-changing experience. Thank you.

You have placed great confidence in me with this promotion; I won't let you down.

I am grateful to you.

Dear Sheila:

Your letter came in today's mail, and I just want to express my appreciation for your confidence in my abilities. I'm eager to take the new challenge as director of Region 6.

Already I've spent some time talking with various reps in the area about what support they'd like to see from headquarters. As we discussed, I'm eager to see what changes I can make there.

Please know that I appreciate this opportunity you've given me.

Cordially,

GUIDELINES AND ALTERNATE PHRASES

ANNOUNCE THE PROMOTION OR TRANSFER, INCLUDING NEW POSITION TITLE, EFFECTIVE DATE, AND REPORTING LINE.

We are pleased to announce. . . .

Jack Jordan will be assuming the new position of vice president of marketing, effective May 1, reporting directly to Michael Crock. We are so pleased to have him take the reins of leadership for our Eastern division.

OUTLINE THE MAJOR NEW RESPONSIBILITIES.

COMMEND THE EMPLOYEE ON PAST CONTRIBUTIONS IN OTHER POSITIONS.

My personal regards to Jackie as she assumes this position in the style of her many past successes.

Myrl has had many successes. In her first year here, she was instrumental in. . . . During the last two years, she has successfully completed. . . .

USE A PROUD, CONFIDENT TONE TO MOTIVATE OTHER EMPLOYEES TO HIGHER ACHIEVEMENT.

We are so pleased to provide these opportunities for advancement for such high achievers as Chris.

We look forward to great things from Sylvia in this new job. She is an idea waiting to happen.

Our eyes are on Phil. We're expecting even more successes in this new position.

To All Employees:

We are very pleased to announce the August 1 promotion of Darrell Ray to vice president of human resources development, reporting directly to me.

In his new position, Darrell will be coordinating all personnel and training functions for all geographical divisions. His number-one priority will be recruitment for senior executive positions as we continue our expansion and reach our goal of becoming the largest eyewear manufacturing and retail operation in the world.

Darrell has been with us for the past ten years, serving in varied capacities in the personnel area. He joined us when we had only three stores open in the area and has successfully taken us through the "swamps" of opening an additional 22 stores. Darrell has worn all kinds of hats during these past years, developing personnel policies, compensation packages, and training courses. The training courses, as those of you who've been trained know, have received excellent evaluations and have enabled us to move forward with new stores at an almost unheard-of pace.

Please join me in congratulating Darrell on his accomplishments and his promotion. We're looking forward to even greater leadership from him in this new position.

Sincerely,

GUIDELINES AND ALTERNATE PHRASES

STATE YOUR APPROVAL OF THE PROMOTION OR TRANSFER IMMEDIATELY.

GIVE THE EFFECTIVE DATE, THE SALARY, MAJOR NEW RESPONSIBILITIES, AND ANY NEW REPORTING LINES.

COMMEND THE EMPLOYEE FOR HIS OR HER PAST PERFORMANCE.

Your participative management skills are just what we've needed in that department for the past two years.

Particularly, we've appreciated your attitude through the difficulties last year. We think this shows the kind of perseverance we need in an executive headed for senior rank.

Your employee record says that you have continued to upgrade your skills on various machines, and we want to commend you on your farsightedness in this preparation for advancement.

I've noted your ease in dealing with difficult customers, particularly on the Pullman and Monroe accounts. We think these interpersonal skills deserve recognition.

EXPRESS CONFIDENCE FOR THE EMPLOYEE'S FUTURE.

You have a great future here, Joan.

We know you will meet the needs in this new department, whatever they may turn out to be this next year.

Keep up the good work and let us hear of your successes.

We'll be eager to read your first reports.

We have every confidence that you can turn this project around.

We feel you are the right person for the project, and we will be behind you all the way.

Dear J.W.:

I am pleased to agree to your assuming the additional responsibilities for supervising Teeben Heather Associates, effective July 1. Robert McNair will report directly to you after that date. You will continue to manage the Western Division, which includes responsibility for the ongoing work in Alaska and in Canada.

We suggest that you continue to keep your office in Seattle. Your compensation will be $78,000 annually, with the normal scale for bonuses.

As we have discussed most recently in my office, your record is exemplary; the early completion of the Ferguson facilities has put us ahead of our projections by over $500,000.

We welcome you to the new challenge and have complete confidence in your abilities to increase our profits by at least 14%, as our marketing projections state. Looking forward to your first quarter.

Regards,

GUIDELINES AND ALTERNATE PHRASES

THANK THE EMPLOYEE FOR HIS OR HER INTEREST IN ASSUMING MORE RESPONSIBILITIES.

GIVE YOUR REASONS FOR REFUSING THE PROMOTION OR TRANSFER. POINT OUT ANY WEAKNESSES OR IMPROVEMENTS THAT WILL INCREASE THE EMPLOYEE'S CHANCE FOR PROMOTION.

All promotions have been put on hold for the next six months.

I simply have no more budget to work with this year.

We feel that a promotion at this time would be premature—that is, until you have gained more experience with the System AZ2 and are able to make service calls unaccompanied.

MEET THE EMPLOYEE'S NEED FOR RECOGNITION IN ANOTHER WAY, IF POSSIBLE, SUCH AS A TITLE CHANGE OR PARTICIPATION IN ANOTHER EMPLOYEE BENEFIT PROGRAM.

STATE ANY CONDITIONS THAT MAY CHANGE YOUR MIND—SUCH AS A MERGER, A NEW PRODUCT LINE, AN UNEXPECTED VACANCY, A NEW SKILL, IMPROVED PERFORMANCE IN SOME AREA.

Should you receive this additional training, please bring that to our attention.

If the new product gets the go-ahead, we will be in touch again and resume these discussions about how you can work with us then.

If we do have a vacancy that calls for the skills that you can bring to the job, we will be happy to discuss this kind of promotion then.

COMMEND THE EMPLOYEE FOR HIS OR HER PAST CONTRIBUTIONS TO THE COMPANY OR FOR PERSONAL STRENGTHS OR SKILLS.

Thank you for your past contributions to our efforts here in Harrisburg.

We think you've done a fine job for us over the past two years.

We've noticed and appreciated your contributions in your present position, an important one in our estimation.

Thank you for serving the organization so well in your current position.

Your skills have been just what we've needed in your present position. Thank you for your energy and enthusiasm for the tasks there.

Dear John:

A few days ago you asked me to consider promoting you to assume the position vacated by Tom Post. We appreciate your interest in the growth of the company and in your own managerial skills and development.

In order to assure myself that our annual review of responsibilities and compensation had been done properly, I asked two other managers individually to help me look at your compensation package in relationship to your responsibilities, your performance, your results, and the way you support the company's goals. Then they were to compare their findings with the compensation of select peers, subordinates, and superiors.

We all independently came to the conclusion that you are well compensated within the WAC structure, which we are satisfied is a good one. We are pleased with your progress but do not feel that adding other responsibilities would be appropriate until the $3.5M backlog is reduced. This reduction in backlog will be a grand achievement as far as we're concerned. If you think that we have overlooked some other valuable contributions on your part and would like to pursue this further at the end of the year, I'll be glad to do so.

Thank you for your willingness to persevere with a difficult situation.

Sincerely,

Dear Chuck:

We've spent much time in the past few weeks reviewing your situation and your request for a promotion, and we do appreciate your interest in understanding how you fit into the company's goals.

The principal objectives we have for your current position are outlined below:

- To find a sufficient quantity of steel to meet our requirements and to do this at the lowest possible price
- To see that the plant continues to function at our optimal requirements
- To report clearly to management what we are doing to increase productivity and reduce cost

The importance of your position to the company will be measured by your effectiveness in meeting the above criteria. It's important to both you and the company to know whether you can function effectively on that basis and if you plan to devote your best efforts to do so.

Please let us know your thoughts about this immediately so that, if you are unwilling to continue in your present position, we can develop alternate plans to see that these very important functions are carried out.

Sometime in the future our emphasis may change, and we will look for greater expansion and diversification. I can't predict when that may be. But we are now satisfied that our present operations are under good control and are giving us all the return we can expect.

I'll look forward to having your response about continuing in your present position. We hope you'll agree that this position still holds a challenge for you. We have seen your management skills grow and appreciate your past efforts.

Sincerely,

Dear Marietta:

Thank you for being patient with me while I found time to review your request for promotion to administrative assistant in the executive suite.

I want to commend you on your efforts to participate in all the training courses offered in-house for clerical staff. Continuing education is a must for all of us to be adequately prepared in this high-tech industry. Accordingly, we feel strongly that whoever assumes the position of administrative assistant should have a CPS certification. Such recognition assures us and our customers that all of our projects will be handled with the utmost professionalism.

If somewhere in your personnel file we have overlooked a notation of your CPS certification, please call that to our attention immediately. Or should you make plans to work toward that certification, let us know when you have completed and received that designation.

We are very pleased with the fine work you're doing in your current job and have had nothing but glowing commendations from your present supervisor. Because of this excellent performance, we would like to ask you to consider transferring to the purchasing department to learn a new area of the business. If such a transfer interests you, let Bill Hargroves (ext. 3456) know immediately.

Cordially,

GUIDELINES AND ALTERNATE PHRASES

BEGIN WITH A STARTLING STATEMENT, STATISTIC, QUOTE, OR AN ANECDOTE AS A LEAD-IN TO HOOK YOUR READER'S INTEREST IN YOUR ARTICLE OR BOOK TOPIC.

GIVE THE PROPOSED TITLE OF YOUR ARTICLE OR BOOK IDEA.

OUTLINE THE CENTRAL IDEA OF YOUR ARTICLE OR BOOK, YOUR UNIQUE APPROACH, AND THE INTENDED AUDIENCE.

ESTIMATE THE LENGTH OF YOUR MANUSCRIPT AND THE APPROXIMATE COMPLETION DATE.

I estimate the manuscript to be about 2,000–2,500 words. Is that acceptable for your journal?

The manuscript can be easily divided into a three-part series of about 1,500 words each. Would that be satisfactory?

The article of 4,000 words is accompanied by two full-page graphs.

As I have outlined it, the book will be roughly 70,000–80,000 words. I can complete the manuscript about nine months from the time we sign a contract.

MENTION YOUR QUALIFICATIONS FOR WRITING ON THE SUBJECT.

I have had 20 years' experience in designing. . . .

As a senior executive of Exxon and with six years' previous experience at General Motors, I feel that I've seen. . . .

For the past six years, I've been a consultant on these issues to numerous Fortune 500 companies, including IBM, Procter & Gamble, and General Electric.

I have both an undergraduate and a graduate degree in psychiatric nursing from the University of Michigan.

Our company was the first to use this manufacturing system with such phenomenal success. Our productivity increased by 52 percent over a six-month period.

ASK FOR PERMISSION TO SEND MORE MATERIAL.

Would you be interested in seeing the complete article?

May I send a more detailed outline of the paper?

I'd like to send the complete manuscript if you're interested.

Do you think your journal readers would be interested in such a success story?

I'd like to give you the complete picture on this important research. May I forward the information to you?

INCLUDE A SELF-ADDRESSED, STAMPED ENVELOPE FOR ANY MATERIAL THAT YOU WANT RETURNED OR SIMPLY FOR A FASTER REPLY TO YOUR LETTER.

Please simply answer in the margin and use the enclosed envelope to let me know of your interest. This is a timely subject that I'd like to get before your readers immediately.

I've enclosed a self-addressed envelope for you to return the manuscript in case you are unable to use the article in an upcoming issue.

A stamped envelope is enclosed.

Dear Ms. Skinner:

In a recent survey conducted by Professional Secretaries International, 68 percent of the 2,000 secretarial respondents reported difficulty in working with their bosses as the number-one cause of job dissatisfaction. Here's how the secretaries most frequently defined those difficulties with regard to their bosses: constantly changing priorities, inadequate instructions, unwillingness to delegate, and lack of time-management skills.

I'd like to submit a 2,000-word article entitled "What Your Secretary Would Like to Tell You," detailing these secretary-boss difficulties. My basic approach will be how-tos for the boss:

- Suggestions for communicating priorities to subordinates through daily two-minute, stand-up meetings
- Four steps to giving adequate instructions and verifying that the instructions are understood
- Two reasons bosses don't delegate and how to overcome those hang-ups
- Twenty time wasters where the secretary is directly affected and tips for improvement

This article will be based on information from boss-secretary interviews done as a follow up to a recent survey at our company, where I am training manager for the pipeline division. I have developed and taught supervisory-skills courses for the past ten years at Hewitt International and QRT Associates. My other publishing credits include articles in Training and Development Journal and a management-skills column in our company newsletter.

Would you be interested in seeing the article? I could complete it in about three weeks from your go-ahead. A self-addressed, stamped envelope is enclosed for your convenience in replying.

Sincerely,

GUIDELINES AND ALTERNATE PHRASES

MENTION THE REASON FOR YOUR REQUEST FOR REFERENCE.

INCLUDE DATES OF PAST EMPLOYMENT, IF APPLICABLE.

OUTLINE THE DUTIES THE NEW JOB ENTAILS SO THE READER CAN MAKE SPECIFIC, APPROPRIATE COMMENTS ON PERSONAL QUALITIES, EXPERIENCE, AND SKILLS.

The job will require excellent communication skills.

I'd appreciate your offering an opinion on my management philosophy and the way I interacted with senior management to "sell" our departmental ideas.

Punctuality, dependability, and a pleasing disposition are of prime importance in this job. In your opinion, does John have these attributes?

We expect the person we hire to have good analytical skills and to be self-motivated on long-term projects.

ASSURE THE READER OF CONFIDENTIALITY IF YOU ARE ASKING FOR A REFERENCE ON A PROSPECTIVE EMPLOYEE.

Of course, we appreciate your frankness and will hold the information in confidence.

We can assure you that your opinions will be kept confidential.

This information, of course, will be only for our own use.

THANK THE READER FOR THE FAVOR.

Thank you for your trouble.

Thank you for providing this help. We'll be happy to return the favor for you if we are ever in a position to do so.

Please let us know when we can provide you with a similar reference.

John, please know how very much I appreciate your giving this reference for me. I want this job very much.

Dear Mr. Murphy:

Ms. Carol Meyers, one of your former engineers (1984-1988), has applied for an engineering position in our Atlanta office and has given your name as a reference.

Would you be so kind as to complete the attached form, commenting on her ability to work with little supervision and her ability and willingness to work under pressure with sometimes short deadlines?

Of course, we will hold your comments in the strictest confidence. If you'd rather respond by phone, please call me collect at 123/456-6789. Thank you for any help you can give.

Sincerely,

Dear Mr. Tartar:

Our conference has been asked to prepare the required character report on Ralph Schell, a member of the bars of New York and Pennsylvania, who is now applying for admission to the bar of Texas.

We wish to verify the position that Mr. Schell has held as vice president and general counsel with your organization (1986-1988). We also will appreciate any facts and opinions concerning Mr. Schell's qualifications for being admitted to the Texas bar. Would you please comment on his general knowledge of the law and the ethical standards he displayed while in your employment.

Thank you for your assistance in verifying the information supplied to us by Mr. Schell.

Sincerely,

Dear Fred:

I have recently applied for a consulting position with Barker Management Consultants and am hoping to begin developing some performance-appraisal video programs and some negotiation-skills packages.

Would you please write a letter of reference for me about the work I did while under your supervision (June 19-- to August 19--)?

Let me outline briefly what the new job entails so that you can comment appropriately on those qualities and skills that will have a bearing on my new situation. In this position I'll be interacting with clients to analyze their needs and then turn my research into a training product. Additionally, I'll have to work well both independently and also with several team members to coordinate the video and print components of the packages. Finally, my organizational skills will be of paramount importance in writing these programs.

Thank you for taking the time from your always busy schedule to help me in this way. I will appreciate it most sincerely.

Cordially,

GUIDELINES AND ALTERNATE PHRASES

RECOMMEND THE INDIVIDUAL OR COMPANY.

We have no hesitancy whatsoever in recommending that you consider Turner Engineering for the project you outlined in your letter.

It is a pleasure to recommend Bill to you.

With eagerness and all sincerity, we can recommend to you Gerald Forde for the position as geologist.

We can offer only the highest recommendation for accountant Carol Lyons, who was previously employed at our firm for six years.

I heartily recommend Bill Frazier to you. We would eagerly rehire him if a vacancy developed.

INCLUDE THE FACTS OF THE EMPLOYEE'S WORK OR YOUR ASSOCIATION WITH THE COMPANY YOU ARE RECOMMENDING: DATES OF EMPLOYMENT, POSITION TITLES, MAJOR RESPONSIBILITIES, CONTRACT PROJECTS, OR PROFESSIONAL ASSOCIATIONS.

GIVE YOUR OPINION ABOUT QUALIFICATIONS, EXPERIENCE, OR ATTRIBUTES OF THE INDIVIDUAL OR THE COMPANY. THE MORE SPECIFIC YOUR COMMENTS ARE, THE MORE HELPFUL AND MORE CREDIBLE THE RECOMMENDATION. IF YOU DON'T KNOW THE INDIVIDUAL OR COMPANY WELL OR CAN'T OFFER A HIGH RECOMMENDATION, YOU MAY CHOOSE TO COMMENT ONLY VAGUELY.

The company seems to be very strong financially and has an excellent reputation for timely completion of its work. Needless to say, we consider the company one of our most valued customers.

I find Ms. Tate to be friendly, reliable, and diligent.

While he was with us, Mr. Baubaum carried out his responsibilities in a very forthright manner. He met our deadlines and easily achieved and exceeded the goals we set for him.

She handles customers well—on the phone, in person, and in writing.

Charles has been active in the community, participating frequently in civic fund-raisers with great success.

Bryan has a fine family and is quite well known in financial circles because of his successful CPA practice here.

Her sales skills would be enviable among the most successful in the nation.

Bob is a responsible, conscientious employee.

VERIFY THE REASON FOR THE RESIGNATION OR TERMINATION OF THE EMPLOYEE OR THE WORKING ASSOCIATION.

Due to the economic situation in our industry, we had to lay off several of our valued employees such as Bill.

Donna simply outperformed the job. Not even six months after we hired her, we realized her skills far exceeded the requirements of the job. We hated to lose her but didn't want to stand in the way of her advancement.

We had to eliminate Sharon's department altogether as one of the economic realities of our declining market share.

Ms. Jones left our company to accept a position with a larger CPA firm.

Our records show that Ms. Michaels left her engineering position here to move to California to be nearer her family.

SUMMARIZE AGAIN YOUR RECOMMENDATION AND BEST WISHES.

We think Joan will prove to be a valuable asset to your organization.

Don has my highest regard. You will be very lucky to have such an employee.

We think you'll be very pleased to see how Don James performs.

Dear Mr. Sheraton:

I am eager to comment on Sharon Tatum's performance as a senior professional in the training industry.

Sharon joined MacIntosh Company in May 19-- to plan and implement a number of resource and organizational development programs, which were badly needed. After two successful years in that capacity, she was promoted to training manager, a new position established under the operations division. She served in that capacity until June 19--.

The continuing recession in the energy-services industry forced us to reduce our critical support functions to lower our operating costs; thus, Sharon was terminated during these staffing cuts.

I have worked closely with Sharon since she joined our company and have the highest respect for her, both personally and professionally. She is highly self-disciplined and dedicated to her work. Additionally, she always supports the goals and principles of the organization.

Under Sharon's leadership and direction, MacIntosh's training programs have been substantially improved despite limited resources. Some of her most noteworthy programs include the establishment of a highly successful new performance-appraisal system and the development of a skills inventory for managers.

I highly recommend Sharon for any position in the training field.

Sincerely,

Letter of Reference

This letter will introduce Donna Stewart, a senior human resources professional. Donna joined Hammerly Inc. (a chain of 34 retail outlets across six states) in October, 19--, as a human resources representative. She has been under my supervision since that time.

Donna has been actively involved in all human resources activities. She has demonstrated particular strengths in worker's compensation and unemployment insurance activities, group health administration, selection interviewing, and forms/policy development. She is completely knowledgeable of COBRA, as well as the provisions of work eligibility verification. During the ten-month expansion that added 28 stores and more than 400 employees to Hammerly, she frequently supervised all human resource functions while I was traveling.

I have the highest personal and professional regard for Donna. She is a unique blend of natural ability, directness, common sense, congeniality, and sincerity. She is completely loyal and totally trustworthy. She smiles readily and interacts effectively at all levels.

Upon the occasion of my resignation, I recommended that Donna assume all of my duties and responsibilities. I did so because of her demonstrated competence, her dedication, and her desire to assume additional responsibilities.

Without reservation or qualification, I recommend that Donna receive every consideration for any position in the human resource field.

Sincerely,

Dear Stafford:

Marilou Davis at Shorwood Construction Company has asked me to write you concerning Barton-Teal Inc.'s bonding capabilities. We are currently bonding this company through Graham Universal, Inc., and they have the capacity to bond single jobs up to $500,000.

All of our six years' experience with Barton-Teal Inc. has been very satisfactory, and to our knowledge this company has a history of timely and successful completion of its jobs.

We know of no reason why you should hesitate to award a contract to this firm.

Sincerely,

To Whom It May Concern:

Efficient in administrative tasks. Knowledgeable. Excellent people skills. If these attributes are important to you in your business, I highly recommend Jean King.

Ms. King has worked for me since 19--, first as my secretary while I was comptroller at Hrogon Company and most recently on a contract basis at my CPA firm. During this time, she has continuously exhibited the qualities noted above. She is thoroughly familiar with computer software such as LOTUS 1-2-3, Multi-Mate, and Wordstar. She is particularly adept at typing and putting together lengthy reports with complex attachments and compiling slides and other graphic presentations for proposals to clients.

If you'd like to discuss her credentials in more detail, please feel free to call me at 713/344-5995.

Sincerely,

Ladies or Gentlemen:

I have known Henry Appleby for nearly 20 years, during which time he has served as general counsel for Blayton Associates. Mr. Appleby has represented the company in all legal actions before various courts and other tribunals, and he has advised and handled the day-to-day legal matters that have arisen in the company.

In my opinion, he has advised and represented us well, and I can recommend him to you wholeheartedly.

Sincerely,

GUIDELINES AND ALTERNATE PHRASES

VERIFY THE FACTS OF THE INDIVIDUAL'S EMPLOYMENT OR THE COMPANY'S ASSOCIATION WITH YOU, INCLUDING DATES OF EMPLOYMENT AND TITLES OR OTHER RELEVANT FACTS ABOUT A JOINT PROJECT.

STATE THE REASON FOR THE EMPLOYEE'S TERMINATION OR RESIGNATION.

Our files show that Mr. Hightower gave no reason for his resignation when he left our firm.

Mr. Hightower's resignation letter states that he left the company to return to the West Coast.

Mr. Hightower left our employment to join Hill Associates in Austin, Texas.

KEEP IN MIND LEGAL SAFEGUARDS. ADDRESS ANY WEAKNESSES WITHOUT MALICE. ACKNOWLEDGE THAT THE EMPLOYEE MAY RESPOND OR PERFORM DIFFERENTLY IN ANOTHER SITUATION.

Charles is an extremely knowledgeable individual and perhaps would be more challenged in a situation such as yours.

Under other conditions with another supervisor, perhaps Denise would have a different outlook on her job.

As long as the job did not require much heavy lifting, I think Gerald would make an excellent employee.

Dear Mr. Smith:

William Stablather held the position of systems engineer with our firm from May 19--
to February 19--. During this period he was promoted twice with appropriate salary
increases.

Mr. Stablather left our company to seek employment in the computer retail area.

Sincerely,

GUIDELINES AND ALTERNATE PHRASES

ACKNOWLEDGE THE REQUEST IN A NEUTRAL TONE.

I received your letter asking for a recommendation on Harold Snow.

As you requested, I've reviewed your employment record for the two years you were with our company.

I am happy to hear that you think you've found a job of interest to you in the Houston area.

The prospective job you mentioned in your recent letter sounds perfectly suited to your interests and aptitudes.

STATE YOUR REFUSAL IN A POSITIVE MANNER.

I don't feel that I know you quite well enough to comment on the qualities the new position would require.

I wasn't in a position, while you were employed here, to observe your work firsthand and, therefore I feel hesitant to give unknowledgeable opinions.

Perhaps you might prefer to contact your direct supervisor about the new position. I think she could probably give a more accurate judgment of your work than I.

WISH THE FORMER EMPLOYEE SUCCESS IN THE JOB SEARCH.

Good luck with the new job.

I hope you find something you really enjoy.

I am glad this new job interests you. Best of luck with it.

We hope this new job meets your needs.

I hope this new job provides the challenge you are seeking.

Best wishes as you seek employment in Colorado.

Dear Jack:

I received your phone message asking that I write you a letter of recommendation as you seek a new job in the New York area.

Through the five years that we worked together, as you remember, we did not often see eye to eye on the department's goals and accomplishments. Therefore, perhaps you could find someone who could write you a stronger letter of recommendation than I could. I will, of course, verify your years of employment here and salary history if you'd like the new company to contact me for that information.

Best wishes in your job search.

Sincerely,

Dear Barbara:

I'm pleased you thought of me in seeking references for your new position. However, in thinking of our association here, I'm reminded that because we worked together for such a short time I feel incapable of offering any meaningful evaluation of your work. Would you please forgive me for not being able to be more helpful to you?

I do hope you find a job that you enjoy.

Sincerely,

Dear Ms. Bono:

Shirley Jackson in our department took your phone message asking that I write you a letter of reference for the prospective sales job.

Because your work with us was so far removed from anything that a job in sales would require, I am reluctant to pass on any comments that may interfere with your efforts in landing the new position.

I do wish you the best, however, in finding a position that allows you the flexible work schedule you have always wished for. Good luck in whatever job you decide to pursue.

Sincerely,

G U I D E L I N E S   A N D   A L T E R N A T E   P H R A S E S

THANK THE READER FOR THE RECOMMENDATION.

MENTION THE GOOD RESULTS.

I got the job I was wanting.

You were successful—your excellent reference cinched the job for me.

I have begun work as a systems engineer, working on exactly the kind of applications that I was trained to do.

Although I haven't heard of their final selection for the job, I greatly appreciate your kind words and will save the letter for other possible uses.

OFFER TO RETURN THE FAVOR.

May I help you in some way?

Let me know if I can ever give someone you know a referral and assistance in this way.

I want to show my appreciation in some small way. May I take you to lunch when you're in New York again?

Dear Martin:

Thank you so much for taking the time to write the letter of reference. Your words were so glowing that I thought the company might believe I walked on water! But good news--I start to work October 15.

This is the job I've been waiting for, and I'll not forget your part in helping me land it. Let me know when I can return the favor.

Best regards,

Dear Cheryl,

We did it. And I do mean we. Your comments were apparently exactly what the new marketing director at Perfield wanted to hear. Out of the 200 candidates orginally considered for the position, I am one of four who have been invited back for a third interview.

Although that interview is still two weeks away, I didn't want to let another day go by without thanking you for taking the time to write the letter of reference. Although I can't imagine how I might help someone of your position in a similar way, I do want you to call on me for any other favor--perhaps some information or special tickets to an event you may want to attend when traveling in New York? I'd love to hear from you for any reason or favor at all.

Thank you for making me look so well qualified for the job.

Cordially,

Dear Ms. Wyatt:

Thank you for responding to the request for a reference from Hewett-Martin, Inc. Evidently, you did an excellent job in communicating with them and your opinion was highly valuable to that company. I began my job as research assistant for Mr. Franks almost immediately.

I still remember the excellent working relationship in your department and count it as extremely beneficial experience that has enabled me to progress in my career.

Thank you again and please write or phone if I can help you in any way.

Sincerely,

GUIDELINES AND ALTERNATE PHRASES

REMIND THE READER OF YOUR PAST ASSOCIATION, IF NECESSARY.

OUTLINE BRIEFLY YOUR SERVICES OR PRODUCTS AND THE TARGET CUSTOMER OR CLIENT.

MENTION ANY MUTUAL BENEFIT OF WORKING TOGETHER.

After our long airport discussion two weeks ago, it occurred to me that you and I might work out a mutually beneficial business relationship through referrals. As I see it, we have different but related products to sell to the same customers.

I think we could make those rabbit-chasing phone calls pay off handsomely with a win-win referral arrangement.

REQUEST REFERRALS AND THANK THE READER.

If you have occasion to mention our company, we will greatly appreciate it.

Thank you in advance for any referrals that you might send our way.

We will appreciate your passing on this information to anyone you think could benefit.

If you have an opportunity to refer us to someone, we will very much appreciate your taking the time to do so.

If any of your acquaintances express an interest in our products or services, be sure to let them know of us. We will thank you.

Should any of your friends, family, or business associates mention interest along these lines, please let us know and we will appreciate the opportunity to follow up with them.

Dear Ms. Wilson:

I enjoyed seeing you again after so many years. I'm glad to hear that my old employer, Hereford Inc., has continued your contract with them because there is certainly a need for your services there.

As I told you, I left Hereford in 19-- to start my own consulting firm specializing in personnel services for smaller companies. We assist organizations throughout the entire process of personnel activities--from recruiting to termination and outplacement. I've enclosed a complete listing of our services so you can see for yourself where we get involved in the process.

I will appreciate referrals to any of your clients or acquaintances who might have need of our services. Perhaps I could even offer some free "friendship" advice to you in a personnel situation. Looking forward to seeing you at other chamber events.

Cordially,

GUIDELINES AND ALTERNATE PHRASES

STATE YOUR REASON FOR MAKING THE REFERRAL.

We no longer provide such services, but we can highly recommend. . . .

Because he is eager to meet you I gave him your phone number and suggested he call you about your specific needs at Harwell.

After our long discussion last week about your new sales campaign, I ran into a former employee (Alan Caraway) whom I think you should meet. He may be just the person who can give your marketing team the focus it needs.

OUTLINE THE POSSIBLE BENEFITS TO YOUR READER.

INJECT AN ENTHUSIASTIC TONE.

I hope this works out well for you.

Perhaps this is just the company you need to get the project off dead center.

Let's hope you both find a discussion profitable.

Mark is the kind of fellow who begs for a problem to solve!

Dear Mr. Farmington:

Thank you for your letter requesting more information about financial planning. I'm sorry to say that we have not yet added that line of services to our firm. But I can recommend Bayars International to you, an organization that I consider to be the best in the city.

Several of my friends and I have worked with Mark Bottoms there (344-6886) and consider him to be highly knowledgeable in investment strategies and opportunities. His firm is an independent one that bases its fees on an hourly rate rather than on commissions from investment recommendations.

I suggest you give Mark a call for the help you requested in your letter.

Sincerely,

REMINDERS AND FOLLOW-UPS

NOTE IMMEDIATELY THAT THE LETTER IS A FOLLOW-UP ON EARLIER CORRESPONDENCE OR AN EARLIER COMMITMENT.

Just a reminder to you that. . . .

I wanted to follow up with our earlier decision to. . . .

Just a note to confirm that you will be. . . .

As a follow-up to our phone conversation, I wanted to get back to you about our agreement to. . . .

INCLUDE ALL THE KEY DETAILS OF THE ORIGINAL LETTER IN YOUR REMINDER, MAKING IT UNNECESSARY FOR THE READER TO RETRIEVE PAST CORRESPONDENCE FOR THE COMPLETE PICTURE.

CALL ATTENTION SPECIFICALLY TO ANY NEW OR CHANGED DETAILS THAT SUPERSEDE EARLIER COMMUNICATION.

Please note that we had originally. . . .

This location is different from the one we had previously discussed on the phone.

There's been a CHANGE! Please re-mark your calendars. . . .

REQUEST CONFIRMATION, IF NECESSARY.

The enclosed form is for your convenience in replying.

Would you please phone me before May 6 if we can count on you to participate?

If we don't hear from you by May 6, we will assume that you will be unable to join us in this effort.

Would you please have your secretary drop me a note or phone if you plan to attend?

AVOID A NAGGING TONE.

Dear Holland:

Recognizing your very busy schedule, I'm sending you this note as a reminder that you were going to select a list of the executives who will participate in our upcoming management seminar on August 4-5. Enclosed is another consensus form for your convenience in checking off the names.

Holland, if it's possible for this list to get to us prior to July 1, we could distribute the pre-reading assignments in plenty of time for those traveling managers to complete the work without undue hardship.

I'm sincerely looking forward to working with you on this project.

Regards,

Exhibitors:

Only a few days are left in the 19-- Expo seniority selection period--the special time we set aside for you as senior exhibitors to select your booths for the March 2-5 Delstar show.

I just wanted to remind you that on October 1 we will begin assigning the booth spaces on a first-come, first-served basis to all those companies on our waiting list. Seniority will "hold no special privileges" at that time.

So if you're looking for excellent booth space at a great show that can pay big dividends, send me your signed contract and deposit today.

Thanks. We're all looking forward to a great show!

Sincerely,

Dear Colleagues:

The Renal Journal Club will meet on TUESDAY, OCTOBER 12--not Monday as previously announced in the newsletter--at 7:30 p.m. in the Cedar Room at Capper Hospital. The topic this month will be "Vitamin and Mineral Supplements for Renal Patients."

Let me remind you that we need confirmation of attendance (call Sharon Wilemon, ext. 2456) from anyone who will need us to make reservations for overnight lodging.

See you on TUESDAY, OCTOBER 12, for an informative meeting.

Cordially,

REPRIMANDS

REVIEW FAVORABLE TRAITS AND
CONTRIBUTIONS TO THE COMPANY IF THE
EMPLOYEE HAS PERFORMED WELL IN THE PAST
AND IF YOU WANT TO CONTINUE THE POSITIVE
ASSOCIATION.

While we appreciate your thoroughness in
your administrative tasks, your attendance record has been unacceptable.

Jean, over the years we have counted on you
as the backbone of our department—your expertise in the audit responsibilities has been invaluable. But we've noticed in the last year
that your performance in other areas has
slipped. In fact, your attitude about assigned
duties to be coordinated with other teams has
been almost adversarial.

We have appreciated your willingness to adapt
to changes in the environment as Hyatt-Bleyl
has expanded to new quarters. However, since
the last move, we have noted. . . .

DOCUMENT SPECIFIC DETAILS OF THE
PERFORMANCE PROBLEM OR SERIOUS EVENT
OR CIRCUMSTANCE THAT WARRANTS THE
REPRIMAND. COMMUNICATE EXACTLY WHAT
PERFORMANCE, ATTITUDE, OR DECISION YOU
WANT CORRECTED.

EXPLAIN THE SERIOUSNESS OF THE POOR
PERFORMANCE.

This habit of leaving equipment unattended in
the hallways has become a safety hazard.

Your attitude has become a barrier to others
of our staff when they must call on other departments for cooperation in meeting tight
deadlines.

This failure in planning results in delays of up
to three or four days when orders come in.

SHOW CONFIDENCE, IF YOU CAN, THAT THE
SITUATION WILL IMPROVE.

I, of course, expect that the next audit of the
manuals will show significant improvement.

With the personal problems you mentioned to
me earlier now behind you, I assume you'll
have no further cause for such absences.

We feel that we can count on your cooperation in correcting this problem.

If you think there is need for further discussion on the details of this problem, please let
me know immediately. We will be eager to
help you remedy the situation.

Thank you for your cooperation. We don't expect any further difficulty on this issue.

Thank you for your willingness to make these
improvements. We look forward to a new attitude and a growing success rate.

ON A SECOND OR THIRD WARNING, RECALL
PAST WARNINGS AND GIVE NOTICE OF THE
NEXT ACTION IF PERFORMANCE OR ATTITUDE
IS NOT IMPROVED.

Your immediate supervisor has counseled you
previously about this problem, and we want
to point out, therefore, that any recurrence
will be cause for immediate dismissal.

This is the second warning, John. If we do not
see immediate improvement, we will be forced
to terminate your employment with us.

Any recurrence, Amy, will mean that we must
ask for your immediate resignation.

We hope you agree that these warnings should
be sufficient: Any failure to attend classes regularly and upgrade your training in the future
will be grounds for dismissal.

The future is in your hands. You must bring
your performance up to the acceptable level or
you will be subject to discharge at the end of
your probationary period.

If we must bring this behavior to your attention again, you will be dismissed immediately.

Max,

We greatly depend on your projections for each week's work scheduled through your shop. Without knowledge of your staff's work plans, the other departments are severely hampered in meeting their production quotas.

During the past few months, there has been a steady decline in your attendance at the weekly production meetings. On the mornings you have attended, you have frequently arrived late.

On two occasions, your attendance at the meeting was so vital that we had to cancel the meeting rather than keep everyone waiting for your arrival and input. As you may realize, your absence or tardiness or, of course, any resulting last-minute cancellation greatly inconveniences the other department heads in scheduling their work day.

From now on, I need you to confirm to me in writing each month that you plan to attend the meeting and that you will be there promptly at 9:00.

T.H. Hill

Dear Harriet:

As our company policy states, we do not accept advertising for "intercepting equipment" such as in the attached ad copy submitted to the artist yesterday. It is your responsibility, as well as that of all salespeople, to see the copy and make a judgment before accepting it from the customer.

Cable, microwave, and/or satellite interception is an invasion. You can refuse this kind of advertising without any explanation to the customer. (See the back of our frequency or bulk advertising contracts for the following refusal clause: "The publisher reserves the right to edit or reject any advertising placed under this contract.")

We have discussed this kind of advertising, and I have returned copy to you on two other occasions during the past few months. Continued disregard of this company policy could result in serious consequences with regard to your employment.

I hope you'll see the personal benefit in cooperating with us on this advertising policy.

Sincerely,

Dear Mr. Montgomery:

We have noted that on several past occasions you have been out of your assigned work area. On November 7 you were counseled individually, and also as part of a group in the monthly staff meetings, about this problem. You have been instructed to inform your supervisor of any changes in the routing of your work orders before you leave the office.

On January 27 one of our customer-contact clerks received a call from a customer informing us that your vehicle #8488 was parked by her house at the railroad tracks on Hogan Street from 1:00 p.m. to 2:45 p.m. Your progress report indicates that you were in the Cypress area at 1:30 p.m. on this date.

On January 28 Robert Maxwell and I observed you on Terra Avenue at 3:00 p.m. Your progress report indicates that you left a Forest Cove customer at 2:50 p.m. on this date.

We want to inform you that being out of your assigned work area and falsifying your progress reports will no longer be tolerated. In the future, if necessary, we will take severe disciplinary action, up to and including immediate discharge.

Your future here is in your hands. We hope you'll decide to correct this problem without further action on our part.

Sincerely,

GUIDELINES AND ALTERNATE PHRASES

STATE THAT YOU ARE RESIGNING YOUR SPECIFIC POSITION/TITLE AND THE EFFECTIVE DATE.

As we have discussed, I am offering my resignation as systems analyst, level 1. I want to make the resignation effective date as convenient for you as possible, but no later than March 1.

Please consider this letter as my resignation as office manager, effective March 1.

I will be leaving my position as general counsel on August 31.

After six long months of contemplation on my future advancement in HyPower, I have decided to resign my geologist position, effective sometime in October—at your convenience. The decision has been quite difficult for me because I truly have enjoyed the relationships I've built here.

I offer my resignation as training coordinator with HyPower. My last day will be March 1, unless you have a replacement who can assume the responsibilities sooner.

STATE YOUR REASON FOR LEAVING. YOU MAY BE AS VAGUE OR AS SPECIFIC AS YOU WISH.

I have been concerned about the limited opportunities for advancement. As you know, I've always been one to thrive on change and growth.

I have decided to seek a job that will allow me more freedom to use my problem-solving skills on nonroutine matters.

As you know, my training is in the financial area, and I've had limited opportunities here to make contributions of that kind.

As we have discussed, because of changes in my personal financial responsibilities, I have had to seek a position that offered a higher salary—although I understand your budgetary constraints.

I really haven't decided completely what kind of job I want to pursue, although I am interested in the possibility of going into business for myself.

I plan to move back to the Midwest to be near my elderly parents, who have had serious health problems the last year.

Rush-hour traffic and my two-hour daily commute have become a growing frustration for me, and, therefore, I have located a position nearer my home that will allow me more time with my family.

I have accepted a position with HyPower as their director of marketing.

EXPRESS APPRECIATION FOR PAST TRAINING, EXPERIENCE, OR RELATIONSHIPS.

The friendships I've developed here will be difficult to leave.

I appreciate your supervision and your genuine concern for my well-being and professional growth.

Your personal management style has allowed me just the flexibility I've needed in a job.

Your confidence in me through the years is one of the things I have valued most during my tenure here.

Please understand how much I have enjoyed working with you under such pleasant circumstances.

I thank you for your constant attention to my needs, both personal and professional.

The communication skills you've practiced here are some that I plan to continue in my new position.

I've learned much from you. I feel that I owe my success in getting this new job to your personal contributions to my professional growth.

Thank you for such a pleasant association over the past ten years. I have fond memories of you and the others on the staff.

Dear Mr. Symond:

Please accept my resignation as associate chemist at the GERT Institute. I plan to leave my job here on September 30, 19--, taking a few days of annual leave just prior to that effective date.

As you know, my primary interest has been in the oil and gas industry, and, therefore, I've accepted a position with Fury Refining, Inc. that should put me back in touch with my "first love."

Although I'm eager to accept the challenges in this new position, there is regret in leaving the Institute. You and the organization as a whole have treated me very well over the past three years. I won't forget the friendship and professional growth I've experienced as an employee here.

Best wishes to all of you for years of expansion here.

Sincerely,

Dear Malcolm:

After months of reviewing the outlook for the company in the wake of this economic downturn, I see no other alternative than to resign my position as chief financial officer with HyPower. Needless to say, after 12 years of service, this decision was not an easy one.

Please make my resignation effective January 31, which is the end of my scheduled vacation. I will turn over all company books and settle my accounts prior to that date.

I look back on the experience gained and the friends made with much regard. The association with HyPower has been a valued part of my life.

Good luck to you in the years to come.

Sincerely,

Dear Vernon:

I am offering my resignation as operations manager of the Leolya plant, effective May 15. As of now, I'm not quite sure where I'll be looking for employment and am toying with the idea of turning one of my life-long hobbies into a profit-making enterprise.

Frankly, Vernon, I was deeply disappointed that the vacancy of general manager was filled by someone from outside the company. Through years of excellent performance appraisals, I was led to believe that I was in line for that position. Under the circumstances, I think you'll understand my decision to resign.

I do appreciate the management training I've been given here; it has indeed prepared me well for almost any general business career I decide to pursue. My best wishes for the company's continued growth.

Sincerely,

GUIDELINES AND ALTERNATE PHRASES

OFFER YOUR RESIGNATION FROM A SPECIFIC POSITION ON A SPECIFIC DATE, IF POSSIBLE.

STATE YOUR REASONS, IF YOU CAN DO SO SINCERELY AND TRUTHFULLY WITHOUT REPERCUSSIONS. IF YOU PREFER, OMIT ANY STATEMENT OF REASON ALTOGETHER OR GIVE A VAGUE, GENERAL COMMENT.

I plan to pursue my investment interests.

My wife has accepted a position on the West Coast, and I will be joining her there as soon as possible.

I believe this decision is in the best interest of the entire marketing department.

AVOID A HOSTILE TONE AND THE URGE TO "GET EVEN."

Dear Dr. Sherbon:

With this letter, I offer my resignation from my position as researcher at ChemWare, Inc., effective October 1, 19--. My decision has been made after months of deliberation, and I now feel that this is the right decision for me.

Thank you for your interest in my career and for the experience I've gained through my affiliation with the company.

Respectfully,

Barry:

I have accepted a job as assistant purser on a large cruise ship and will be leaving my HyPower position as accountant/level 2, effective at the end of this week.

I lost nearly everything when I filed bankruptcy, including both my cars. And with the creditor hassle, I will never be able to buy another car in my name even if I have the money. Therefore, I had to find a job where I didn't really need any transportation.

Additionally, as I'm sure you can imagine, I was very distressed about the bankruptcy proceedings and felt that I could not concentrate on doing my usual thorough, dependable job for you or the company.

My long-range plans are very indefinite at this point. I may go back to my profession as an airline pilot if the right situation opens for me.

Sincerely,

Dear Ms. Howard:

Please accept my resignation as administrative clerk in the accounting department, effective Friday, May 6, 19--.

Sincerely,

GUIDELINES AND ALTERNATE PHRASES

EXPRESS REGRET IN ACCEPTING THE RESIGNATION.

Your resignation has come as a surprise—a disappointing one at that.

We accept your resignation with great misgivings; how will we ever replace you?

We regretfully accept your resignation as comptroller, effective October 1.

We are so sorry to hear that you are leaving the company.

THANK THE EMPLOYEE FOR HIS OR HER CONTRIBUTIONS.

I can say with all sincerity that you have made invaluable contributions to the organization. You have. . . .

Thank you for your long years of service in the personnel department. I can enumerate project after project that originated as your idea and came to fruition through your leadership.

We have appreciated so much the way you have handled the projects we've assigned—your timeliness, thoroughness, and professional attitude toward the customers.

SUGGEST ANY NECESSARY ALTERNATE DATES FOR THE EMPLOYEE'S DEPARTURE.

Although we regret that you are leaving and appreciate your thoughtfulness in giving us two weeks' notice, we feel that won't be necessary. Because you have so adequately trained Barry Howell, he is now ready to move into your position at the end of the week.

Would you consider delaying your effective date to May 6 in order to allow us to interview several out-of-town candidates? We are hoping this won't be a problem for you since your letter of resignation indicated no immediate new-job plans. Please let me know if this date would be equally acceptable.

WISH THE EMPLOYEE WELL ON HIS OR HER PLANS.

We wish you every success on your new assignment.

Best wishes with your plans.

We hope all goes well with your relocation.

I hope your husband is immediately successful in finding appropriate work as he moves to accompany you to the Atlanta area.

The job should be just what you enjoy. Accept our every best wish for your future success.

We hope the plans work out just as you have envisioned.

If we can help you get established in your new business, let us know. We'd be glad to pass on referrals in your area.

If I can ever give you a reference, please call on me.

We'd be happy to supply you with an excellent reference if you need one.

Dear Margaret:

It is with regret that I accept your resignation as a systems engineer. Your positive attitude and willingness to take on new challenges and responsibilities will be missed.

During the short 18 months that we have worked together, you have made significant contributions to the Mesa unit:

- Completion of an office TRV study
- Significant participation in the branch office automation for Barker Banks
- Development of a "packaged" slide presentation to customers on the System/260

The sensitivity, professionalism, and enthusiasm you demonstrate have resulted in a business-partner relationship with your customers and very positive comments from customer executives as well. Thank you for all these efforts and a job well done.

I do have one concern: Would you consider working two weeks longer than you indicated in your resignation letter? This position is going to be difficult to fill with someone of your calibre, and we want adequate time to hire the best.

I feel that I speak for everyone here at Mesa when I say that we will miss you. We all wish you the very best in your move back to New Hampshire and know that you will find another job immediately.

Sincerely,

Dear Bryant:

Thank you for giving us such adequate notice of your decision to leave the company. From a selfish perspective, I am really sorry to hear that you have accepted a new position in Denver. I do hope the new job allows you to use your skills to the fullest. You have been an excellent employee who has produced many dollars for the company.

I have developed high personal respect for you and your abilities, and I know we will feel the loss deeply.

With best personal regards,

Dear Dave:

Opening my mail was disappointing today--I received your letter of resignation. If we must accept your decision to leave--and I guess we do--your suggested effective date of October 1 will be fine.

Please accept our heartfelt appreciation for the contributions you've made to the organ-ization, and specifically to our division here in Baltimore. The Drummond account, Blackwell account, and the Fitcher account have all been directly your responsibility, and they couldn't have been handled any better. As you are well aware, you have had our utmost confidence in building these largest and most profitable relationships.

Let us know if we can pass on any referrals to you in Los Angeles. Our very best wishes to a star performer. We'll be looking forward to tracking your career through our mutual industry acquaintances.

Cordially,

GUIDELINES AND ALTERNATE PHRASES

BE SPECIFIC ABOUT WHAT JOB YOU WANT, REFERRING TO HOW THE POSITION CAME TO YOUR ATTENTION.

I am very much interested in the Boston plant manager's job advertised in the July 6 *Wall Street Journal*.

In a conversation last week with Dr. Sylvia Brown, I learned about an opening in your research and development department. Upon her recommendation, I'm enclosing my resumé.

I recently learned of an opening for an administrative secretary in your accounting area. Would you please consider me for that position.

SUMMARIZE YOUR EDUCATION, KEY WORK EXPERIENCE, AND SKILLS OR TRAITS THAT SPECIFICALLY APPLY TO THE JOB.

I've had 12 years' experience in. . . .

As an engineer at Exxon, I had full responsibility for designing. . . .

EMPHASIZE BENEFITS OF YOUR EXPERIENCE TO THE EMPLOYER RATHER THAN BENEFITS YOU EXPECT TO GAIN.

Such a job calls for persistence and self-discipline—both of which are just part of my makeup.

That first impression on the phone with a client is crucial to the sale; I have always taken such calls very seriously.

Long hours, travel at a moment's notice, and attention to detail present no problem whatsoever to me.

I would be eager to see that you had the monthly financial information on a timely basis and in a form you could easily interpret and immediately use.

The work you want done in the international setting, of course, directly relates to my experience at Huffco.

AVOID MENTIONING SALARY UNLESS THE AD OR INTERVIEWER ASKS YOU TO DO SO.

I'd be happy to discuss salary during our interview.

My salary requirements are negotiable, and we can discuss those as we review the exact nature of the job.

My salary requirements are flexible, depending on the chance for advancement in the company and the cost of living at the work location.

If there's a good connection between the job and me, I feel sure that we can also get together on salary.

SUGGEST AN INTERVIEW.

May I talk with you further?

I will welcome the opportunity to respond to more specific questions you may have in a personal interview.

No letter, of course, can adequately convey all the details of my experience, but if the above qualifications are in line with the job you're trying to fill, I'd appreciate a personal interview.

I'll call in a couple of days to see when we might get together to discuss the job and my qualifications in more detail.

I would be happy to fly to Houston for an interview at your convenience. I really want to work for an organization with the reputation yours has in the industry.

Would you please phone me at 344-6789 so that we can talk further about the jobs?

I'd very much like to join your organization. I'll hope for a positive response for an interview when I phone you Thursday.

Dear Mr. Maxwell:

We met about five years ago at a Chamber of Commerce awards banquet. Because we had such a lively conversation about the changing world marketplace, I have kept up with your company through the media. Especially, I've admired Arcon International's remarkable progress in the last two years since you've become chief executive.

I am writing to you because your company's plans for future growth may create the need for someone of my training and expertise--to organize and manage your international business. If so, you may be interested in the enclosed resumé, detailing my experience during the last 15 years:

- I have conceptualized and developed energy and energy-related projects on four continents, comprising total assets of $300 million.
- I have acquired four manufacturing companies in Japan and combined them into one operation, losing no key executives in the reorganization. Sales from this new organization increased from $5.7 million to $12 million and net profits tripled, from $500,000 to $1,500,000.
- I reorganized a Venezuelan company, recruiting and installing professional management. In 15 months, I reduced the work force by 42% and increased sales from $4 million to $5 million. Return on investment jumped from 12 percent to 29 percent.

My affiliations during these experiences have been with Conoco, Exxon, and Shell Oil. During my work with them I rose from plant supervisor to regional marketing manager, to general manager, to vice president. Presently, I am a vice president with T.H. Davis Company, responsible for worldwide business development.

I have two degrees (engineering and marketing) from MIT, and I speak four languages fluently.

Your company's growth has been very impressive, as you well know. I'd very much like to explore areas of possible mutual interest and to discuss further details of my experience in a personal meeting. If you think I could contribute to your organization, please telephone me at home after office hours at 713/333-4444.

Respectfully,

Dear Ms. Jason:

I was pleased to learn during our telephone conversation today of a possible opening in your organization. The plans sound challenging for the upcoming year; I definitely would like to be considered as an instructor and curriculum developer.

As my enclosed resumé indicates, the teaching of writing has often been a major focus of my training objectives for past employers (Whitley Inc. and IBM). I believe I have developed original content and an instructional approach that have produced excellent, measurable results in short, fast-paced courses. Your plans to design courses in additional subject areas particularly excite me. Further, I am just as interested in implementing the overall instruction plan as I am in research and course development.

For your review, I have enclosed a project proposal and a brief course outline that I think will help you characterize my approach and organizational methods.

May we talk again about how I can help you with your 19-- plans?

Sincerely,

Dear Mr. Whitney:

I have recently moved to the Boston area and am interested in work as a technical writer.

In addition to ten years' experience in writing computer documentation, I have a broad scientific background (BS and MS degrees) and believe I could contribute effectively on a variety of subjects.

May I come by your office to discuss my qualifications and your specific needs for a technical writer? Please suggest any time that would be most convenient for you.

Sincerely,

Dear Mr. Graham:

I am writing with the thought that you may from time to time need a larger resource base to complete a client project. I am available for such co-consulting work and sales efforts. My experience has been broad, including a position at the highest operational level in the U.S. Navy. There I designed and coordinated all safety and health programs, focusing heavily on drug and alcohol abuse.

My specific qualifications and areas of expertise include:

- Extensive knowledge of governmental compliance standards in the area of environmental safety
- Training design for safety and health education
- Nontherapeutic counseling
- Management of physical and psychological conflict
- Interracial and intercultural communication

I have attached my resumé. If these qualifications are of interest to you, I welcome an opportunity to meet you personally.

Sincerely,

Dear Ralph:

It was good to talk with you on the phone and very kind of you to offer to act as "point of contact" for me. Enclosed is the resumé--a copy of the one I'm sending to the manufacturing company looking for a consultant on the problem they have in San Francisco.

For your further information, I would be interested in any assignment your organization might have in the negotiation of mergers and acquisitions. To date, I've helped more than 30 companies through those murky waters and have the tenacity such reorganizations require.

Sincerely,

GUIDELINES AND ALTERNATE PHRASES

MENTION THE ENCLOSED RESUMÉ, GIVING THE PROSPECTIVE EMPLOYEE'S NAME AND INTEREST IN A POSITION.

LEAVE THE READER A GRACEFUL WAY TO IGNORE THE REQUEST IF THERE IS NO INTEREST IN THE INDIVIDUAL.

If you think the benefit might be mutual, you might want to give Joan a call.

If you have any interest here, I suggest that you follow up.

If you can pass the information on to the proper person, I think Joan would like to talk with you further.

What do you think? Might he be what you need for your new marketing strategy?

EXPRESS APPRECIATION FOR ANY ASSISTANCE THE READER MAY BE ABLE TO GIVE, IF YOU ARE MAKING THE REQUEST AS A PERSONAL FAVOR.

Thanks for the favor.

Thanks for any help you may be in a position to provide.

I'll appreciate whatever you can do to see that John gets to talk to someone there.

Thank you for passing this information on to the manager of that department. I hope things work out for both John and your organization.

I have no personal interest in your hiring this consultant, but I do think he sounds like a "good fit" for your needs.

Dear Reza:

Henry Sloane is a recent graduate of the University of Texas and is anxious to join a progressive organization where he can have an excellent future in sales. Naturally, I thought of Toasten Foods.

So, would you please forward the enclosed resumé to the appropriate person in your organization. I think he'll be the kind of high-calibre employee any manager would grab. I'll appreciate whatever you can do to get him an interview.

Sincerely,

Dear Rita:

At our last meeting you mentioned that you had lost your CFO to a competitor. A friend of mine--whose judgment I trust--has sent me the attached resumé of Mike Burns, with a strong recommendation on his competence and effectiveness. Until recently, Burns was vice president of finance at Perryton; he is currently comptroller of its parent company, RWW.

I am told he might be interested in relocating. Perhaps one of your people or your search firm might want to talk with him.

I was pleased that you were able to attend the retirement luncheon--I wish we could have visited longer. My best personal regards.

Cordially,

Dear Mr. Kennton:

I have just reviewed the kind of resumé I hate to put aside without taking some action: Mark Abbott has eight years' experience in direct-mail marketing and quite a list of sales feats to his credit. However, because we have recently decided to stop all our direct-mail efforts, we have no place to use his expertise. The thought struck me that you perhaps could use such a person.

Rest assured that I have no personal interest in your speaking with him, but because such resumés cross my desk so seldom, I hated to pass him by without calling someone's attention to his potential.

Mr. Abbott's resumé is enclosed, should you have any interest in contacting him.

My best regards,

GUIDELINES AND ALTERNATE PHRASES

MENTION ANY EARLIER CONTACT SUCH AS A REFERRAL OR THE READER'S RESPONSE TO A PRODUCT/SERVICE MAIL-BACK CARD.

I understand you are considering the purchase of a new computer system. Since you seem to be unhappy with your current computer vendor, I hope that you'll want to explore all the alternatives before you make another purchase. Were you aware that we offer. . . .

Thank you for stopping by our Expo booth last week in Detroit. It was nice to visit with you about your specific interest in custom binders.

We received your card expressing interest in more information on investments particularly suited to IRAs.

Thank you for taking the first step toward learning about our latest investment recommendations. We received your card asking for further printed information.

Harry Butler and I had lunch a couple of weeks ago and he suggested that I get in touch with you about your possible interest in our accounting services.

As I'm sure you've heard, our company is now part of Buford Manufacturing and as such we have been "looking over each other's shoulders" for our customers' interests in broader issues. Therefore, I thought I would drop you a note to let you know. . . .

SUMMARIZE THE KEY BENEFITS OF YOUR PRODUCT/SERVICE THAT WILL BE OF INTEREST TO THIS SPECIFIC CUSTOMER.

ADD AN AIR OF INTRIGUE TO THE DETAILS OF YOUR PROPOSAL.

I think that you will find that we've added quite a few new services that can assist you in fulfilling your aims for 19—.

I think I can share some market research with you that will be quite thought-provoking.

I hope I can stimulate your thinking in an exchange of ideas, including what I learned on the international front during my recent trip to the Far East.

It was an exciting show. I'm sorry you missed it, but then I hope to be able to fill you in on what's new in the marketplace when we can sit down together for a few minutes.

I think my most recent experience with another, smaller client could be helpful to you on this project. On that job, we ran into the same issues you're contemplating now in your own situation.

MENTION THAT YOU WILL BE CALLING TO TALK FURTHER ON THE PHONE OR TO SET AN APPOINTMENT.

I'll be calling when I get to Boulder and will be delighted to set up an appointment at your convenience.

If you are not attending the convention but are interested in discussing these services, give me a call to arrange a convenient appointment.

I'll be in New York October 12–14 to assist another client company in relocating to West Gables this fall. While there, I would welcome the opportunity to visit with you further about the new developments, which I think may be of interest to you. I'll call when I arrive.

Paul, I'd really like you to take a long look at this equipment. If you're interested, would you phone me this week (345-6882) so we can arrange to get together?

Carrie, let me know if I can answer other questions. In fact, I'll phone you next week. So if you'll just keep a running list of things that come to mind as you browse through the enclosed information, I'll set aside all the time you need to answer them.

Jim, I'll be in touch with you in the near future and would appreciate a shot at your business.

Dear Ms. Tunbow:

When Fred Grimes and I visited with you last summer about the Boston construction project, you expressed interest in our Management Diagnosis program.

You may recall that this program involves one day of administration with your top management team to develop a composite of their thinking about the company's present situation and to identify 20 crucial issues for future growth. Feedback of what your team has said in the form of a written report follows in ten days.

The program is designed not only to complete what is generally considered a management audit but also to develop the best attitude within the team about the future.

I will appreciate an opportunity to pursue our previous conversation about this program. I'll give you a call in the next week or two and see if you still have some interest in this kind of help.

Sincerely,

Dear Carl:

Many of our customers are caught between the increasing demand for new data processing equipment and shrinking budgets.

If you find yourself in the same situation, I'd like to remind you of our leasing terms. These long-term leases can be structured for up to five years, and the firm monthly payment protects you from any price increases.

By installing your equipment under a lease contract, we can replace your 245 with a 390 and save you over $500 each month. Other new features and options are detailed on the enclosed brochure.

I'll be calling you on May 5 to discuss this unusual opportunity to "have your cake and eat it too"--new equipment at a lower price.

Sincerely,

Dear Mr. Burton:

Have you given any serious thought to your future requirements for accounting software? Having worked directly with some of your employees (Darrell Graham, Bob Holland, Eva Plume) prior to joining Universal Software, I am somewhat familiar with your company and its needs.

I'm enclosing literature on our newest software programs and would like to schedule a meeting with you to conduct a free needs analysis. I think you'll find this exercise to be quite helpful as you plan for your future software needs--specifically in cost planning and order processing.

May I visit with you further about this? I'll phone next week.

Sincerely,

Dear Neighbor:

I recently moved into Suite 480 and thought this letter might be the best way to introduce myself without infringing on your valuable time. If you're around my way, please drop in; I would enjoy meeting you personally.

We operate a small public accounting firm with concentration in manufacturing management consulting, tax planning, and complete small-business services. If I can ever be of assistance to you or any of your clients or associates, particularly in "untangling" the new tax laws, I hope you will keep me in mind. I certainly will do the same when I have had a chance to learn more about your business objectives.

I look forward to meeting the person behind the company.

Cordially,

Dear Ms. Grayson:

Do you find yourself in need of a secretary, but your cash flow says "no" to hiring a full-time one with experience? Does your company just not have enough work to keep a full-time secretary busy? If so, I have the solution for you. Now you can have the benefit of an experienced secretary without having to pay for idle time. Let me explain.

The services I can provide are endless. With over 20 years of office experience, I can offer quality word processing, typing, and many other related services at a very afford-able rate.

I've enclosed letters of reference from some of my small-business clients, and I hope to add your company to that list of well-served businesses. I'll phone you in a couple of weeks after you've had time to assess your needs to discuss how we can help you use your time and cash flow more profitably.

Sincerely,

GUIDELINES AND ALTERNATE PHRASES

THANK THE READER FOR TAKING TIME OR MAKING THE EFFORT TO TALK WITH YOU ON THE PHONE OR IN A PERSONAL INTERVIEW.

Thank you for a most enjoyable chat last week about your upcoming software decisions.

I appreciate your courtesy in spending so much time with me discussing your future plans. After our meeting, I feel as though I can really research the exact kind of equipment your setup calls for.

I enjoyed our brief visit last week and want to thank you for taking the time to meet the newest member of our sales team.

Thank you for taking the time to see our demonstration of the laser printer last week. We were very much impressed with your organization, and we also hope you were equally impressed with our printer and support service.

Thank you for allowing me to introduce myself on the phone the other day and for hearing our story.

Thank you for talking with me this morning and giving me an update on your activities. We value your business and look forward to continuing our strong relationship.

I want to thank you for the opportunity to meet you last week and discuss with you the options for new telex equipment. As we discussed, I am now prepared to back up some of my claims about. . . .

I appreciated the opportunity finally to be able to meet with you yesterday after our many visits on the phone. Customer feedback is important to me; I thought our discussion was informative and useful and hope you felt likewise.

Please accept my sincere thanks for the candid interview we recently had. With your comments, I feel we have a better perspective on your needs.

REEMPHASIZE THE KEY BENEFITS OF YOUR PRODUCT/SERVICE TO THE CUSTOMER.

SUGGEST THE NEXT ACTION STEP.

Please give some thought to how we might schedule this work. I'll check back with you in a few weeks.

I'll look forward to the call from your CFO that you promised.

As you suggested, I plan to call Barney Malone in your accounting department to see if we can talk further.

I suggest that you circulate some of the information I left with you, and then if there's interest from your staff, let me know.

Should you have absolutely no interest in the fabric, I'll appreciate your phoning to let me know. Otherwise, I'll be investigating the pricing arrangements we discussed.

We look forward to submitting our recommendations to you in the very near future.

Please let me know what other information you need to make your decision. I'll phone again Friday.

Would you please let us know when you're ready to see a proposal?

If you do decide not to attend the conference, I'll phone you again next month to give you a personal demonstration.

Please add us to your list of bidders. We're eager to get your business.

I'm making a calendar note to call you again in the fall to see if you might be free to attend another seminar like the one you just missed.

Would you give me a call after you've had time to investigate your needs further?

We look forward to the additional relationships with your firm. Bill Jordan and Susan Green will be talking with you further.

Dear Mrs. Grace:

It was certainly a pleasure talking with you today, and I would like to thank you for giving Brooks International the opportunity to be of service.

As I promised, I'm enclosing a copy of The Savvy Investor, which will give you a brief history of our firm. Particularly, note Chapter 7 for the investment strategies we were discussing today. Let me reemphasize that the research techniques we use are un-matched anywhere--in a matter of hours, we can have a report to our customers on all major stock purchases or sales by corporate officers of a particular company.

We're looking forward to providing this investment research to you. I'll phone again next week to see if you've come to a decision.

Sincerely,

Dear Mr. Peach:

Thank you for talking with us last month when we conducted our telephone survey in the Brighton area. You expressed some interest in our custom packaging processes.

Therefore, I'm enclosing a data sheet and photos of recent designs for other clients. Note the quality of the reinforced spines on the boxes and the way the logos have been imprinted so as to give you maximum use of the front covers.

I'll be back in touch in a few weeks to see which kind of packaging best suits your needs at Brighton. In the meantime, however, if you have an immediate need or question, call me at 467-3444.

Regards,

Dear Ms. Cook:

After your meeting with Bill Shore last week, he passed on your name to me because of your interest in the upcoming INDEX Expo. Thank you for taking the time to consider this important event in your marketing efforts.

As you're probably aware, a show's measure of success frequently focuses on quantity of attendees rather than on quality. Ours will be different. The series of events that we have planned will emphasize an environment conducive to actually making the sale on the spot. In the enclosed literature, you'll note the larger booth spaces and the opportunity to schedule additional space in our "Product Aisle" to let your prospective customers get their hands on your products.

A second key difference in this show will be the very focused way we've gone about selecting our mailing list for pre-show publicity. All in all, we estimate that 70% of our buyers will be customers who "have checkbooks in hand."

Your time is valuable, as is ours. If you're interested in participating in the show, simply return the enclosed card, indicating which events will be of most interest to you. When I receive your card, I'll be in touch again with the specific contract forms or other information you need.

Cordially,

GUIDELINES AND ALTERNATE PHRASES

EXPLAIN THAT A NEW SALESPERSON IS TAKING OVER THE ACCOUNT AND COMPLIMENT THE FORMER ONE.

We regret to say that Carrie Jones has transferred to our Midwest Division but are very eager to have you meet Sam Wade, her replacement. As you know, Carrie had the energy and enthusiasm to meet every obstacle in servicing your needs. We think Sam is her match.

GIVE THE NEW REPRESENTATIVE'S QUALIFICATIONS (EDUCATION, EXPERIENCE, OR PERSONALITY) FOR HANDLING THE BUSINESS.

EXPRESS CONFIDENCE THAT THE GOOD RELATIONSHIP WILL CONTINUE.

We know you'll give John the same warm welcome you always extended to Frank Towers.

We've assigned one of our finest reps to handle your special needs because your business is so very important to us. We look forward to continuing to serve you as you've come to expect.

Dear Ms. Thomas:

Effective February 1, Bob Hutchins will become our ETG sales representative for commercial accounts in Preston County. As you may have heard, Glenda Rapon has moved into our public relations office. I know you two enjoyed working together because she has spoken so fondly of servicing your account over the last two years. But I'm sure you'll agree that with her winning personality and excellent communication skills our PR department is exactly the place for her.

We think you'll equally enjoy getting to know Bob and working with him on your investment needs. He has a graduate degree from Purdue and six years' experience in our Shreveport branch in handling accounts with the same interests and investment strategies as yours. In fact, we're getting calls from his Shreveport clients who are chagrined because of his decision to move to our area! Nevertheless, that's our problem. . . .

Bob will be calling you in a few weeks to arrange a convenient time to meet with you. He's eager to get thoroughly acquainted with the ways we can serve you best.

Cordially,

GUIDELINES AND ALTERNATE PHRASES

GRAB ATTENTION IMMEDIATELY—CREATE A DESIRE IN TERMS OF THE READER'S NEEDS OR INTERESTS.

DETAIL THE BENEFITS OF THE PRODUCT/ SERVICE TO THE READER, NOT THE FEATURES.

TELL HOW THE PRODUCT/SERVICE DIFFERS FROM WHAT ELSE IS ON THE MARKET.

Ours is the only product on the market that can. . . .

Independent research studies show that our product. . . .

To our knowledge, no other firm in the city offers. . . .

USE LANGUAGE THAT'S SPECIFIC AND CLEAR.

PAY ATTENTION TO EYE APPEAL—USE SHORT PARAGRAPHS AND SENTENCES, EASY-TO-SKIM- AND-RECALL LISTS, INFORMATIVE HEADINGS, AND ADEQUATE WHITE SPACE.

MAKE THE PRODUCT/SERVICE EASY TO INVESTIGATE OR SAMPLE.

For a free demonstration, sign this letter and return it to me.

We will be happy to leave a copier with you on a free 30-day trial basis.

We've enclosed our complete four-color catalog to give you an opportunity to see the designs we have available.

ASK FOR A RESPONSE/REACTION.

Simply return the enclosed postage-paid card.

Phone us collect to let us know of your interest.

Our toll-free number is. . . .

I'll be calling you later this month to talk further about. . . . Please have any questions ready and I'll be happy to explain the differences between. . . .

Dear Ms. Grogan:

We would like to refer your company to some of our clients.

We are a conference meeting site and recently have expanded our services to act as a consultant "clearing house" for corporations who frequently use our facilities for meetings. Clients often come to us to ask if we have heard of firms that present programs on this or that topic. We'd be pleased to add your name to the list and distribute your promotional material to appropriate inquiries.

What's in it for you?

- Opportunity to make your presentation to some of the largest corporations in the nation
- Leads sent to you on all those who have asked for your area of expertise
- Contact name and phone number of the "right" people who can make a decision about your service

What's in it for us?

- Promotion of our "full-service" meeting site
- Interest from you and your clients in our meeting site

We hope you'll agree that it makes sound business sense for us to develop a good working relationship. If so, please send us several copies of your promotional material so that we can promote you properly.

If you have a chance to visit our facilities, please call me (234-5663) and give me an opportunity to show you around personally.

Sincerely,

Dear Mr. Crawford:

Are you paying too much for group health insurance? We can help you through the maze of carriers when it comes time to price group insurance coverage by doing the shopping for you. This service costs you nothing.

Mettle and Associates is an insurance brokerage firm that specializes in employee-benefit design. With ten years' experience in the field, we pride ourselves on the ability to offer quality health coverage at very competitive rates. With your protection in mind, we deal only with A-rated carriers. And unlike some other agents, we aren't tied to one company for our commission; we can act independently in your best interest.

Let us do the leg work for you--we'll make a cost comparison at no obligation to you. At the bottom of the page, simply fill in the name of the appropriate contact person in your company, along with his or her phone number, and we'll go to work for you.

Sincerely,

Dear

Is a loyal employee who's been consistently productive worth five minutes of your time?

Five minutes . . . for me to show you how you can recognize loyal service, outstanding performance, or a great idea . . . with the most wanted employee award: Accutron by Bulova . . . the only quality timepiece made in America.

As your local Bulova Territory Manager, I'd like to tell you about the experience of many companies, large and small, including . . . IBM, Texaco, Goodyear, Equitable Life, Western Electric, Eaton, and divisions of General Motors . . . companies who thought enough of their employees to let them select their own service awards.

Result: More than 80% of employees chose Bulova timepieces over all others.

Bulova products represent prestige and quality. To your employees, they say "thank you" more meaningfully than any other award you could give.

But whether you currently have an awards program or not, the material I'll bring you will prove extremely useful in your employee planning.

I will call in a few days for an appointment. If it's not convenient for you to see me personally, perhaps another member of your management team would be available.

Very truly yours,

Reprinted with permission courtesy of Herb Seligman and Bulova Watch Company.

GUIDELINES AND ALTERNATE PHRASES

SUMMARIZE WHAT YOU ARE PROPOSING; THIS SUBMISSION LETTER BECOMES THE "EXECUTIVE OVERVIEW" FOR SOME READERS.

EMPHASIZE KEY BENEFITS OF DOING BUSINESS WITH YOU.

ANTICIPATE AND ANSWER SPECIAL QUESTIONS ABOUT THE PROPOSAL ITSELF: ARE THERE OMISSIONS, CHANGES, EXPLANATIONS, OR EXCEPTIONS TO WHAT YOU'VE STATED IN THE ATTACHED DOCUMENT?

Please note on page 4 of our proposal that. . . .

We can change these maintenance terms if you prefer a firm- rather than a floating-fee arrangement.

Let me remind you of our volume discounts (detailed in the Cost Section of our proposal).

EXPRESS APPRECIATION FOR BEING ASKED TO BID OR SUBMIT A PROPOSAL.

Thank you for working with us on this study.

We appreciate the opportunity to provide this quote.

We're appreciative of the opportunity you've given us to learn more about your organization. We readily see why you're still number one in the industry.

Dear Mr. Hightower:

With the data you provided us about the University Bookstore, we recommend installation of our 458 Zeno system. Using this system, you should be able to accomplish the following:

- Reduce inventory by approximately $125,000
- Improve inventory turnover to an industry level of 3.5
- Cut staff by approximately 50%
- Eliminate repeat bad checks
- Reduce customer check-out time

If you prefer to lease this equipment, the cost will be $2,300 monthly. In about 18 months, the system would pay for itself.

We can schedule your staff for training classes immediately and can assure you that they will be successfully operating the system in a matter of hours.

You also mentioned a delivery date of May 6. Although we ordinarily cannot arrange shipment on such short notice, if that date becomes critical in your decision-making, I assure you that I will do everything possible to meet your deadline.

Full details of all these applications and benefits, along with a cost analysis, are included in our enclosed proposal. Thank you for allowing us to evaluate your needs and for considering our system. We are eager to make you a satisfied user and look forward to doing business with you.

Sincerely,

G U I D E L I N E S   A N D   A L T E R N A T E   P H R A S E S

MENTION THE "REASON" YOU'RE WRITING—AN ARTICLE OF INTEREST, A FREE GIFT OR DEMONSTRATION, AN UPCOMING EVENT OR VISIT.

I was sorry you missed our Expo booth last week!

The enclosed article seems written just for your situation. Have you seen it yet?

Bob, just a note to remind you of our plans to be in Atlanta May 9–11. If you have a spare moment, I'd like to buy you dinner and see what you've been up to in the last six months.

AVOID MAKING THIS SOUND LIKE A SALES LETTER.

CHOOSE A CONVERSATIONAL, "CHATTY" TONE.

BE BRIEF.

Dear Marvin,

I have just received a cable from our branch office in Tokyo informing me of your intent to open a Farfield International office in Japan. As I'm sure you realize, culture shock can be a problem for those employees transferring from the states. If there's anything I or my staff can do personally to make the move into the Japanese market easier for you, please call on me.

As soon as vacationers return to work and get settled in again, I am hoping to get to Fort Worth to visit your new headquarters.

Best regards,

Dear Denny:

Since our discussion the other day on the phone, I have give more thought to your underwriting process. You said that your company does not require bonds from construction firms building your projects. Although I'm sure your management has given this careful consideration, you might want to reconsider the option of bonding as a mechanism for transferring the risk in that Hydon project.

I'm enclosing an article I found while thumbing through my files. It answers many of the key questions you asked the other day. Does this make sense in your situation?

Cordially,

Dear Don:

On behalf of RiteWrite Software, I want to thank you for attending our north Denver office demonstration on Thursday. I hope you picked up some tips on making your own office more productive.

I'll give you a call sometime next month and see if you're free for lunch.

Cordially,

Dear Don:

Bill Gardner, president of United Forrester-Smith, and I are planning a trip to New York the week of October 7. He will just have arrived from London. Perhaps we can get together with you while there and discuss some of our international activities and you can tell us some of your latest adventures in Latin America. Surely there's mutual interest somewhere among all these travel and war stories.

The choice of days is yours. I'll phone when we get to the hotel.

Thanks,

Dear John:

Attached are the tabulations covering the last big Harris County overpass. Thought this might be of interest to you because it gives you an idea of the "going" prices.

After this job is well under way, maybe we should go out and visit with the contractors to give you a better idea of how these structures are being built on Texas freeways. See you soon.

Regards,

G U I D E L I N E S   A N D   A L T E R N A T E   P H R A S E S

EXPRESS APPRECIATION FOR PAST BUSINESS FROM THE CUSTOMER.

We haven't talked with you in quite some time, and I wanted to let you know that we've missed your business.

Frank, you've been an excellent customer through the years. And now that it has been 18 months since we've heard from you, we're distressed. An excellent customer like you is hard to come by these days.

For three years we've appreciated such an excellent working relationship with your staff. They have always been efficient, courteous, and helpful.

STATE THAT YOUR REASON FOR WRITING IS TO REGAIN THE CUSTOMER'S BUSINESS, AND ASK WHY HE OR SHE IS NO LONGER USING YOUR SERVICES/PRODUCTS.

We've been waiting for another call from you . . . and waiting. Frankly, we're downright worried that we've done something to lose your business. Would you let us know if there's some problem?

Let me be honest in my reason for writing, Bill. We have very much valued your business over the years, and we're concerned about why we haven't heard from you recently. Would you be frank with me?

I'm writing from a purely selfish motive—we value you as a client. You have always asked for the best service and paid our fees promptly, and we've appreciated that. May I ask why you stopped doing business with us?

This letter is prompted by one thing—we have missed your business and such a solid working relationship with your people. Have we inadvertently done something to lose your confidence?

MAKE IT EASY FOR THE CUSTOMER TO REPLY.

I've enclosed a questionnaire and would appreciate your completing it; it will let us know how we need to improve our services to you.

Would you phone me (234-5567) personally to let me know if there is something about our product or service that needs attention?

Could I impose on you to jot me a note on the bottom of this letter to let me know if there is some problem with your account or our service?

The enclosed, stamped card is for your convenience in letting us hear from you. We will appreciate your letting us know how you feel.

MAKE AN EFFORT TO SELL. ENCLOSE (IF APPROPRIATE) OR OFFER TO SEND A NEW CATALOG, BROCHURE, ORDER FORM, FREE SAMPLE, OR OFFER OF DEMONSTRATION.

Until we hear from you otherwise, we're going to assume that you have not called simply because you haven't needed our services. We've, therefore, enclosed a brochure that will outline some of our new financial advisory services. Please let us know if we can serve you again.

We hope that we haven't heard from you simply because you've been involved in other projects and that there's no problem with our service. Under that assumption, I'm extending an invitation to a May 1 public seminar introducing some of our new management videos. (See the attached brochure for details.) We'd like to see you again.

Dear Mr. Browne:

We haven't talked in a while. For the past three years, I've enjoyed those opportunities about two or three times a year to sit down and discuss with you your ideas for new employee benefit packages and then work with you in implementing them.

But looking back over my calendar, I notice that it has been quite some time since we've worked with you. From other sources, we know that your firm is still growing and expanding into new markets, and we congratulate you on your continued success.

Have you had any difficulty in administering the compensation package we've designed? If so, please call me collect (409/234-5532) and I'll continue to work with you on any necessary changes. We've missed working with you lately, and we want you to know that we value the opportunity to see that you have been thoroughly satisfied with our past help.

We have some new market research available around which we've designed new early-retirement packages. I'd very much appreciate the opportunity to discuss how we can work together again on your employee benefits.

Cordially,

GUIDELINES AND ALTERNATE PHRASES

THANK THE CUSTOMER FOR THE ORDER.

We appreciate your confidence in once again ordering from us.

Thank you for giving us another opportunity to serve you. We have received your response card and order for 250 customized, gold-stamped binders.

GIVE THE DETAILS OF THE RATE INCREASE OR POLICY CHANGE.

We want to explain one new policy with regard to. . . .

We have a new policy to enable us to better serve you. . . .

There has been one change in policy since you last ordered from us. . . .

As you may recall, we haven't had a price increase in the last four years. However, our increased production costs have now made it necessary to raise prices on our fans. The model you ordered is now $456.

REEMPHASIZE KEY BENEFITS OF YOUR PRODUCT OR SERVICE.

ASSUME THE CUSTOMER WILL CONTINUE TO DO BUSINESS WITH YOU.

Thank you for the order, and as soon as we hear from you with further details, we'll be glad to fill the order.

Let us know if you agree to these terms and if we can process your order immediately.

We are ready to ship your merchandise immediately—just let us know your preference on the new discount arrangements.

Thank you for doing business with us.

Please let us know if you'd prefer that we return this check or if you will send another for the difference in price.

We look forward to working with you on this project.

Dear Ms. Walters:

We have received your order for a subscription to Foursome magazine. We appreciate your order, but there is one problem: In January our rates increased. A one-year subscription is now $46--still quite a bargain, we think, for hours of fun in daydreaming about country weekends.

Therefore, I'm returning your check #3445 for $32, along with a current subscription form and return envelope.

We hope these terms are satisfactory to you, and we look forward to having you as a regular reader. As soon as you can send us another check (or let us know to bill you), we will begin your subscription and get your first issue in the mail.

Thank you.

Sincerely,

Dear Mr. Jackson:

We have received your request for reservations during the ARWA convention and are looking forward to the pleasure of welcoming you personally to the Beachfront Hotel.

For each reservation that we accept, we are now requiring a first and last night's prepayment. The first night's prepayment will serve to guarantee that your accommodations will be available on the check-in date; the last night's prepayment will guarantee your accommodations through your departure date.

Many hotels in the city, along with ours, are experiencing very high cancellation rates and no-shows on conventions that have asked us to set aside blocks of rooms. Additionally, inaccurate arrival and departure dates have caused many of our loyal guests to be inconvenienced.

In order for the Beachfront Hotel to continue to provide the excellent service for which we've become noted, we have established this new reservation policy to minimize any such inconveniences to you.

When you receive our confirmation, please review the accuracy of your arrival and departure dates and then forward your check to the Reservations Manager.

We are confident that this policy will allow us to serve all our guests in a more efficient manner and that we will be able to honor your reservation to make your stay with us trouble free. Thank you for choosing to be our guest May 6-10.

Cordially,

Dear Don:

Thank you for your August 9 printing order for the manuals, letterhead and envelopes, business cards, and mailing labels. Congratulations--it looks as though your business is continuing to grow.

We noticed on your order that you also asked to have all printing plates and veloxes for the manuals returned to you, as usual. However, about three months ago, we initiated a new policy that the plates cannot leave our offices after a completed job. As you may be aware, we do price our work so competitively that sometimes we have to depend on repeat business to make a profit on particular jobs. Therefore, our decision to keep all plates is our effort to encourage reprinting jobs here and to build loyalty from our customers so that we can continue to give them the lowest prices.

Since you've been doing business with us for so many years, we hope this new arrangement won't cause any inconvenience to you. Unless we hear from you otherwise, we will be processing your order and completing your work in the customary, speedy fashion.

Thank you for giving us another chance to meet your printing and stationery needs.

Sincerely,

GUIDELINES AND ALTERNATE PHRASES

WELCOME THE NEW CLIENT OR CUSTOMER WITH A SINCERE "THANK YOU."

We welcome you as a new customer and look forward to the opportunity you have given us to serve you.

Please accept my sincere appreciation for your first order.

Thank you for the recent confidence you have placed in us in moving your account to our company.

Welcome. We want to express our sincere appreciation in having a chance to serve your future banking needs.

REEMPHASIZE ANY BENEFITS YOU CAN PROVIDE THE NEW CLIENT OR CUSTOMER.

As you know, our staff is on call 24 hours a day to serve your every need.

Throughout the country, we have the capable, thoroughly trained, and dependable employees who will do everything possible to meet your account needs.

Our products have been tested in a highly competitive marketplace for the past 28 years. We know you will be pleased with the results.

Please be assured that I want you to call me personally so we can meet your needs in any special circumstances.

LOOK FORWARD TO A MUTUALLY REWARDING FUTURE.

We're celebrating what we hope will be a long, mutually rewarding business association.

We are eager to serve your next project.

We look forward to working together through the years.

Thank you for giving us the opportunity to call on you about your future software needs.

Dear New Client:

We want to welcome you to the Alex Jones Equity Fund. We appreciate your investment and plan to work hard to achieve our primary goal of capital growth.

Since the initial offering, we have been committing assets to our new target markets. But we are in no hurry. We plan to assess our selection carefully during the next few months, contemplating a volatile market and desiring success over speed in becoming fully vested.

As a new investor, you will receive our quarterly reports of the Fund's portfolio and a summary of the Fund's performance by month.

We have every confidence that you will agree that our Fund is a real opportunity, and we look forward to serving your investment needs.

Sincerely,

Dear Mr. Howard:

We at Today-Tomorrow Travel want you to know that we appreciate your business and will continue to do all we can to ensure that your company receives personal and professional service from all our staff.

Our personal profiles on each traveler in your company will enable us to give you the fastest service available and to meet your individual preferences whatever they might be--from a nonsmoking hotel room to a special-color Lincoln rental car.

We are very proud that you've chosen to give us your business, and we're pleased that you're in Houston.

Thank you,

Dear Ms. Harper:

Your account has been active a little more than one year now, and we would like to express our appreciation for your prompt payment each month.

Too often, our attention gets focused upon the problem accounts, and we forget to recognize the achievements of those we value most.

We know it is not always easy to maintain an ongoing record of prompt payments. Your account performance, however, is outstanding, and it's good credit customers like you who make our business a pleasure.

Thank you again; we look forward to our next occasion to serve you.

Cordially,

GUIDELINES AND ALTERNATE PHRASES

THANK THE READER FOR HIS OR HER INTEREST IN DOING BUSINESS WITH YOU.

We appreciate your taking the time to write us about. . . .

We are pleased to learn of your interest in. . . .

Thank you for the confidence you've shown in our firm by contacting us about your interest in. . . .

EXPLAIN TACTFULLY WHY YOU ARE DECLINING TO DO BUSINESS.

Major factors in our decision in this case are time and short deadlines. We simply cannot. . . .

We are concerned that we will have difficulties in. . . .

SUGGEST THAT IT MAY NOT BE IN THE BEST INTEREST OF THE READER TO DO BUSINESS WITH YOU.

We think that you'll agree on the sticky issues of. . . .

You probably are as aware as we are, if not more so, of the dangers in. . . .

In these matters, we would want you to be completely satisfied, and we simply cannot guarantee our services under these circumstances.

REFER THE READER TO ANOTHER FIRM THAT MAY BE ABLE TO PROVIDE THE PRODUCT OR SERVICE.

If you're still interested in pursuing this project, you may want to contact Belling-Well International in London.

We know that there are probably several other firms in the state that can do this sort of thing for you. Perhaps you can check the directory published each year by. . . .

We suggest that you call Hartford Inc. to see if they might be able to serve your needs in this situation better than we could.

EXPRESS APPRECIATION FOR THE CONTACT.

Thank you for writing us.

Thank you for having your representative call on us.

We appreciate your interest in discussing the matter with us.

Dear Mrs. Dori:

Thank you for writing us about representing your agency in the public-speaking and seminar markets.

After our telephone conversation June 5 in which you mentioned working with several other agencies on these same objectives, I do not believe that it would be in the best interest of either of us to sign an agreement on these projects. As you know, to market speakers appropriately we do many elaborate brochures and spend a great deal of money on telemarketing services. To get the necessary return on this investment, we need to have our clients agree to an exclusive arrangement for representation. And because we also understand your desire to continue to market your own services, we think you'll agree that neither of us would be completely satisfied with any contract we might draft.

We do know of other agencies that don't require exclusive contracts--Buckingham Associates in Dallas is one. Perhaps you may want to contact that organization.

Thank you for your interest in our agency and best wishes in all your speaking and seminar efforts.

Sincerely,

PRAISE THE SALES STAFF'S CONTRIBUTION TO THE ORGANIZATION AND SHOW APPRECIATION FOR THEIR SUCCESSES.

GENERATE ENTHUSIASM ABOUT NEW PRODUCTS OR SERVICES THAT THEY MAY NEED TO CALL TO THEIR CUSTOMERS' ATTENTION.

SUPPLY INCENTIVES—TANGIBLE OR INTANGIBLE.

Mr. Burke has asked for a list of all the sales reps who have exceeded their own quota by 20 percent for this quarter and we're definitely in that group! I think such recognition of our department certainly puts our division in the national limelight. I'm proud of your efforts.

Anyone who reels in at least two new clients will receive a pair of season tickets for the sport of your choice.

I'm counting on this month's extra effort as a personal favor.

Remember that the sliding-scale commission formula is in effect on this new product. Here's your chance for extra bucks this month.

EXPRESS CONFIDENCE IN THEIR FUTURE SUCCESS.

Let me see you pull out all the stops again.

You can do it.

Keep up the good work.

The whole organization has its collective eyes on you with these new products. Let's show 'em what you can do.

I know you'll do your usual great job with this new line.

Here's to exceeding our quota by 20% this month!

You've got what it takes; let's put the competition away.

I've always counted on you—even in the rough times we've had before. This is no exception. Your perseverance, your dedication, and your skill in all kinds of difficult situations will see us through the present circumstances.

Thank you for making us look good once again.

KEEP THE TONE UPBEAT AND INFORMAL.

Dear Kevin:

I'm very pleased to see the success that you recently have had with Berzone Model 34. As you can now see, persistence pays off. We've got an excellent product with none of the installation problems our competitors seem to be experiencing.

Now that you are a member of the 10 Group, what could be better than to be a member of the elite 20 Group. I know you have set this as one of your goals, and if you continue as you have recently, this goal should be reality in short order.

Thank you for your efforts on the Berzone series.

Regards,

To the Service Personnel:

You're doing it again! You're out in front.

Our money-back guarantee and free evaluation services on the Graton Series are major opportunities for you to continue to prove to your customers that Belton has a superior quality rewind.

I've enclosed a kit that contains full information on our money-back guarantee policy and evaluation services. Please review the kit carefully so that you can give all the details to your customers. In the final analysis your aggressive participation in the program is key to its success.

Right now, we've got the jump on our competition. But this is not to say that competitive terms and products might not be around the corner. The way to beat out the others is simply to tell our quality story to your customers as fast as possible.

I'll be in touch with each of you personally to see how many calls you've been able to arrange for this next two-week period. I know of no other sales force I'd rather be motivating than you. I have every confidence that you are again going to be the winners in this product line.

Sincerely,

To the Best Sales Force in the Industry:

Yes, I meant every word of that opening. Our second quarter results show a 39% increase in gross sales for the new Selton fans and lighting fixtures. I don't know what you've done differently in your presentations to customers, but keep doing it!

Of course, the new Selton product line can't be oversold. I think the new slimmer line has hit the market at just the right time and the manufacturer's rebate is the icing on the cake. As an additional incentive to get your customers to make an immediate decision, remember to mention that the rebate offer expires August 15.

Thanks for the big push on these products; your enthusiasm shows. Let's go for a 50% increase next quarter and ring everybody's bell around here.

Regards,

GUIDELINES AND ALTERNATE PHRASES

GET ATTENTION FOR YOUR CAUSE.

EXPLAIN WHO YOU ARE AND SPECIFICALLY WHAT YOU WANT; AVOID VAGUE GENERALITIES.

POINT OUT EITHER PERSONAL OR CORPORATE BENEFITS FROM INVOLVEMENT IF THEY ARE NOT APPARENT.

Today's students adequately trained become your future employees.

Our children deserve to live in a community that protects their rights to participate in sports events and other extracurricular activities in order to learn the basic skills of life.

We think that such a contribution will enrich your own life. In buying food for at least one child for a month, you perhaps will be better able to instill in your own children gratitude for what parents such as yourself routinely provide for their loved ones.

USE TESTIMONIALS FROM PROMINENT PEOPLE WHO HAVE HELPED THE CAUSE OR FROM RECIPIENTS OF THE MONEY OR SERVICES, IF POSSIBLE.

Bob Jones and Art Wilde have asked me to express their personal appreciation for your help in this way.

A recent unwed mother who stayed with us until after the birth of her baby had this to say about what the center meant in her life. . . .

ASSURE THE READER THAT ANY AMOUNT IS WELCOME.

We will appreciate any amount you can contribute and can assure you of its wise use.

We hope you can contribute $100 to our cause. If not, we welcome any amount you feel that you can afford.

Any size gift is appropriate—$5, $10, $25. Simply do what you can to help.

THANK THE READER FOR HIS OR HER HELP WITH SINCERE WARMTH AND PERSONAL GRATITUDE.

My heartfelt thanks for your support.

We will appreciate whatever you can give to help these mentally handicapped people lead self-supporting lives.

Thank you for your help in this way. Without your contributions, many abused teenagers would be on the streets tonight.

Please accept my personal gratitude for a generous gift toward the day we will conquer this dreaded disease.

Dear Friend:

Truly exciting things are happening on this campus:

- Establishment of a <u>$1 million endowment</u> for BCU <u>student career testing</u> and <u>educational loans</u>
- Development of a <u>master plan</u> for the campus
- BCU's first <u>Celebrity Golf Tournament</u>
- Top rating of BCU's <u>baseball team</u>
- <u>Record enrollment</u> for our spring semester

We invite you to help make possible yet another exciting event: meeting our annual gifts goal for the tenth consecutive year! We have received $2,500,000 toward our goal of $3,500,000 for fiscal year ending May 31.

Your gift--any gift of $15, $40, $100, $500, or more--will be so very helpful; it will be an investment in the lives of today's BCU students and tomorrow's work force.

Please accept our gratitude for your generosity.

Sincerely,

Dear Chamber of Commerce Member:

How would you like to take three of your favorite friends, business associates, and employees to see Mike Scott and the Houston Astros five times next season? Suppose you love the idea but would prefer going to five Houston Oilers games instead?

Suppose we threw in a fabulous dinner for you and your guests either before or after the game? Suppose you and your guests got to meet, obtain autographs of, and have pictures taken with your favorite Astros and Oilers? Suppose the entire program was a business deduction?

SUPPOSE YOU COULD ENJOY ALL OF THE ABOVE AND, ALSO, STRIKE A BLOW AGAINST OUR NATION'S NUMBER ONE GENETIC KILLER OF CHILDREN AND YOUNG ADULTS--CYSTIC FIBROSIS?

Well, "Have we got a deal for you!" We at the 65 Roses Sports Club, in conjunction with the Houston Astros and Houston Oilers, are very pleased to offer you this wonderful, unique and somewhat priceless opportunity. For a contribution of $1,200 you will receive either an Astros or Oilers package.

More importantly, you will take pride and pleasure in the fact that you are an active member of the nation's most successful nonprofit sports-related activity, the 65 Roses Sports Club, benefitting the Cystic Fibrosis Foundation.

Each 65 Roses Sports Club membership is limited to 65 members and will sell out quickly. Memberships will be sold on a first-come, first-served basis. To reserve your membership, call the 65 Roses Sports Club at (713) 523-9044.

Sincerely,

To All Faxton Employees:

Through the United Fund campaign you and I have the opportunity to voluntarily support over 160 human-care services that help to make our city and county a better place to live.

The United Fund activity that is most familiar to us is the annual campaign, but it is important to realize that the United Fund does far more than just raise money. Through volunteer efforts from your fellow citizens, the United Fund ensures that services and funds are adequately administered and that your contribution goes as far as possible.

The importance of the United Fund in our community hasn't lessened. People still need emergency aid in time of crisis and support throughout ongoing hardship and handicaps. No matter how much government does, there still is and always will be the need for voluntary contributions. The United Fund is one of the best ways I know to ensure that the volunteer voice is strong.

The amount you give and how you give is a personal matter--something only you can decide. For your convenience our company provides a payroll-deduction option each pay period.

Giving to the United Fund is a community responsibility in which all of us with jobs should share. I want personally to encourage and thank you for your decision to support this effort in the most generous way possible.

Sincerely,

GUIDELINES AND ALTERNATE PHRASES

EXPRESS INTEREST IN AND APPRECIATION FOR THE ORGANIZATION AND THE CAUSE.

Through the years, we have encountered many success stories from those you've helped to find life-changing skills.

Bert Hawkins, a long-time sponsor and one of our employees, speaks very highly of your efforts on behalf of the Boy Scouts of America.

We appreciate your contacting us about your need for financial help in restoring the Hican Building and the mental health center. We are pleased to contribute.

STATE WHAT SPECIFIC AMOUNT IS ENCLOSED OR WILL BE FORWARDED.

DISTINGUISH BETWEEN A PERSONAL CONTRIBUTION AND A CORPORATE ONE.

Although my company cannot contribute at this time, please accept my personal check for $50.

My organization is pleased to enclose a check for $500 toward your worthy efforts.

On behalf of our organization, I am enclosing our corporate check for $375.

WISH THE ORGANIZATION SUCCESS IN ITS ENDEAVORS.

We have every confidence you'll meet your goals.

We wish you every success in these efforts.

Thank you for your commitment to this project; I wish you success.

460

Dear Mr. Sanders:

We are very pleased about your establishing the Echert Scholarship Fund. Such an effort accomplishes two wonderful purposes: a memorial to a marvelous civic leader and a method to contribute to the education of deserving students.

Our company check for $1,000 and my personal check for $50 are enclosed. We sincerely thank you for the opportunity to contribute to someone's life in this way.

Best wishes in building the program and providing greater resources for future years.

Cordially,

GUIDELINES AND ALTERNATE PHRASES

BEGIN WITH A NEUTRAL OPENING, STATING THAT YOU HAVE CONSIDERED THE REQUEST.

We have received your letter about support for the local YMCA summer program.

Thank you for writing us to present your fund-raising goals for the rebuilding of Hague Street.

The project for restoring Milton Square to attract tourists has interesting possibilities.

We admire your dedication and tenacity in your ongoing efforts on behalf of the local Heart Fund.

AGREE ON THE WORTHWHILE EFFORTS OF THE ORGANIZATION MAKING THE REQUEST.

We hear from time to time about the successes you are having in your counseling centers.

We agree that these people are very deserving.

We are happy to learn that your organization has taken on the responsibility to see that something is done about these community problems.

Your efforts with these deserving groups should be appreciated by all of us who want our children to grow up in a safe, healthy community.

GIVE YOUR REASONS AND STATE THAT YOU WILL NOT BE ABLE TO CONTRIBUTE ON THIS OCCASION.

We have asked our committee to review all the requests we have received from excellent organizations such as yours, and the members have chosen to support those they feel most worthy. We regret that we have contributed our available funds elsewhere this year.

As you are probably aware, so many fine organizations such as yours come to us for fi-

nancial help each year. And we find great difficulty in deciding on which causes are most deserving. This year we have allocated most of our funds to the three local drug rehabilitation facilities.

Because we've already overextended our budget for charitable causes this year, we simply cannot help you out this time.

Over the years, we've done our best to continue to support those organizations that have pursued goals we think most important in the community. This year has been no exception. We have contributed to each of these again and feel that we are continuing to do our part to improve the community in this way.

WISH THE ORGANIZATION SUCCESS IN ITS ENDEAVORS.

Yours is an excellent organization, and we wish you every success.

Thank you for contacting us about this opportunity; we hope to help you out at a later time.

We wish you the best in your fund-raising efforts. Yours is a worthy project.

We know many benefit from your services each year; we hope you'll continue to be able to keep up the excellent work.

Thank you for spending such time and effort in improving the community. We wish you success.

Without organizations such as yours, our community would not be the nice place to live that it is. We hope you will have every success in meeting your service objectives this year.

We wish you the very best in meeting your financial goals for this worthy cause.

Dear Ms. Coats:

Thank you for contacting us about your efforts in establishing halfway houses for abused spouses and their children.

With all of the requests for donations, some time ago we established a committee to consider all corporate giving and to administer our approved budget for charity. The committee members have reviewed our corporate charitable decisions for the year and find that it will be impossible to contribute to your organization at this time.

We want you to know, however, that we think you are doing very commendable work in the community. And we often feel frustrated by the impossibility that we face here in not being able to contribute to every worthwhile opportunity, such as the one you are chairing. We wish we could have had a more positive answer for you.

On behalf of the community as a whole, thank you for the help you are giving these abused families.

Sincerely,

GUIDELINES AND ALTERNATE PHRASES

BRIEFLY PAVE THE WAY FOR YOUR REQUEST FOR SUGGESTIONS.

We've said it before and we'll say it again: Our employees make the company what it is. And we are again asking for your help.

In an effort to update our library and its usefulness to you as employees, we need your input on the kinds of periodicals most beneficial to you in performing your jobs.

We need your help once again.

May we count on you? Do you have five minutes to spare?

As you are well aware, we have undertaken to reach some goals that most of our competitors would think are impossible. And we need your suggestions for reaching them.

BE AS SPECIFIC AS POSSIBLE IN WHAT KINDS OF SUGGESTIONS YOU WANT.

We'd like you to respond to the enclosed questionnaire about your perceptions of waste in your own department.

We ask that you simply telephone Marg Atwell (453-6687) with your comments about cost-cutting measures you've taken in your own department.

We'd like you to attend the upcoming cocktail hour in the lower lobby and visit with our senior managers about what you perceive to be our biggest challenge in 19—.

Would you drop a brief memo to Marcell Whitley, our training coordinator, telling how many seats your department should be allocated if budget were no problem.

MAKE IT EASY TO RESPOND; REMEMBER THAT THEIR COOPERATION IS VOLUNTARY.

The questionnaires do not need to be signed.

You can drop your suggestions into designated boxes at each elevator bank.

We will keep all comments confidential; please feel free to be as frank as possible.

These letters will be opened only by the administrative assistant in that department and forwarded to us in a batch with all names removed.

We've set up a special number and operator just for your calls on Friday.

POINT OUT HOW INDIVIDUAL EMPLOYEES AND THE ORGANIZATION AS A WHOLE CAN PROFIT FROM THE SUGGESTIONS.

To the Southern Region Sales Staff:

Help--or at least help us help you!

From what several of you tell us, you are beginning to feel very comfortable using the new closing techniques we introduced. Your attitude and efforts have been super!

But here's where we need help: The greatest stumbling block in closing more sales is effectively handling a customer's objections. I'm working currently on a program to handle these new objections and want to make sure my ideas are right in line with the "real world" of your marketplace.

Would you take a few minutes to jot down the most difficult objections you are hearing. Specifically consider M-Text, Nu-Deltron, and DexNdiasti. Please have your ideas to me by March 14.

For everybody who sends me a list of at least 20 objections, dinner at the next staff meeting is on me.

But most important, we think our united efforts to come up with the best script for handling key objections will make you even more successful. Keep closing.

Regards,

GUIDELINES AND ALTERNATE PHRASES

SUMMARIZE THE PROBLEM OR SITUATION.

MAKE YOUR SUGGESTION TO CORRECT THE PROBLEM OR IMPROVE THE SITUATION.

BE AS SPECIFIC AS POSSIBLE, WITH DETAILS TO CONVINCE THE READER THAT THE MATTER NEEDS ATTENTION AND TO CONVEY THE APPROPRIATENESS OF YOUR SUGGESTION.

KEEP YOUR TONE HELPFUL RATHER THAN ADVERSARIAL OR JUDGMENTAL.

Do you agree that this might solve the problem?

What do you think of the idea?

Does this suggestion merit further consideration?

Are you interested enough in the idea that I should gather additional information?

May I meet with you to discuss this further?

Shall I do some further research on this?

I bring this situation to light only to offer my help in finding the best solution to the problem.

I'm sure you are aware of the problem, but I wanted to let you know of my concern and interest in improving the situation.

Dear Mr. Dowsaki:

I'm writing to express concern over the rapidly changing marketplace. In my opinion, we are becoming noncompetitive because of inflexible policies regarding our credit terms. Recently we lost a $210,000 sale to BloGar, Inc., because our credit terms (30 percent down payment) were not competitive with those of Whitley Associates.

I strongly believe in Universal's products, prices, policies, and people, but I think we must be more flexible in dealing with the customer.

May I make some specific suggestions to this end? I suggest that Universal:

- Review its credit policies in light of the terms now offered by our competition
- Communicate to its salespeople the reasons behind our credit policies so that they may present them to the customer more effectively
- Assign a person at the local level who can authorize changes to policies in "exceptional" situations

I've attached a memo to my immediate supervisor detailing the circumstances of the BloGar situation mentioned above. This memo will illustrate the difficulties and delays in getting authorized approval for special customer situations.

I think I speak for all salespeople when I say that our first concern is making the sale. I hope you'll agree that the above suggestions make sense in this changing market.

Sincerely,

GUIDELINES AND ALTERNATE PHRASES

EXPRESS APPRECIATION FOR THE SUGGESTION, INITIATIVE, AND INTEREST SHOWN.

We appreciate your interest in writing to us.

Thank you for taking the time to put your ideas on paper for us.

We appreciate your initiative in suggesting a change in upholstery fabrics for our interiors.

We always enjoy hearing from our customers, and your letter was no exception. Your suggestion for the new plants around the building has merit in a climate such as ours.

STATE WHAT ACTION YOU PLAN TO TAKE ON A GOOD SUGGESTION.

Let me forward your idea to the responsible manager and she will be in touch shortly.

SUMMARIZE THE BENEFITS GAINED AND YOUR APPRECIATION FOR A SUGGESTION YOU CAN USE.

We think this idea should save us almost $10,000 next year alone. We commend you for this farsightedness.

You are so right in your analysis of the situation. We can certainly count on at least an extra hour's productive time each day. We appreciate your calling the matter to our attention.

We will not lose sight of what you have contributed to the company in a way that you have probably considered "a small matter." We don't. It's an excellent idea, and you deserve much credit for this.

Dear Walter:

Marge Caldwell and I were pleased to talk with you last week about the problems you see in the marketing campaign we have planned to launch this spring. We appreciate your usual candid appraisal of the reactions you anticipate from field employees.

We have given careful consideration to the concerns you raised and have passed on our notes of the discussion to the responsible vice president. After he has time to review them, I will get back to you about how we can put these changes into effect with your people.

Please keep me informed about any other developments in your research--both formal and informal.

Regards,

Dear Mel,

Thanks for your August 6 letter with copies to Roger Tamson and Phil Lewis. We appreciate the time you took in writing us about this lead with Aramco. Dedicated employees like you keep us on our toes.

Our people will certainly follow up on the possibility of working with Aramco in connection with the canal construction. A contract with them could mean a substantial part of our 19-- revenue.

Thanks,

Dear Mr. Benton:

Thank you for writing us about changing our operations to remain open for 24 hours a day. The idea has come up for discussion from time to time, but we have never been quite able to measure the customer's need for such coverage. You raise some provocative points in your letter, however, and we definitely plan to give the around-the-clock scheduling more careful attention. In fact, we are now toying with the idea of sending out a questionnaire in our monthly statements to find out more ways we can improve services to our customers.

We take your letter as a welcome show of loyalty and interest. Thank you for letting us hear how we can better meet your needs.

Cordially,

GUIDELINES AND ALTERNATE PHRASES

REPEAT ENOUGH DETAILS OF THE SUGGESTION SO THAT THE READER KNOWS YOU HAVE GIVEN IT PROPER ATTENTION.

IF YOU CANNOT USE THE SUGGESTION, EXPLAIN UNDER WHAT CONDITIONS YOU MIGHT RECONSIDER.

Should we have need of an outside legal firm, I'll keep the name of your acquaintance on file in my office.

If the situation seems to be changing in the next few months, I'll get in touch with you for more details about your idea.

If our budget does call for an increase a couple of years down the line, I'd like you to bring this to my attention again then.

If we do decide to eliminate the Ohio division, this idea would make perfect sense at that point. Keep it in the back of your mind for that occasion.

If sales should pick up, however, in the next year, we would want to reconsider these value-added suggestions. They do have merit.

THANK THE READER FOR OFFERING THE SUGGESTION.

Bill,

I received your letter about the last closing meeting. Although the meeting you attended in St. Louis may not have been as productive as we all would have liked, we are attempting to identify and resolve problems associated with this area of responsibility. To do this, we need the insight and cooperation of MIS and all the accounting units; therefore, I think that to eliminate the closing meetings completely would be premature at this time.

But let me assure you that we are trying to make the format as productive as possible. And as encouragement for the future, let me emphasize that when all the closing structure falls into place, we likely will have no further need for these monthly meetings.

I appreciate your interest in the closing project, and please continue to advise me of any other concerns about our progress.

Cordially,

Dear Mr. Fitzroberts:

Thank you for your nice letter of March 2, suggesting how to avert the coming economic depression in the oil and gas industry.

We sincerely hope, as I'm sure you do, that such a downturn will not materialize. I've given your conclusions serious thought; however, I believe that we have spent as much time and money as we can justify in following these public-work projects.

Thank you for thinking about our welfare.

Yours truly,

Dear Mr. Jordan:

Thank you for your letter concerning the use of actual customers in our advertising commercials.

Dreyton has not recently used non-actors in our television ads. We last did this several years ago when we used actual Dreyton service station dealers to play the role of dealers.

I will forward your letter to our advertising department to make our representatives aware of your availability should they use "real customers" in future commercials.

Thank you for your interest in our company and your kind remarks.

Cordially,

THANK YOU/For Award, Bonus, or Benefit

EXPRESS YOUR GRATITUDE FOR THE AWARD, BONUS, OR BENEFIT.

What a surprise! I am so appreciative of. . . .

I want to thank you sincerely for your recognition of my work.

Thank you so much for the recognition you have offered in this way.

I was so pleased to learn of the . . . award.

Your selection of me for the . . . award is such a great and unexpected honor.

I had no idea that I was in the running for the . . . award. I'm so thrilled.

PRAISE THE ORGANIZATION'S WILLINGNESS TO PROVIDE THIS RECOGNITION.

BE MODEST IN TONE.

I feel certain others were more qualified for this honor; nonetheless, I'm thrilled that you have selected me.

I don't know how my name got in the hat, but I do appreciate your recognition.

Thank you so much; I'll do my best to represent our organization according to the standards this award represents.

Though I feel quite undeserving of this award, I certainly appreciate your thoughtfulness in presenting it to me.

Dear Members of ARD:

Thank you very much for selecting me to receive the Newman Award at our December meeting. This is one of the most memorable events of my professional career. To be recognized by you, my peers--experts in your own companies--is a highlight that I will remember over and over with gratitude.

I appreciate all that each of you has contributed to my professional growth and skills. Many of you have served as my role models during the years since we began our company. In fact, your "corporate" advice has been very much responsible for the successes we've had along the way.

I sincerely thank you.

Cordially,

Dear Herbert:

I was very pleased to receive your letter advising me that the continued improvement in the company's earnings permits the company to increase retired employees' death benefit to $10,000.

Because I had decided that I couldn't afford to convert any of my insurance at the time of my retirement, this is most welcome. Please extend my thanks to the board of directors.

My best wishes for another good year at Philboro.

Sincerely,

Dear Mr. Harper:

I want to express my appreciation to you for the most generous bonus at the end of the year. The company's outstanding growth record makes me very proud to be a part of the team, and the bonus represents to me your confidence in my abilities and my future with the company.

I do realize that not all organizations value their managers' personal dedication to the extent that Herrington Inc. does. Therefore, I feel quite pleased to work for executives who put real incentives behind the lip service some organizations give to considering their employees as their most valuable asset.

My work here is extremely rewarding. Thank you.

Sincerely,

THANK YOU/For Gift or Donation

EXPRESS APPRECIATION FOR THE SPECIFIC GIFT OR DONATION, AVOIDING THE SOUND OF THE "FORM" THANK-YOU LETTER.

MENTION AT LEAST ONE SPECIFIC USE OR BENEFIT, IF POSSIBLE, FOR THE GIFT OR DONATION.

Through your gift, used to purchase bullet-proof vests, the city police can now feel safer and better serve the public.

Such support will assist in our continuing effort to maintain an independent private institution of the highest quality.

The landslide victory and the clear mandate from the people could not have been achieved without sufficient funds to carry out the election plans. We thank you.

Dear Mr. Alfred:

Your Cross pen and pencil set arrived in my office today. Thank you so much. Some-how I have managed to lose the last two I've had--perhaps because I find them so nice to use and consequently carry them around in every available pocket.

You were thoughtful to remember me in this way, and I do wish you the best with your research project.

Sincerely,

Dear Margaret:

Thank you for the copy of The New Secretary: How to Handle People As Well As You Handle Paper. I'm very anxious to read it and lower the level of my ignorance! The table of contents tells me that this is a book I'll want to share and to recommend to others in the office. It is a book I would have dearly loved to have had available when I was just getting my feet wet.

I appreciate your thoughtfulness in sending it.

Cordially,

Dear Mr. Hines:

Thank you very much for your March 2 letter enclosing a check for $2,000 from your corporation to the Resomm Arts Campaign. Our first project, using your money, will be to begin restoration of the Hoffine Museum.

It has been most gratifying to observe the response of companies such as yours to the appeal of this campaign on behalf of the arts in the community. Particularly, I was encouraged by the statement of your intention to increase your support next year.

We commend you for such farsightedness and your generosity in supporting the community and us.

Sincerely,

GUIDELINES AND ALTERNATE PHRASES

EXPRESS YOUR APPRECIATION FOR THE SPECIFIC SERVICE RENDERED.

Thank you for making it possible to free Mark from his regular schedule to participate in our fund-raising efforts.

We want to express our sincerest thank you for your time and emotional energy in participating in our recent interview of experts in the insurance industry.

MENTION SPECIFIC DETAILS OF THE READER'S CONTRIBUTION OF TIME, EFFORT, AND REPUTATION.

Lianne volunteered two full weekends to the project—time that I'm sure could have been spent in more personal pursuits.

The participants' comments on the evaluation forms indicated that the seminar was highly informative and worthwhile. The ideas should specifically help us in our proposal writing.

Your reputation is well established in our state, and your personal involvement alone drew much attention to our cause.

SUGGEST THAT THERE HAS BEEN SOME PERSONAL BENEFIT TO THE READER.

We hope that in some small way, you yourself have found satisfaction in serving this campaign.

We know that you, too, are proud of the contribution on behalf of your family and your fellow employees.

We hope you, too, will reap the benefits of your efforts on behalf of the city. Acts of graciousness and generosity such as yours often have a way of returning to the benefactor.

Dear Charles:

I know there has been a great deal of personal effort that you expended in serving on the various top committees and task force of the International Business Committee of the Chamber of Commerce during the past five years.

To thank you adequately is impossible. You spent long, long after-business hours on the various projects. You took great care to see that protocol was followed in each situation and that no other board members felt slighted in the decisions made. Finally, your business experience and personal communication skills were invaluable.

I do hope you have gained some inner satisfaction in knowing that through your efforts you have made the city a better place to live and work.

Thank you sincerely for all the wholehearted assistance.

Cordially,

THANK YOU/For Hospitality

GUIDELINES AND ALTERNATE PHRASES

MENTION THE EVENT OR CIRCUMSTANCE DURING WHICH YOU WERE TREATED SO WELL.

———————————

BE SPECIFIC IN WHAT YOU ENJOYED, GIVING DETAILS OF THE INDIVIDUAL'S THOUGHTFULNESS.

———————————

OFFER TO RECIPROCATE IF POSSIBLE.

———————————

I look forward to getting together with you at our club soon.

I'll be phoning next month to see if I can take you to lunch.

Marge will give you a call in October to see if we can meet for dinner at the conference—as my guest this time.

It was nice of you to think of us; we'll be in touch soon to see if you can join us for dinner and dancing.

We plan to stay in touch and be of service to your staff in any way we can.

486

Dear Sharon:

Thank you so much for permitting me to drop by your home to tape the script for my audition for the training video. I never expected you to go to so much effort in preparing such delicious snacks and in having arranged your schedule to give me so much of your time.

The tape is just perfect for my purposes--your personable way of speaking has made learning the dialect so much more enjoyable and certainly much easier. My drama character, Gloria, is blossoming into a true-to-life Texan, thanks to you.

Most sincerely,

Dear Joan,

I appreciate so much your hospitality in including me in the Alejando party last weekend. As you know, these sessions provide a unique opportunity for a banker to meet new people and continue contacts with existing construction friends. (I trust you don't mind my using your hospitality to this end.) I must add that I took particular pleasure in meeting Bob Hart, an interesting fellow from Peru. It seems that we have many mutual friends there.

You always give such attention to your guest lists in an effort to make us all comfortable--not to mention the lavish buffet.

Thank you again for including me. I'll look forward to having you join me as my guest sometime soon.

Best regards,

Dear Benton:

The reception for Dr. Harris and his wife provided just the opportunity I'd been wishing for to renew all my acquaintances with Universal. Some of the attendees I met for the first time, of course, because you have continued to lead Universal to success after success--all of which require additional staff. And I must say, after having talked with some of them at length, you have hired some of the best in the industry.

But the most enjoyable part of the evening was swapping "remember whens" with familiar faces. It was so thoughtful of you to invite my wife also. Because she had accompanied me to so many company functions in the years I was with you, she met and visited with nearly as many old friends as I did.

I don't want to let the renewed relationship lapse again. Could we count on meeting you for dinner at Tony's the weekend of August 6? I'll phone you later in the month to see what your schedule looks like.

Cordially,

THANK YOU/For Referral or Reference

GUIDELINES AND ALTERNATE PHRASES

THANK THE READER FOR THE REFERRAL AND FOR CONFIDENCE IN YOU AND/OR YOUR ORGANIZATION.

SUMMARIZE THE OUTCOME, OR THE ANTICIPATED OUTCOME, OF THE REFERRAL.

LET THE READER KNOW YOU UNDERSTAND THE TIME AND EFFORT INVOLVED.

I understand that you had to make three long-distance phone calls before you finally got to speak to the right person in referring our company. That's persistence and I thank you.

Some of that time you spent I'm sure was after hours. Please know that I appreciate your personal sacrifice in spending time away from your family on my behalf.

OFFER TO RECIPROCATE OR EXPRESS YOUR GOODWILL IN ANOTHER WAY.

Will you please let me know if I can ever return the favor?

Please call on me to help you in some small way.

Please keep my new work number and call on me whenever I can help you make contact with a prospective client.

May I take you to lunch next Thursday as a very small token of my appreciation? I'll phone you.

Joy,

Thank you so much for giving our name to Netmart in Philadelphia. Mr. Tom Sizemore from their marketing staff called this morning, expressing an interest in our services, and we plan to visit their headquarters next week to show them what we have to offer.

I realize that you had a very hectic time simply following up on all the leads your trade-show booth turned up for your own company. With your own work load, to take the time to write Netmart suggesting they contact us was "above and beyond the call" of professional friendship.

Thanks so much. I'll be looking for an opportunity to return the favor.

Cordially,

Dear Earl:

I want to thank you personally for your interest, support, and encouragement in my recent job search. I've accepted a position with T.J. Samson and Associates in San Diego.

I'll be joining their company as vice president of marketing with responsibilities in the five-state western region. Primarily, we sell oil-field engineering and inspection services and related products.

Your advice was particularly helpful in the interviewing process. Let me know if I can help you, your friends, or your associates in any way. I don't want to get too far away from your network!

Sincerely,

Dear Dr. Wright:

Thank you very much for giving me so much of your time yesterday morning. I did follow up on your suggestion and your introductory phone call on my behalf. I'm happy to report that I got the position. I begin my work this coming Friday.

Getting this weekend job means that I will be able to go on with my college program as planned and, at the same time, to get experience that should prove helpful in my studies and future career. I can't thank you enough.

Respectfully yours,

GUIDELINES AND ALTERNATE PHRASES

EXPRESS YOUR THANKS FOR THE READER'S THOUGHTFULNESS IN LETTING YOU KNOW YOUR EMPLOYEE'S OR YOUR OWN EFFORTS WERE APPRECIATED.

I sincerely appreciate your warm message regarding our Christmas bonus and have passed on your comments to the board.

We were so pleased to be able to grant the benefits you mentioned in your letter. Your contributions through the years have not been forgotten.

Thank you for letting us know of the excellent service you received from Mae Templeton in our Akron office.

It was so thoughtful of you to take the time to write us about how pleased you are with our financial services.

We are happy to know you were pleased with the year-end bonus. It is our way of saying thank you for working productively and efficiently during the past year so that all would benefit.

MENTION THE PLEASURE THE THANK-YOU NOTE GAVE YOU.

I highly respect your expertise and opinion, so you can imagine my delight over your letter.

It's so nice to hear that our employees really do go the extra mile as we encourage them so often.

Your letter made my day.

What a way to start the day—a warm, complimentary letter from a valued customer. Thank you so much for letting us know how you feel.

Thank you so much for writing. We've taken your comments to heart.

TELL THE READER THAT YOU HAVE PASSED ON THE GOOD COMMENTS TO THE OTHER PEOPLE INVOLVED.

We have sent Joe Hartwell a copy of your letter.

The marketing department was also pleased to hear your response.

We have taken the liberty of passing on your letter to the organization as a whole. In fact, your commendation will provide just the incentive our employees need to continue to put forth their very best efforts on our customers' behalf.

BE SINCERE.

Dear Ms. Peppersen:

Now and then the mail includes a letter that brings special warmth to the day. It is especially nice when someone is helpful in a situation such as you described in your letter, and I am very glad that Frank Golightly and Don Davis from our company were so accommodating. As you point out, the interest shown and service provided make real friends for us at Telget and are the kinds of actions that make us particularly proud of our employees.

I am pleased to forward your letter to our field office; the manager there will provide an opportunity to recognize Mr. Golightly and Mr. Davis for their outstanding representation. No doubt they will appreciate, as well as be encouraged by, the time and trouble you took in writing your kind remarks. In addition, I have asked that a subscription to our in-house magazine be forwarded to you for your future needs.

Thank you for taking the time to write. We sincerely appreciate your thoughtfulness and your business.

Cordially,

TRANSMITTALS

GUIDELINES AND ALTERNATE PHRASES

STATE WHAT YOU HAVE ENCLOSED, LISTING EACH ITEM SPECIFICALLY EITHER IN THE BODY OF THE LETTER OR AFTER THE SIGNATURE LINE BESIDE THE ENCLOSURE NOTATION.

POINT OUT THE ACTION YOU WANT THE READER TO TAKE OR GIVE YOUR REASON FOR SENDING THE DOCUMENTS.

We need your immediate approval before we can go further.

The enclosed Hite contract is simply for your review; it has already gone to the customer.

We are sending a list of these entries simply to verify our records. Would you initial those that also appear in your files?

Please distribute copies of this safety poster to your staff at the local branch.

If the attached listing is correct, you do not need to take any action. If there is an error in your address or any corresponding notations, please make the appropriate corrections and return the form to us.

SUMMARIZE OR REPEAT KEY INFORMATION IN THE ATTACHED OR ENCLOSED DOCUMENT.

EXPLAIN ANYTHING UNUSUAL THAT YOU THINK THE READER WILL QUESTION— OMISSIONS, EXCEPTIONS, CHANGES, SURPRISES.

We have not included the ratings here because. . . .

Note that on page 2, we have omitted four entries. These omissions are to indicate. . . .

Please note that the figures for May are exceptionally high.

Within two weeks we will forward. . . .

ADD THE NAME AND PHONE NUMBER OF THE PERSON TO BE CONTACTED WITH ANY QUESTIONS. REMEMBER, HOWEVER, THAT THE TRANSMITTAL INFORMATION SHOULD BE COMPLETE WITHIN ITSELF. THE READER SHOULD HAVE TO CALL THE CONTACT PERSON ONLY WITH EXCEPTIONAL SITUATIONS OR QUESTIONS.

ASK THE READER TO ACKNOWLEDGE RECEIPT OF THE LETTER, IF NECESSARY FOR YOUR RECORDS.

Please initial this form and return it.

Please call Sharon Love at ext. 2347 if you will be unable to distribute these bulletins before the meeting.

As soon as you receive this note, enter the dates on your calendar and call Kevin Black with your reservations.

Please sign this letter, make a copy for your files, and return the original to me.

(Note: For transmitting bids or proposals, see "Sales and Marketing.")

Dear Mr. Mattox:

Enclosed are Piedmont-Jenter's answers to the three interrogatories in the Caddy-Seuter v. Fillmore and Piedmont-Jenter suit.

In all cases, we believe that we are not liable for the damage because the operators of the equipment were not wearing appropriate safety gear and were not following approved standard operating procedures when the injuries occurred.

Please review these answers and then inform me when you set the plaintiff's deposition and the doctors' depositions.

Sincerely,

Harold P. Steward
Vice President

Enc: Interrogative #1
        Interrogative #2
        Interrogative #3

Ladies and Gentlemen:

On behalf of American Enterprises, Inc., a Maryland Corporation, we enclose the following documents for filing under the Securities Act of 1933 and the Investment Company Act of 1940:

(1)   One manually signed and three conformed copies of a Notification of Registration on Form N8-A

(2)   Ten additional copies of the Registration Statement, without exhibits

(3)   A certified check for $1500 payable to the Securities and Exchange Commission in payment of the Securities Act of 1933 registration fee and the Investment Company Act of 1940 registration fee

We expect to file a pre-effective amendment to the Registration Statement after receiving comments from your staff on this filing. The amendment will include a pro forma balance sheet and will have cross-references and other blanks filled in.

We request selective review of the Registration Statement. The fund now being registered will employ investment objectives, policies, and techniques similar to those of American International Fund, Inc. The primary difference between the two funds is that the investment policy of the registrant will limit the maturities of the portfolio securities to not more than five years.

If you have any questions about this filing, please call Kenneth Woods at 214/445-6667. Would you please acknowledge that you have received this filing by stamping and returning the enclosed copy of this letter.

Yours truly,

Kenneth Waites
General Counsel

ds

Enc

Dear Ms. Silcot:

Please review the attached set of four guidelines and give me any suggestions you may have for revisions. We'd like to have your comments by July 1. I apologize for the short deadline, but we want to put the guidelines into effect as soon as possible.

These guidelines are arranged in the usual format (subject, forms used, purpose, procedures) and cover procedures for the following topics:

- Inventory packages
- Motor-fuel analysis
- Tire, battery, and accessory analysis
- Upline litters and reconciliations

I will be back in my office on Friday (ext. 2345) if you have questions about any of these. Thanks for your review and help.

Sincerely,

Sylvia Shores
Research Assistant

tr

Enc

WELCOME/To New Employee

GUIDELINES AND ALTERNATE PHRASES

SHOW ENTHUSIASM AND PLEASURE IN THE READER'S DECISION TO JOIN THE ORGANIZATION.

GENERATE EXCITEMENT ABOUT FUTURE JOB ASSIGNMENTS AND CHALLENGES.

Of course, we think ours is the best bank in the city, and we think you will, too, especially after you begin work here. Our employees have built the fine reputation we enjoy.

We think you and Bob Harris are just the two people to turn our company to the future in account management.

We expect another great year—we're projecting real growth of about 28% again.

OFFER ANY SPECIFIC HELP YOU CAN TO ACQUAINT THE READER WITH THE COMMUNITY OR THE WORK ENVIRONMENT.

AVOID HAVING YOUR WELCOME SOUND LIKE A FORM LETTER SENT TO ALL NEW EMPLOYEES; BE SPECIFIC AND PERSONAL IN YOUR COMMENTS.

I hope you and your two boys can get immediately involved in the Grayson Golf Club.

Although the weather in Houston is somewhat muggier than Boulder, you can always look at the bright side—your skin will look young forever!

You're going to have about a 30-minute commute from your Westwood subdivision. Unless you've heard of a better route, I suggest taking I-10 into downtown.

Why don't you ask Marge and the girls to join us for lunch sometime during the first few weeks? I'll be eager to meet them.

500

Dear Jean:

Welcome aboard! I'm sure you're going to be a valuable asset to our team in Miami. With your help, we're going to get that new software line off to a commendable start.

I'm sure you have some questions about what you are supposed to do and how you should do it--but take it easy and you'll do fine. There are lots of folks around here who will help you out with their great wisdom!

As I'm sure you know, to be a successful salesperson, you need a plan. Therefore, our plan for the next two weeks is as follows:

Week of 2/10--This week should be spent familiarizing yourself with our shop operations. Move about the shop, ask about equipment with which you're unfamiliar, ask about how things are done and why. Introduce yourself to the operators. Locate the pricing book and skim through it (we'll discuss that the second week). Then spend the rest of the week calling your old accounts to tell them you've moved. And it wouldn't hurt if you want to drum up a little business from your old accounts.

Week of 2/17--You and I will spend the week together discussing how to manage your time and territory, how to use the pricing book, and how to make effective sales calls. Then we will put what you have learned into practice.

I'm looking forward to getting to know you better and meshing our skills into a very successful team. I'm equally confident that the community will welcome your husband and boys. In fact, why don't you let the boys meet you here after shop hours some evening? I think they'd probably like to see the heavy equipment.

If you have other questions before you report your first week, feel free to call me here or at home (233-4598).

Best regards,

GUIDELINES AND ALTERNATE PHRASES

WELCOME THE POTENTIAL CUSTOMER OR CLIENT TO THE COMMUNITY.

We hear that you are moving to the community and want to extend our welcome.

Welcome to you and your family as you "migrate" north to Ohio.

We are pleased to learn that you are moving to Nehmann.

We understand that you have accepted a position with Tramart Associates and will be moving to the Wichita area soon. We congratulate you on joining that prestigious firm and welcome you to the city.

INTRODUCE YOURSELF AND YOUR SERVICE OR PRODUCT BUT AVOID MAKING THE LETTER SOUND "PUSHY."

INCLUDE AN INVITATION TO CALL OR VISIT YOU, MENTIONING ANY FREE SAMPLE, FREE DEMONSTRATION, OR NEWCOMER DISCOUNT AVAILABLE.

We encourage you to use the enclosed coupon for a 20% discount on your initial appliance purchase with us—our way of getting to meet you and introduce you to our excellent products and services.

Drop in for a free makeup and consultation. Simply bring this card with you for a free lipstick pencil—your choice of colors.

Of course, our financial consultants bill on an hourly rate, but we'd like to visit with you for the first hour with no charge—simply acquainting ourselves with your financial objectives. Call Sue Dunnaway at ext. 4560 for an appointment at your convenience.

Dear Mr. Poston:

We have received word that you and your family will be moving to Newell next week. Welcome! We've enclosed a small packet of information--maps, directories of schools, churches, libraries, and important phone numbers--that should help you find your way around.

We also wanted to let you know that our bank is offering excellent real estate loan rates--9-10% on conventional mortgages. These rates do continue to change regularly, so we encourage you to call Diane Osborne (234-5777) the next time you come to town and set up an appointment to see how we can help you save some money on your home mortgage.

Again, welcome. We want to make your transition to our community as easy as possible.

Cordially,

Dear Ms. Fairbaxter:

I wanted to tell you how pleased we were to have had an opportunity at the Hilman Shrimp Fest to welcome you and your husband to Louisiana. We are glad you could join us in this quarterly "fling" that we host to meet newcomers to the city.

We also want to offer our CPA services to you: complete bookkeeping services for small businesses, tax preparation and related consulting, and financial investment and management counseling. Although we are located in the northwest part of Shreveport, we draw clients from all over the city.

Please stop by at your convenience to talk with me or one of our senior partners about your financial needs. Thanks again for enjoying Louisiana's finest shrimp with us.

Sincerely,

Dear Mr. and Mrs. Dennison:

On behalf of all of us at Cedar Point Bank, I would like to welcome you to our community. We feel confident that you and your family will enjoy your new home and all the advantages available here in the Cedar Point area.

We would also like to do business with you and your family. By presenting this letter when you come in, your first check order will be free; and when you open a savings account, we will add $25 to your initial deposit.

Our bank is conveniently located just south of the I59 and Loop 612 intersection, on property adjacent to Newcastle Mall.

Our objective is to provide the finest banking service available in our community. To accomplish this goal, we have the most experienced staff, the finest on-line data processing support, 24-hour automatic teller machines, and the most extensive lobby and drive-in hours available in the city.

Most of our staff live in the local area so someone around here can answer most questions you may have. Just ask for Melinda Garrett, Mark Brighton, or me.

We want to be your bank. We pledge to merit your trust with excellent professional service provided with personal concern.

Sincerely,

GUIDELINES AND ALTERNATE PHRASES

MAKE THE STOCKHOLDER FEEL A PART OF THE COMPANY.

———————

We welcome you as a company owner.

We're pleased to have you as a stockholder and voting decision maker in our growing organization.

———————

INFORM THE STOCKHOLDER ABOUT REPORTS OR OTHER DOCUMENTS YOU ARE ENCLOSING OR WILL BE FORWARDING REGULARLY.

———————

INVITE THE STOCKHOLDER TO ASK QUESTIONS OR OFFER SUGGESTIONS ABOUT THE COMPANY'S OPERATIONS.

———————

We welcome your questions, ideas, and suggestions for improving our services and products.

Let us know when we can provide further information to you.

If you discover ways we can improve our operations, please feel free to pass along those ideas to us.

Dear Mr. Grafton:

We are pleased you have purchased common stock in Fullerton-Ramsey. As one of the company's owners, you will be kept informed about your investment. Enclosed is our latest financial statement. You will also begin to receive copies of our annual and quarterly reports.

The annual meeting of shareholders is held on the last Tuesday of May. We will solicit proxies from shareholders who are unable to attend the meeting in person. You will receive a report telling you what happened at the meeting whether or not you attend. We hope you will find our financial and other reports helpful in following the progress and activities of your company.

Fullerton-Ramsey is currently paying quarterly dividends of $1.02 per share. Dividend checks will reach you about the 15th of March, June, September, and December. If you prefer to apply your dividends toward the purchase of additional stock, you may participate in the Automatic Dividend Reinvestment Service described in the enclosed brochure.

We are happy to have you join our group of owners.

Sincerely,

Appendix A
To the Letter Checklist for Form

ATTENTION LINES

An attention line is optional. Use it primarily when you are addressing a company but want to direct your letter to a specific person to handle your message or request. An attention line immediately conveys to the person opening the mail that yours is a business letter rather than a personal one. Therefore, if the person named in the attention line has moved to a new position or is absent for other reasons, the letter will be handled by someone else.

Place the attention line two lines below the inside address. You may or may not use a colon after *Attention*. Do not underline it or use all capital letters:

Acme Steel Company
12345 Arkansas Lane
Arlington, Texas 76015

Attention: Mr. Samuel P. Horne

Dear Gentlemen or Ladies:

The attention line is being used less and less frequently in business today. Unless the letter has been marked "Confidential" or "Personal," the letter is assumed to be about company business and automatically routed to the appropriate person handling the request in the other's absence.

ADDRESSES—INSIDE AND OUTSIDE

Be sure you spell a person's name correctly. Some recipients don't read letters that arrive with their name misspelled—they assume the letter can't be important or the writer would have been more careful.

Equally offensive is an inappropriate title. When you address someone, use either the title or degree but not both:

Howard E. Wyatt, D.D.S.
Dr. Howard E. Hyatt

Two or more men are addressed as *Messrs.,*

which means *Misters.* Do not use first names with this abbreviation:

Messrs. Smith, Wyatt, and Fury

Two or more women are addressed as *Mesdames, Mmes.,* or *Mses.* Do not use first names with these abbreviations:

Mses. Farb, Lionel, and Gray

When addressing couples, give both appropriate titles:

Dr. and Mrs. Harold Wright
Mr. Harold Wright and Dr. Margaret Wright
Drs. Harold and Margaret Wright
Dr. Margaret Wright and Mr. Steven Jones
Mr. and Mrs. Harvey Adams-Quinn

Ms. Margaret Wright
Mr. Steven Jones

In selecting a title, always notice the way an individual identifies himself or herself. For example, some who hold honorary degrees do not use their titles; others do. Some married women prefer *Mrs.*; others prefer *Ms.* If you do not know the title the individual prefers, use the standard *Ms.* or drop the title altogether:

Miss Sarah Gray
Mrs. Sarah Gray
Mrs. Ken Gray
Ms. Sarah Gray
Sarah Gray

Place the inside address at least two lines below the date. If the position title is short, you may place it on the line with the name. If it is long, place the title on the second line:

Ken Green, President

Ken Green
Vice President of International Operations

When the position or department title continues to a second line, indent that carryover line two spaces.

The comma before the abbreviations *Jr.* and *Sr.* is optional. Follow the recipient's preference if you know it:

Michael J. Smith, Jr.   Michael J. Smith Sr.

With the outside address, make sure the typing is correctly spaced and easy to read. Avoid unusual typescript that mailhandlers find difficult to read at a glance.

When you use both a street address and a post office address, the postal service will deliver your letter to whichever address appears directly above the city-state-zip line.

In an outside address, place an attention line directly below the company name.

Type the name of foreign countries in all caps on the envelope.

Spell out all numerical names of streets if they are ten or below. Use figures for all residence numbers except *One*. Use a space, a hyphen, and a space to help the reader easily distinguish the street number from the residence number:

127 Ninth Avenue, North
127 E. 15 Street
5 Park Avenue
One Wingren Plaza
556 - 91 Street

"Boilerplate" Paragraphs

With the advent of the computer came "boilerplate" paragraphs—used both effectively and ineffectively. Certainly, one of the great benefits of the word processor is to reuse standard paragraphs in letters that we frequently write.

But boilerplate paragraphs become ineffective if writers use them when a letter calls for original comments for a specific audience. Most boilerplate paragraphs must be general to be widely useful. At best, boilerplate writing creates the impression that you don't care about your individual reader. Simply because you insert a person's name throughout a boilerplate document, don't think readers mistake it for an original letter, tailored to them specifically.

At worst, boilerplate language with its broad generalizations confuses the reader. Take this example that many people use as a closing line in correspondence: "If I can answer any further questions or be of any assistance, please do not hesitate to call." Questions about what? What assistance? How can the writer help?

Your writing is much more effective when you can take the time to be specific: "If I can answer any further questions about this Maxim contract, please call me next week. Perhaps I can get further clarification on Subsection A from John Turner, if you think that would be helpful."

There is, of course, a place for form correspondence. But when you want to impress your readers that you care about them specifically, choose a model and then add your personal touch.

Complimentary Closings

The closing should match the formality or the informality of the salutation, the tone of the letter, and the relationship or rapport between the writer and reader. Listed below are several closings that may be appropriate on occasion:

Very Formal
  Respectfully yours,
  Yours respectfully,
Formal
  Very truly yours,
  Yours very truly,
  Yours truly,
Less Formal
  Sincerely yours,
  Yours sincerely,
  Sincerely,
  Cordially yours,
  Yours cordially,
  Cordially,
Informal
  Regards,
  With kindest regards,
  With my best regards,
  My best,
  Give my best to Mary,
  Fondly,
  Thanks,
  See you next week!

COPY NOTATIONS

The old *cc* (meaning carbon copy) is still standard, although the copy may be a photocopy or another reproduction. Type the notation flush left below the signature block or, if there is one, after the enclosure notation. You may also write out *Copies to:*.

If you do not want your reader to know that you are sending a copy to another person, do not add the *cc* line on the original letter. Instead, type *bcc* (blind carbon copy) only on the copy of the original letter:

cc: Sarah Smith
cc Sarah Smith
cc: Dr. Howard Stewart
    12337 Rocky Lane
    Houston, Texas 77070
Copy to: Sarah Smith
Copy to Sarah Smith
Copies to: Sarah Smith
            Howard Jones
            William Toast

DATE LINES

Place the date at least two lines below the letterhead. The line may be flush left, flush right, or centered below the letterhead.

Date the letter according to when it was dictated or written, not when typed. Do not abbreviate a month or use *nd, st,* or *th* on numerals. Also, do not use numerals for the month. Not: 6/23/89.

Either of the following date orders is appropriate; however, the latter is primarily used by the government, the military, and those outside the United States:

December 10, 19--
10 December 19--

ENCLOSURE NOTATIONS

Type the enclosure notation flush left at least two lines below the signature block (or below

the typist's initials if you include those). If you are sending more than one enclosure, always identify each specifically either in the enclosure notation or in the body of the letter. This notation warns the reader if something has inadvertently been omitted from the packet of information:

Enc
Enc.
Enclosures 3
Enclosures: Hite contract
            Check for $458
Enclosures
    1. Draft of absentee policy
    2. Invoice #459990

ENVELOPES

Address your envelope so that it looks balanced and uncrowded. Start the first line a little below the center of the envelope. Make sure the address is legible and complete. Why delay your correspondence for days while someone in the mailroom tosses it aside to "check the suite number later"?

If you want to add any special instruction on the envelope such as "Personal," "Please forward," or "Confidential," put it on the left side of the envelope so that it is clearly visible when someone reads the address:

Confidential
                Ms. Susan Johnson
                Harris International
                3445 Tartarn Blvd.
                Houston, TX 77070

FORMATS FOR TYPING

Almost every secretarial typing book will show several typing styles with different names, but most are variations on the following two: block and indented. The variations are based on the indentation of the date, subject line, body paragraphs, and signature block.

APPENDIX A

BLOCK STYLE

Date

Name of Recipient
Title/Department
Company
Street Address
City, State, and Zip Code

RE

Dear Name:

Subject:

_____
_____
_____

_____
_____
_____
_____

_____
_____
_____

Sincerely,

(Handwritten Signature)
Writer's Name
Title

dm   (typist's initials—If the writer is also the typist, you may
      omit this notation.)

Enclosure

cc   Dr. Joseph Hardy

PS:

514

INDENTED STYLE

Date

Name of Recipient
Title/Department
Company
Street Address
City, State, and Zip Code

RE

Dear Name:

Subject:

_____

_____

_____

_____ _____

Sincerely,

(Handwritten Signature)
Writer's Name
Title

DDB/cm

Enc

cc

P.S.

IDENTIFICATION INITIALS

The purpose of the identification line is for the writer's company to trace who originated or typed correspondence. The identification line may contain the writer's initials or simply those of the typist. If the writer has typed his or her own correspondence, no identification line is necessary. The initials can be divided by either a slash or a colon:

> dms
> DDB:dms
> DDB/dms

MAILING METHODS

If you want to specify mailing instructions such as "First Class" or "Overnight Express," type those instructions on the envelope two lines below the stamp.

PERSONAL PRONOUNS

The choice between the personal pronouns *we, I,* and *you* has become troublesome for many writers. Let clarity, courtesy, and tone be your guide.

If you are speaking as a company representative in an authorized capacity to conduct business, then you can correctly say either of the following:

> We will reimburse you for these legal expenses.
> Exxon will reimburse you for these legal expenses.

If you are speaking just for yourself, use *I:*

> I found the brochure very informative.

You may appropriately mix both *I* and *we* in the same letter as clarity dictates:

> We are pleased to offer you the position of sales director, and I'm looking forward to our Tuesday morning meeting.

What about the general rule you've heard about not using *I* in your letters? The idea—to put the reader's interest ahead of your own—is good. But the application of the "you" approach may create a pompous or artificial tone that you don't mean to convey. Consider the following pairs of sentences:

> You will be pleased to learn that you have been selected to serve on our advisory board. Your prompt response will be appreciated. (Condescending tone—Oh, yeah?)

> I'm pleased that our board has selected you as the best qualified candidate to serve on our advisory board. I hope you'll agree to serve. (Friendly tone—I'm pleased about your selection.)

> Your book was well written and comprehensive. (Condescending tone—Who are you to judge? I already knew that.)

> I thoroughly enjoyed your book and found an answer to every one of my questions about performance appraisals. (Grateful tone—Thank you for helping me.)

> Again, clarity and courtesy dictate proper tone and pronoun use.

POSTSCRIPTS

Postscripts can be useful for two reasons: 1) to add emphasis to a key point or action item or 2) to make the letter sound informal and personal. The postscript may be handwritten or typed:

> P.S. Just return the enclosed card to see if you aren't pleased with the service you receive!

> PS: Give my regards to the others who had a part in making the program such a success.

REFERENCE LINES

Reference lines help clerks file or route correspondence appropriately. You may have a reference line to refer to your own files and your reader's files. If so, place your reference line below the incoming reference line.

Our reference: Project #234
Your reference: Invoice #3444

RE Order #4558

SALUTATIONS

Always try to address your letter to a person by name rather than title. If you must send a form letter or if you can't find a specific name, you may choose one such as:

Dear Committee Member:
Dear Meeting Planner:
Dear Colleagues:
To All Sales Reps:
To Whom It May Concern:
Dear Sir or Madam:
Dear Madam or Sir:
Dear Purchasing Agent:

If your letter is addressed to a company, the proper salutation is:

Gentlemen or Ladies:
Ladies or Gentlemen:

If your letter is addressed to an organization of only women or only men, use:

Dear Sirs:
Dear Ladies:
Dear Mesdames:
Gentlemen:
Ladies:

If you do not know the gender or the person to whom you're writing, use one of the following:

Dear Kim Krause:

Dear K. Krause:

After formal salutations, use a colon. After informal salutations, use a comma. Whether you use the first or last name and whether you drop the *Dear* make your letter either more or less formal:

Dear Mr. Jones: (most formal)
Dear Joan:
Dear Jim,
Jim,   (very informal)

SECOND-PAGE HEADINGS

When the letter continues to the second page, be careful where you divide it. Carry forward at least two lines of typing on the second page. Also avoid beginning the second page with a single, short line. Do not break the last word on the first page with a hyphen.

At the beginning of the second and succeeding pages, type identifying lines that include the name of the addressee, the page number, and the date:

Baeddle Telecommunications, Inc.
Page 2
June 10, 19--

Harriet Jonnasburg
Page 2
June 10, 19--

Harriet Jonnasburg   -2-   June 10, 19--

SIGNATURES

Always sign your letters in ink and by hand. Do not sign an accompanying title such as *Mr., Ms., Mrs., Dr.,* or *Rev.* Your name and title or other designation may be typed beneath your signature:

Yours truly,
    (Handwritten signature)
Brenda Maxwell, Ph.D.
Research Chemist
Exxon Corporation

Sincerely,
    (Handwritten signature)
John D. Maxwell, Vice President
Friedman, Inc.

Sincerely,
    (Handwritten signature)
John D. Maxwell
Vice President of Marketing

Cordially,
    (Handwritten signature—Cheryl Jones)
(Mrs.) Cheryl Jones

Cordially,
    (Handwritten signature—Cheryl Jones)
Secretary to Howard Wyatt

If you are simply signing or typing and signing (not actually composing) the letter for a boss, add your initials just below and to the right of the signature:

Yours truly,

    (Handwritten boss's name) (Your initials)
Richard H. Gere, Vice President

Again, be sure that the way you sign your name matches the tone of the letter. To a close friend and business associate, you may prefer to sign *Bill* and to a stranger, *William:*

Regards,

    (Handwritten signature—Bill)
William C. Paxton
Human Resources Director

If you are acting as an official of a company, such as a lawyer giving a legal position or a CPA providing company financial information, you may want to use the company name in your signature block:

Yours truly,

Acme Tires International
    (handwritten signature)
Harvey P. Smith
General Counsel

STATIONERY

For most business correspondence, standard 8½-by 11-inch sheets of 20- or 24-pound bond with 25 percent cotton fiber is appropriate. This heavier weight conveys quality and also allows the paper to be handled extensively without damage.

For notes of thanks, congratulations, or condolences to business associates whom you consider close friends, select personal "executive" stationery of a smaller size. Another personal touch is to write your letter in longhand. A handwritten note makes your message sound more personal and warm. In other words, it conveys to your reader that you took extra time to write it rather than simply to have your secretary tailor one of your standard letters.

SUBJECT LINES

Subject lines may or may not be necessary. In *external* correspondence they primarily tell a clerk two things: how to file a document or how to route a document. A clerk can read *Subject: Project #2469-993KLS* and get the paperwork back into the appropriate file. Or the clerk can read *Subject: Exhibitor Information for June 22-26 Expo* and know to forward the letter to the appropriate person in the organization to handle the incoming request.

Subject lines in *internal* communications should carry the above process a step further: subject lines should be informative. Think newspaper headlines. Notice how much more informative each successive subject line gets in the list below. Be as informative as possible in your own:

Subject: Management Development
Subject: Management Development Classes
Subject: Request for Approval on Management Development Classes
Subject: Request for Approval on August 6–10 Management Development Seminar

Instead of *Subject:,* you may also use *Re* or *RE.*

Place a subject line two lines below the salutation because it is part of the body of the letter. Either use all capitals and no underlining, or capitalize the first letter in each important word and underline the complete subject line:

SUBJECT: EXHIBITOR BOOTH SPACE STILL AVAILABLE
<u>Subject: Exhibitor Booth Space Still Available</u>
Re Exhibitor Booth Space Still Available

VISUAL PLACEMENT AND DESIGN

The overall look of your letter says much about your attitude toward your work and your reader. Did you take the time to do things correctly? If so, your care conveys respect toward your reader and adds credibility to the content of your letter.

Your letter should be centered between the top and bottom of the page, with margins of one to two inches all around. The body of the average letter should be single spaced, with double spacing between paragraphs. If the letter is short (fewer than 100 words), you may prefer to double space it.

Short paragraphs are best. A reader's comprehension drops off drastically with paragraphs running over ten lines. Also, look for places where you can use lists to help your reader skim and review key ideas.

Finally, you may choose to add emphasis to a key word or idea (such as a crucial deadline or a benefit) by underlining or bold-printing it. Remember, however, that any such visual device loses its effectiveness when it is overdone.

Appendix B
Form for Customizing and Dictating Letters

You may wish to duplicate this form and keep blank copies in your desk. If you dictate, simply use this form as a guide for your instructions and the letter text.

_____ _____ _____
(writer/dictator's name)   (typist's name)   (today's date)

This letter is a ☐ *rough draft* ☐ *final copy*.

Please use *what kind of stationery or paper?* _____

The layout of this letter is the usual/unusual:

   The margins should be ☐ *1 inch* ☐ *2 inches* ☐ *3 inches*.

   The spacing should be ☐ *single* ☐ *double* ☐ *triple*.

   There will be special effects such as ☐ *headings* ☐ *italics* ☐ *bold print*
   ☐ *columns* ☐ *lists* and I'll tell you when to add these.

We are going to customize letter model #_____

Send copies to the following people (Spell all unfamiliar names and addresses):
_____
_____

The incoming reference line is: _____
The outgoing reference line is: _____
The subject line is: _____
The salutation is: _____

Make the following substitutions in the model letter:
   Sentence 1: Add _____
                    Delete _____
   Sentence 2: Add _____
                    Delete _____
   And so forth:

Make these additional changes: _____
_____
_____

The complimentary closing should be: _____
My signature block should read: _____
Enclosures (List specifically if not listed in the body of the letter):

File this letter on the computer under: _____
                                            (file title)
Keep a paper copy in: _____
                         (file title)
Make a note in my tickler file to follow up on: _____
                                                     (date)
This is the end of my instructions about this document.

ABOUT THE AUTHOR

DIANNA BOOHER is president of Texas-based (Dallas and Houston) Booher Writing Consultants, whose clients include numerous Fortune 500 companies, among them IBM, Exxon, and Tenneco. This is her eighteenth book. Her previous business titles include: *Would You Put That in Writing?, Send Me a Memo, Cutting Paperwork in the Corporate Culture, Good Grief, Good Grammar,* and *The New Secretary: How to Handle People As Well As You Handle Paper.* She has a master's degree in English with a specialization in writing.